THE OUTSIDE-IN
CORPORATION

THE OUTSIDE-IN
CORPORATION

How to Build a Customer-Centric Organization for Breakthrough Results

Barbara E. Bund

McGraw-Hill

New York   Chicago   San Francisco   Lisbon   London   Madrid   Mexico City
Milan   New Delhi   San Juan   Seoul   Singapore   Sydney   Toronto

1 2 3 4 5 6 7 8 9 0 DOC/DOC 0 9 8 7 6 5

ISBN 0-07-145931-6

FIRST EDITION

This publication is designed to provide accurate and authoritative information
in regard to the subject matter covered. It is sold with the understanding that
neither the author nor the publisher is engaged in rendering legal, accounting,
or other professional service. If legal advice or other expert assistance is
required, the services of a competent professional person should be sought.

> — *From a Declaration of Principles jointly adopted
> by a Committee of the American Bar
> Association and a Committee of Publishers*

McGraw-Hill books are available at special quantity discounts to use as
premiums and sales promotions, or for use in corporate training programs.
For more information, please write to the Director of Special Sales, Professional
Publishing, McGraw-Hill, Two Penn Plaza, New York, NY 10121-2298.
Or contact your local bookstore.

Library of Congress Cataloging-in-Publication Data

Bund, Barbara E.
   The outside-in corporation: how to build a customer-centric organization
for breakthrough results / by Barbara E. Bund.
        p.   cm.
   Includes bibliographical references.
   ISBN 0-07-145931-6 (hardcover : alk. paper)
   1. Customer relations—Management.   2. Success in business.   I. Title.
HF5415.5.B86 2005
658.8'12—dc22

                                                          2005021008

This book is printed on recycled, acid-free paper containing a minimum of
50% recycled de-inked fiber.

For Adam

CONTENTS

9. OUTSIDE-IN COMMUNICATION

10. OUTSIDE-IN CHANNELS OF DISTRIBUTION

PREFACE
Outside In,
Not Inside Out

*We've been inside-out for over a hundred years. Forcing
everything around the outside-in view will change the game.*
—*Jack Welch, former chairman of GE*

THIS BOOK GREW OUT of my three decades of experiences with
businesses and businesspeople—experiences as a teacher of
courses for executives and graduate students and as a consultant. I
have been fortunate to teach at MIT Sloan School of Management and at Harvard Business School and also in organization-
specific courses at individual companies.

I have worked with people from hundreds of organizations,
from brand-new start-ups to some of the largest corporations in
the world. I have worked as an individual consultant, and I have
founded and run a consulting practice within a larger firm, focusing on marketing and sales in information technology companies
and also on the use of information and technology in the marketing and sales efforts of companies in other industries.

In the course of this experience, I discovered some bad news.
Few managers actually run their companies from the outside in,
starting with customers and prospective customers and making
sure that all of their strategies and actions are chosen and implemented from a strong customer perspective.

But there is good news, too. Over time, working with my consulting clients and students, I developed a remedy for the problem: *the outside-in discipline*. This good news turns the bad news into an opportunity, a path to competitive advantage. If your rivals get it wrong by taking an inside-out perspective, you can gain a competitive edge by transforming your company into an outside-in corporation, using the insights, principles, and actions in this book.

Let me be very clear at the outset that I was not the first business author to recognize the importance of outside in. Peter Drucker, the father of modern management, was the first to write about the importance of building and running a customer-centered organization. He argued that only by looking from the outside, from the point of view of the customer, could business-people determine what a particular business should be and how it should operate.[1] More recently, author Jeffrey Krames (who, I should note, in the interest of full disclosure, is also the editor of this book) identified an "outside-in perspective" as the most important trait of the most successful modern CEOs.[2]

The primary objective of this book is to help business managers use these and related insights effectively in practice. It is to share the outside-in discipline—to provide a road map for managers to follow in creating and leading outside-in corporations, even in organizations where the unfortunate inside-out perspective has prevailed in the past.

The first chapters describe the bad news in some detail, not to dwell on the negative, but with the goal of clarifying the problem, highlighting behaviors that detract from success, and explaining why I designed the solution as I did. The majority of the book then describes and explores the solution—the outside-in discipline. It explains how to analyze customers, constructing what I call customer pictures to capture the essence of customers' needs and customer behaviors. It shows how to use those descriptions of customers to base marketplace strategies and actions firmly and explicitly on an outside-in (customer) foundation.

Throughout, the book offers action recommendations for achieving the outside-in perspective in the real business world, where managers never have nearly as much hard data about customers as they need, and where everything (including customers) keeps changing. In essence, the goal is to offer a realistic road map to outside in, helping readers in actual companies in the challenging real world of business to achieve and maintain an outside-in perspective, thereby gaining competitive advantage.

ACKNOWLEDGMENTS

Many people contributed to the learning and experiences that enabled me to develop the outside-in discipline: my students, my consulting clients, and my colleagues in academia and in business. I am grateful to them all. I have also been fortunate to teach at MIT Sloan School of Management and Harvard Business School and to work with numerous fine companies. All of these organizations helped shape my understanding.

I owe a special debt to the work of Peter Drucker. His forceful pioneering writings steered me to the outside-in perspective.

In addition, I have been particularly fortunate to have as my editor Jeffrey Krames of McGraw-Hill. He immediately understood the bad news, the good news, and the purpose of this book, and his own writings contributed the term "outside in." He and Lisa O'Connor of McGraw-Hill also provided excellent editorial advice and support.

1

THE BAD HABIT OF INSIDE-OUT THINKING
It's Unfortunately Common

*It is the customer who determines what a business is. For it is
the customer, and he alone, who through being willing to pay
for a good or service, converts economic resources into wealth,
things into goods.*
—Peter Drucker

OF COURSE BUSINESSPEOPLE UNDERSTAND that a company's
success hinges on the customers who buy the company's products and services. But sadly, in practice, few managers design and
operate their businesses with a strong customer perspective, from
the outside in. It turns out to be really hard in practice to base all
marketplace decisions firmly and clearly on insights into what
customers value and how customers behave.

Instead, many people in business have fallen into the habit of
thinking from the inside out, strongly emphasizing the capabilities, people, and processes within their companies instead of the
customers and marketplaces outside. Let's be clear: there are lots
of important things to be done within the company, and there are
lots of techniques and frameworks that can help. Six Sigma and
other quality efforts can be extremely important—provided that
they lead to the manifestations of quality desired by customers, or
allow the lower prices demanded by customers, or are driven by

some other outside reason. Internal team building can be extremely important—provided that it aims to create and foster behaviors that will be effective in the marketplace. And so on.

Sadly, choosing corporate activities, both internal and external, and carrying them out with an outside-in perspective is not the rule. Often, the perspective is inside-out instead. The bad news is that this inside-out habit is so common among businesspeople. Clearly, there's something seriously wrong here.

But there's good news, too. The outside-in discipline is an effective (though challenging) way to overcome inside-out thinking or to avoid the inside-out habit in the first place. And, if you have that discipline, you have a powerful advantage over people who don't—those who haven't been able to kick the inside-out habit.

Before we explore that antidote, however, let's look in more detail at the problem—how it manifests itself and how it gets in the way of success.

INSIDE-OUT THINKING KEEPS TURNING UP

Inside-out thinking turns up in many different companies. It is widespread in entrepreneurial situations, both in completely new organizations and in existing organizations that are pursuing new marketplace opportunities. Plans for addressing such new opportunities often fall short in their analysis and evaluation of the opportunities that the businesses are targeting.

Innovators know that customers who buy the business's products or services are the key to their companies' success. They know that they have to get the attention of prospective customers, give those customers compelling reasons to buy, convince them that they should actually make a purchase, and then deliver lots of benefits to them. Yet many business plans barely mention the customer perspective.

True, business plans generally do present estimates of market size. In fact, they often present rather precise estimates of market size, even for markets that do not yet exist or are not well defined. But they generally do not present clear, explicit analyses of the prospective customers, with consideration of those customers' needs and behavior and with clear explanations of just how the business will meet those needs and fit (or, occasionally, modify) that behavior. They do not explain clearly and convincingly why their planned actions in the marketplace fit (or will fit in the future) with customer needs and customer behavior.

The bad habit of inside-out thinking afflicts people in existing businesses, too. Senior managers in such businesses often feel that they understand their customers, since they've already sold to those customers successfully, often for many years. But those managers are unfortunately not immune to inside-out thinking. Many of them do not think through and then explain their marketplace strategies, including the details of those strategies, in strong customer terms, with all the actions based on customer needs and customer behavior. Their marketing plans or other strategy documents fail to give good, clear customer reasons for the strategies, both overall and in detail.

When senior managers emphasize inside-out thinking, one result is that their subordinates have difficulty fully understanding the organization's strategies. As a result, those subordinates have lowered abilities to execute those strategies effectively, especially when conditions in the marketplace change—as they certainly will.

The bad habit of inside-out thinking shows up even though some famous and highly successful mangers have clearly and publicly attributed their success to avoiding this type of thinking—to understanding and focusing on customers instead. But that fact is also part of the good news. The successes demonstrate that it is clearly worth while to break the inside-out habit and to replace it with something better.

OUTSIDE IN: AN ALTERNATIVE HABIT WORTH HAVING, BUT A CHALLENGE TO KEEP

Some well-known entrepreneurs escaped the contagion of inside-out thinking. Instead, they designed and operated their businesses from the outside in, starting with customers and prospective customers.

One of the big, visible entrepreneurial successes of the late twentieth century was Dell Computer, founded by Michael Dell, who was quite clear about the orientation of his business:

> From the start, our entire business—from design to manufacturing to sales—was oriented around listening to the customer, responding to the customer, and delivering what the customer wanted.[1]

There's no question about it; Dell had an outside-in orientation.

Similarly, one of the big, visible entrepreneurial successes of the early and middle twentieth century was IBM. The company built its early success in computers on providing solutions to customers' problems and on understanding those customers in depth—how they did business, how they made decisions to purchase, what they worried about. IBM's Thomas Watson had stated very clearly how he wanted IBM employees to behave in order to achieve success for IBM. He wanted them to talk about the customer's business, not about machines.[2]

Clearly, the early IBM had an outside-in orientation.

The next part of the story is a lot less positive. It turns out that maintaining an outside-in perspective is a real challenge.

Even companies that begin with a solid outside-in perspective too often lose that orientation as time passes. Managers become complacent. They figure that if they have sold to customers successfully then of course they understand those customers. But sometimes they figure wrong.

IBM lost it. By the 1990s, IBM was no longer an outside-in corporation. It had lost its way badly.

Looking back in 1996, *BusinessWeek* described the IBM of the early 1990s as "distant, arrogant, unresponsive."[3] Despite having introduced so many other corporations to computers decades earlier, IBM had lost its clear focus on the customers' business problems. Louis Gerstner, who was brought in as CEO to address the situation, said that the focus had shifted to inside the company, to a series of intramural competitions.[4]

IBM was no longer an outside-in corporation.

McDonald's lost it, too, although it had started out fine.[5] During much of the second half of the twentieth century, it grew into a large and successful business—a symbol of America. Kids grew up going to McDonald's. Families often chose McDonald's for their meals away from home. Many young males were especially frequent visitors, eating at McDonald's several times a week.

By late 2002, however, McDonald's was in serious trouble. For one thing, consumer needs had changed. Many adults felt that they had outgrown the chain. Consumers had become more health-conscious. Frequently, mothers took their kids to McDonald's because the kids liked the food and, especially, the toys they received, but the mothers didn't eat there themselves.

In addition, according to surveys of consumers, both the service and the quality at McDonald's had fallen dramatically. Ratings of customers' satisfaction with fast-food restaurants by the University of Michigan put McDonald's at the bottom.

McDonald's managers were not listening hard enough to customer complaints, and they certainly were not taking effective corrective action. The company was losing 1 to 2 percent of its customers each year.

At the end of 2002, James Cantalupo was appointed CEO of McDonald's with a clear mandate to clean up the mess. He told McDonald's home-office senior executives in his first meeting with them that the problems were clearly about McDonald's treatment of customers.

McDonald's was no longer an outside-in corporation—and that was its problem.

Now the story turns positive again. It is possible to overcome the bad habit of inside-out thinking and to replace it with outside-in. And the outside-in discipline can bring back success. When some highly talented managers got big-name companies back on track, the managers and the business press both stressed that focus on customers was the key.

Outside in brought success back at IBM.

In 1996, 3½ years after Louis Gerstner took the job of CEO at a troubled IBM, *Business Week* ran a cover story about the company under the headline "How IBM Became a Growth Company Again."[6] Revenues were climbing smartly. The stock price had come back. Other managers again cited IBM as a respected business leader.

It wasn't new moves in technology that put IBM back on track. And the company didn't buy business with drastic price cuts.

Instead, it went back to what *Business Week* called the most basic notion of how to succeed in business: "talking to customers, learning their needs, and figuring out how to satisfy them." And, the magazine added, going back to basics wasn't easy. As it quoted one expert saying, "That sounds simple, but show me companies that are really good at it. It's easy to say but hard to do."

Gertsner himself was quite clear about his philosophy for business success:

> I came here with a view that you start the day with customers, that you start thinking about a company around its customers, and you organize around customers.

And he was equally clear that his job at IBM was to implement that deceptively simple prescription for success. He believed that a big part of his job was to refocus IBM on the marketplace. He told "virtually every audience . . . that we were going to rebuild the company from the customer back."[7]

In other words, Gerstner rebuilt IBM into an outside-in corporation.

The outside-in discipline brought success back at McDonald's, too.

James Cantalupo's prescription for McDonald's was also to focus on customer needs and the customer experience.[8] In fact, he was described as being obsessed with customers. Talking about his decades of experience at McDonald's, Cantalupo recalled his policy of never leaving a McDonald's without talking with a customer.

Cantalupo insisted on measuring customer needs and the customer experience at McDonald's, and he shared the data with the managers of McDonald's restaurants so that they could use the information to improve the situation. He also shared the data with McDonald's product developers, who used it to overhaul the menu. For example, they developed salads that enticed more mothers to eat with their kids.

Results quickly began to improve. U.S. same-store sales began rising in May 2003, just six months after Cantalupo took charge. Both profits and the stock price began rising, too.

Then McDonald's hit some dreadful bumps in the road back to outside-in success. First, Cantalupo unexpectedly died of a heart attack in April 2004. But his successor, Charlie Bell, continued the outside-in focus and the recovery continued. In September 2004, for the first time in 30 years, McDonald's realized two consecutive year-to-year same-store sales gains exceeding 10 percent.

Then there was another major bump: Charlie Bell resigned to fight the cancer he had learned he had soon after taking over. By this time, however, McDonald's was functioning as an outside-in corporation again. Bell explained that the entire McDonald's system was mobilized behind a powerful strategy. In December 2004, *Advertising Age* named McDonald's its marketer of the year.[9]

The example of Tesco Plc shows that the outside-in discipline can bring success to a company whose preceding history was at best mediocre.[10] In the early 1990s, the U.K. grocery chain was losing 1 to 2 percent in market share each year. Terry Leahy, who would subsequently lead Tesco to outside-in thinking, reported a joke that a tobacco company had refused an offer to acquire Tesco, fearing that the acquisition would hurt the tobacco company's image. (I have also seen this story presented as the truth rather than a joke.)

Leahy's first step was a study to analyze the problem. He found that Tesco was known for low prices, for merchandising that simply copied that of up-market grocer Sainsbury's, and for poor customer service. He said that Tesco needed to stop copying Sainsbury's, to target its merchandising to what Tesco's own customers wanted, and to institutionalize listening to customers.

The changes at Tesco consisted not of one big move but instead of what managers called "bricks in the wall"—many incremental steps to respond to customers' needs. The company adopted the slogan "Tesco: The Natural Choice for Ordinary Shoppers," and it made numerous changes to implement that vision. In 1993 it introduced a lower-priced, basic "value" line of products as an additional private label (called an own label in the United Kingdom). After finding out how much customers disliked waiting in lines, in 1994 Tesco introduced "one in front," a policy of opening new registers if there were more than two people in checkout lines. In 1995 it introduced the Clubcard loyalty card, which gave customers a 1 percent rebate. Managers learned how much customers valued exceptionally clean restrooms and responded with another program. They increased the amounts of over-the-counter medications and health and beauty aids that the stores carried. In a joint venture with Royal Bank of Scotland, they added financial services. They kept listening, and they kept adding bricks to the wall.

In a remarkably short time, Tesco had become the leading grocery chain in the United Kingdom, known for its strong focus on customers. It expanded successfully into central Europe and Asia. It introduced a carefully designed online shopping service that both became the world's largest and also earned profits. CEO Terry Leahy's customer focus was legendary. According to the *Economist*, he did "not change as much as a light bulb without pouring over customer surveys and sales data first." A bricks-in-the-wall approach to outside in had turned a very weak company into a star.

These examples show the power of managing from the outside in. Working to achieve and maintain a habit of outside in is worth time and effort. Respected business experts have been talking about the power of focusing strongly on customers, too.

DRUCKER TAUGHT OUTSIDE IN LONG AGO

As long ago as 1954, Peter Drucker was crystal clear about the critical central role of the customer in business success. In *The Practice of Management*, he wrote:

> If we want to know what a business is we have to start with its *purpose*. . . . There is only one valid definition of business purpose: *to create a customer*.[11]

As Drucker said in the quotation that started this chapter, it is customers and their willingness to pay for a product or service that determine what a business is—and whether the business will succeed. Drucker also provided a clear description of the outside-in perspective. He gave a very broad definition of the role of marketing, a definition that has been adopted in this book. Drucker described marketing as the unique, distinguishing function of a business. In fact, he said, marketing encompasses the entire business:

> It is the whole business seen from the point of view of its final result, that is, from the customer's point of view.[12]

In other words, in Drucker's broad definition, marketing is the outside-in view of the business. Drucker added that, according to this definition, both concern and responsibility for marketing must permeate every part of the business.

Thus, in 1954 Drucker made it very clear that the customer is the foundation of a business and that concern and responsibility for marketing (the customer's point of view) must permeate the entire organization. We should all create (and demand) outside-in strategies.

Others followed Drucker. For example, in 1960, Theodore

Levitt published his famous article "Marketing Myopia," which he subsequently described as a manifesto communicating the thinking of Drucker and others.[13]

Famously, one of the examples that Levitt used was the buggy-whip industry. He described that industry as being so fixated on its product that it missed the signs that the product was becoming obsolete. How much better it would have been, he argued, if the companies in the buggy-whip business had looked for other customer needs in the changing transportation marketplace that they could meet profitably.

Levitt went on to say that an industry is a customer-satisfying process, not a goods-producing process. He said that an industry should begin with customers and their needs and then develop backward to the products for those customers. In other words, he argued that industries (and the businesses within them) should work from the outside in.

Despite these clear statements from Drucker, Levitt, and others many decades ago, applying these insights effectively and consistently in the real, complex business world has proved remarkably hard. Falling into a bad inside-out habit has been easy; breaking that habit has not.

An excellent old article by Charles Ames shows that the problem was already quite clear in 1970. Focusing on companies that sold business-to-business, Ames looked at the problems of implementing the marketing concept (what I call the outside-in viewpoint).[14]

Ames argued that by 1970 most executives said that they believed that the marketing concept (the idea of organizing and running a business to be responsive to customer needs) was the only sensible way to go. However, the actions of those executives showed that there was something missing in their understanding of the concept, their ability to implement it, or perhaps both.

In fact, Ames found that many of the executives he surveyed knew that there was a problem. They were disappointed with the results of their marketing efforts.

The president of one business told Ames that he had been spending money and his sales and administrative costs were up. Business results hadn't improved, however, and he didn't believe his organization was operating any differently from the way it had operated before he and his managers had started talking about marketing.

Another corporate president described his company's marketing effort as a total waste. He said all he had gotten so far was an expensive marketing staff with harebrained ideas about advertising and promotion. His organization had executed an expensive campaign of print advertising, but sales hadn't increased at all. The president wondered whether his customers even read the magazines on which his marketing staff had spent so much money.

Ames went on to argue that marketing is a general-management function, a total business philosophy. It starts with customer needs and then creates product and service offerings that meet the needs of selected customer groups more effectively than do competitive offerings.

In other words, Ames argued that an outside-in orientation throughout the corporation was the basis for competitive success. Over the decades, business publications have periodically rediscovered this importance of the customer. With each rediscovery, they have carried articles about the need for more customer orientation in business. Often, they have claimed that practices had changed and that businesses had in fact become customer-oriented. They have given examples of managers who succeeded because they ran their organizations from an outside-in perspective. A few years later, however, the same publications would again lament the lack of widespread customer orientation and again report that practices were changing.

There is lots of evidence that achieving and maintaining an outside-in perspective is a serious challenge in practice. There is evidence of this difficulty in marketing and business plans. Many business managers and investment professionals have agreed with me that inside-out is a bad habit and that an ongoing outside-in perspective would be a big plus for business plans and for businesses.

Interviews with business innovators about their approaches to their markets and customers provided more evidence. For the most part, the interview subjects told me a great deal about their products and very little about their customers. They talked considerably more about their products and the technologies incorporated in those products than about the customer problems or interests that the products addressed. I heard almost no customer insights that went beyond product—almost nothing, for example, about how customers evaluated and bought such products.

Others have made similar observations. In 1991, in describing over 25 years of research in entrepreneurship, Edward Roberts reported that only a small minority of the business plans from high-technology start-ups that he examined presented clear arguments about why customers would in fact buy from the company. Instead, the plans emphasized products and technologies, along with the backgrounds of the founders.[15]

OUTSIDE IN: POWERFUL ANSWER TO HARMFUL PROBLEMS

For one thing, the stubborn persistence of the problem makes it clear that solving it is not easy. If it were, intelligent, energetic businesspeople would have solved it long ago. Businesspeople know, at some level, that customers are the foundation of business success. If they knew how to make customers the foundation in practice for both their strategies and their actions, surely they would have done so.

The solution is nevertheless powerful and important. The examples given earlier in this chapter of successful customer-focused start-ups and successful customer-focused turnarounds give some idea of the power of constructing and running a truly outside-in corporation.

As noted at the outset, the basic objective of this book is to present and explain the outside-in discipline, a way of basing strategies and actions in the marketplace firmly on a foundation of thinking about and understanding customers. This outside-in discipline leads to substantially better marketplace strategies with improved probabilities of success. It leads to competitive advantage. It leads to strategies that adapt and succeed over time.

The fundamental idea is to create and communicate clear, explicit analyses of the customers or prospective customers, considering customers' needs and behavior and providing clear explanations of just how the businesses will meet those needs and fit (or alter) that behavior.

In practice, of course, it's impossible to know as much about customers as we would like. To be useful, the outside-in discipline must be effective despite that challenging reality.

The idea is to create and communicate strategies that rest firmly on a foundation of understanding of customers—and to do so under normal business conditions, in which businesspeople seem never to have nearly as much information about customers and markets as they want.

The remainder of this book presents, explains, and explores the outside-in discipline. First, however, especially because in practice that discipline is not easy, and because customer focus has been a challenge for so long, this chapter takes a big-picture look at the results of the overall, basic problem: insufficient outside-in thinking and action.

The following short list of these unfortunate results came from interviews with senior managers in existing businesses and with innovators in new ones. In those interviews, the questions that turned out to be most useful concerned problems. I asked in general about problems related to customers and markets that the respondents had faced. I also asked them to imagine that they could go back and change or improve the actions they had taken. What did they most wish they had done differently?

On analysis, the responses seemed to fall into three broad categories, which I've called "inadequately articulated strategies," "inadequate communication," and "inappropriate time frame."

OUTSIDE IN TO FIGHT UNCLEAR STRATEGIES

With inadequately articulated strategies, business managers and entrepreneurs made unnecessary mistakes. The managers described mistakes that, in retrospect, they thought could reasonably easily have been avoided. Missteps are inevitable in the marketplace, but it surely makes sense to avoid making more mistakes than necessary.

Sometimes the managers or entrepreneurs themselves had simply not thought carefully enough about how their strategies and actions fit (or did not fit) with whatever they knew about customer needs and customer behavior.

Even more often, though, they had failed to get input from other people who had information and insights that would have allowed the businesses to avoid the mistakes. Some respondents said that others in their organization or other people they knew had information that would have allowed them to avoid the mistakes. The managers or entrepreneurs had not received that information when they needed it, however, and had made the mistakes.

Probing these situations uncovered the fundamental problem: the respondents didn't articulate their thinking and their assumptions. They didn't explain enough to allow others to help them improve their strategies and avoid the avoidable mistakes.

These examples showed the importance of making strategic thinking explicit so that the strategic thinker could think carefully and thoroughly. Even more important, explicitness allowed others to help shape and improve the strategies. I concluded that one impact of the lack of outside-in thinking and management was that marketplace strategies were weaker than they could have been with more thought and more input and that, therefore, their probabilities of success were lower.

Inadequately articulated strategies created additional problems because they were hard to improve over time. Smart innovators in particular and businesspeople in general update their strategies over time. They learn more about customers, competitors, and other important factors, and they should surely use their increased knowledge to update and improve their strategies.

In addition, business conditions (including customers and competitors) change over time, and good strategies evolve (or sometimes change radically) as conditions change. As Michael Dell has said:

> Being in touch with customer needs is . . . always important. But perhaps even more important when needs are changing. . . . [16]

If my respondents had not forced themselves to make their initial assumptions and strategies explicit, they found changes in their marketplaces (or in their understanding of those market-places) unnecessarily difficult to recognize. As a result, they were far less agile than they might have been at adapting their strategies over time.

OUTSIDE IN TO FIGHT INADEQUATE COMMUNICATION

The second major group of problems fell into the category "inad-equate communication." These problems involved communica-tion between the managers or entrepreneurs and their own organizations.

Here's an example. One entrepreneur's company sold its prod-uct through a variety of distribution channels, including catalogs. In the middle of the interview, the entrepreneur pulled out sev-eral catalogs and remarked that one did a very poor job of pre-senting the product.

Then, in response to a series of questions, the entrepreneur ex-plained that it was critically important for the pictures of the product in catalogs to demonstrate the key product benefits clearly. He complained about the difficulty of hiring really good salespeople; he found that his salespeople did not see to it that the catalog pictures were satisfactory. As a result, he felt he had to do too much of the sales job himself.

More probing demonstrated that the entrepreneur was himself quite clear about what he thought it would take to get customers' attention, what would influence their evaluations of his product, and what was the role of a catalog picture. He had not, however, communicated that understanding clearly and in depth to his salespeople. To be sure, he had an awful lot of things to worry about and attend to, so it's easy to see why some tasks would slip. At the same time, the lack of communication about the role of catalog pictures had led to a weaker than necessary performance by the salespeople.

There were similar problems in many situations. Managers and especially innovators complained about not being able to delegate enough, but their inadequate communication was fundamental to their problems. Probing very often established that those respondents had not explained enough of their thinking. Their subordinates did not understand the basic principles and assumptions underlying the business approach well enough to be able to adapt them intelligently to different circumstances.

An experiment that I tried in several rooms full of entrepreneurs (50 or more founders of businesses in each case) highlights the problem of inadequate communication. I asked each entrepreneur to imagine that I was visiting his or her company and speaking with a wide range of employees, as many different types of employees as the company had. In each imaginary conversation, I would ask the employee to tell me briefly who were the company's customers, what it was that the company did for those customers, and, very briefly, how.

My question for the entrepreneurs was: "In your company, would I get answers to my questions that were consistent from one employee to another? I know that I wouldn't get nearly the level of detail and depth from the receptionist that I would get from the head of the business, but would the answers be consistent? Would I be able to tell that you were all talking about the same opportunity and the same overall strategy for attracting and serving customers?"

Each experiment elicited embarrassed laughs from the entrepreneurs, who then began discussing with one another just how inconsistent the results would be in their companies. By and large, the entrepreneurs predicted that I would definitely not get consistent answers to my questions.

Next, I asked if they felt able to delegate as much as they

should or would like to be able to delegate; the great majority said they definitely did not believe they could. I then asked if there might be a strong connection between the lack of consistent understanding and the problems with delegation. Again, the response was a somewhat embarrassed yes.

Inadequate communication is widespread. It happens in part because we're all so busy. It happens because we don't have a good outside-in habit. It shows up in both new businesses and long-established ones.

As my experiment emphasizes, innovators often do not communicate their strategies and translate their visions into terms that others can understand. The results are poor implementation and unnecessarily overworked innovators.

In established businesses, the same basic problem looks a bit different. Frequently, it shows up as unstated assumptions about customers, marketplaces, and strategies.

New employees in such businesses find it extremely difficult to figure out what's going on—why the business operates the way it does. They therefore find it unnecessarily difficult to become effective employees, implementing the strategy well.

Moreover, in such a business, even long-time employees often turn out to have subtly or even fundamentally different ideas about customers and the marketplace. It's therefore unnecessarily hard for them to implement the strategy well together and to recognize what actions do and do not fit with the strategy.

OUTSIDE IN TO FIGHT POOR PREPARATION FOR THE FUTURE

The third major group of problems falls into the category "inappropriate time frame." These problems lead managers to prepare inadequately for the future.

The interviews highlighted the importance of spending a little time looking further into the future in order to make some future marketplace actions much easier or even, in some cases, to make them possible. The decisions that require such advance thinking are, of course, the ones that can take a long time to implement. One example is positioning and branding. Another is channels of distribution.

Looking into the future in this way is especially challenging for entrepreneurs, who must devote much of their attention to immediate concerns—getting the technology to work, finding customers, and so on. It can also be challenging for managers in existing businesses.

The challenge is to think clearly and explicitly enough about customers and the marketplace to be able to select action areas that will be especially important in the future. It then requires spending a bit of time on areas that have especially long lead times.

One example came from a software company. The founder described the struggle to gain market acceptance for his initial product. That struggle had ended successfully, and the product was established.

Unfortunately, however, he had been so consumed with gaining credibility and selling the initial product that he had not thought about whether customers would find it credible for the company to offer other products. He had worked extremely hard to position the company as competent in the area of the original product.

Later, he was ready to apply the company's technology to somewhat different products that would be purchased by the same customers. Those customers, however, had come to identify the company strongly with the original product; they did not consider the company to be a credible player in a different area.

The founder noted, with considerable regret, that the transition to a new type of product would have been much easier if he had spent a little effort positioning the company so that customers would be prepared for the change.

BENEFITS OF THE OUTSIDE-IN DISCIPLINE

Let's look at the flip side of these problems and consider the benefits of creating and managing a corporation from the outside in. The outside-in discipline provides benefits in designing good strategies, in implementing them, and in adapting them over time. While the remainder of the book will explore the approach and the benefits in more detail, we can at least construct an initial general list:

- The outside-in discipline increases the probability of success for a business strategy. It can't guarantee success, and it certainly will not make a poor idea successful, but it can help increase the probability of success by improving more promising ideas.
- The approach helps managers communicate their strategies, translating their visions into terms that others can understand and help implement.
- It also provides a sound basis for responding to changes in the marketplace and in the company's understanding of the marketplace. Such changes, especially in understanding, will inevitably occur. An explicit outside-in explanation of past decisions provides the basis for incorporating new information and adjusting actions appropriately. Absent such an explicit foundation, it is almost impossible to reconstruct the logic of past actions accurately, and therefore it is unnecessarily difficult to respond well to new information and to changes.
- Finally, it helps managers to prepare adequately for the future, doing enough thinking about future strategy that even

time-starved innovators can sensibly spend a bit of time on areas with especially long lead times.

SUMMARY

Too many businesspeople have fallen into the bad habit of inside-out thinking. That bad habit leads to serious problems: inadequately articulated strategies, inadequate communication, and an inappropriate time frame. The results are lowered probabilities of success in the marketplace because of weaker-than-necessary strategies, difficulties in implementing marketplace strategies, and poor preparation for the future.

That's the bad news. The good news is the outside-in discipline, a way to overcome or avoid the habit of inside-out thinking.

The outside-in discipline increases the probability of success in the marketplace. It improves communication and facilitates effective implementation. It provides a sound basis for identifying and implementing needed changes and for preparing for the future.

The outside-in perspective has been the foundation for the success of some outstanding entrepreneurs. It has been the basis for some famous business turnarounds. And we've heard about it from business experts, starting with Peter Drucker.

The outside-in discipline is not easy. It takes effort to learn, and it's discouragingly easy to lose. But the benefits are large enough that it is worth the effort to acquire and to keep the good outside-in habit. The purpose of this book is to explain, explore, and share the outside-in approach.

OUTSIDE-IN ACTIONS

Even now, before the following chapters' more complete discussion, this introduction allows some actions for becoming more comfortable with an outside-in approach:

1. **Practice outside-in thinking by analyzing products and services that your organization purchases.**
    Describe what you and your colleagues need from each product or service. Explain how you go about evaluating possible purchases and then deciding to buy. Describe how well your supplier does or does not meet your needs and your processes. And (an especially useful topic) identify places where the supplier falls short. Try to think of actions by the supplier that would be a better match with your needs and processes.

2. **Practice by analyzing your own and your family's purchases, too.**
    Identify products and services that you buy, especially ones that are problematic because you're not happy with the product, or you dislike the process of buying it, or you have some other serious complaint. Describe what you or your family needs from the product. Explain how you would like the product to be sold. Identify points where the seller falls short. Try to think of things the supplier could sensibly do that would be a better match with your needs and your behavior.

3. **Practice the outside-in perspective in the other direction, going from strategies and actions to the specific assumptions about customer needs and customer behavior that would make those strategies and actions sensible.**
    Consider both examples of marketing to organizations and examples of marketing to end consumers. In each example, notice as much as you can about the seller's marketing strategy: the characteristics of the product, how and where the product is sold, how the seller communicates with its customers, the billing procedures, and so on. Ask what assumptions about customer needs and behavior would make those actions sensible. Look for any assumptions on your list that seem incorrect to

you. And see if you can find some other assumptions about customers that seem to you to be correct but that conflict with the strategies and actions.

4. Begin to get colleagues, including subordinates, to articulate their thoughts about and understanding of customers.

Ask a wide variety of people in your organization what they think customers need and how they think customers buy and use your products or services. Ask them to tell you about the customers they've encountered who seemed the best served and the happiest with your company and about the customers who, in their experience, were the unhappiest. Try to identify just what it was that your organization did to match the needs and behavior of the first type of customer so well and what it failed to do for the second type. Listen rather than talk. Notice especially the inconsistencies and gaps that show up in the responses you get.

5. Begin making a list of people who can serve as good sounding boards for your outside-in thinking.

Include, but do not limit yourself to, people who have special knowledge of your customers and markets or of other customers and markets that might provide interesting comparisons with yours.

2

THE OUTSIDE-IN DISCIPLINE
A New Discipline—For a New Habit

What is our business is not determined by the producer but by the consumer. . . . The question can therefore be answered only by looking at the business from the outside, from the point of view of the consumer and the market.
—Peter Drucker

SURELY, AS THE PREVIOUS chapter said at the outset, success in the marketplace comes from customers who purchase your product or service. More specifically, marketplace success for a business requires a set of elements and events:

- There must be some customers or prospective customers.
- Those customers or prospects must have certain needs.
- Your offering must satisfy those needs sufficiently well.
- The customers must decide to do something about their needs (rather than continue to live with the current situation).
- They must select your offering from among whatever alternative solutions they perceive.
- They must pay enough so that your business is adequately profitable.

In other words, customers must have a need, must become aware that they could do something to address that need, must do whatever they consider appropriate to learn about and evaluate alternatives, must decide that they should in fact make a purchase, must select your offering, and must pay you. (Then there are the additional steps in which the customer actually uses your product.)

Thus, customer behavior is rather complex, involving numerous steps. Even so, these statements generalizing customer behavior seem straightforward, even rather obvious. People basically know that success requires these elements.

But unfortunately, as discussed in the previous chapter, achieving and maintaining a customer perspective turns out to be really hard in practice. The bad inside-out habit is all around us. In designing, organizing, and running a business, it's difficult to keep the focus firmly on these elements of success.

The main purpose of this chapter is to introduce the *outside-in discipline*, the way to break the bad inside-out habit or to avoid it in the first place. First, however, let's spend a bit more time looking at inside-out. There are two reasons for doing so. I want to explain my theory as to why inside-out is so common and why outside in is so difficult. In addition, I want to provide some insights into why I designed the outside-in discipline (and this book) as I did.

THE MANY FACES OF INSIDE OUT

Inside-out thinking and action show up in many different places and in many different guises. Let's start with GE, certainly one of the most successful and respected companies in the world. Jack Welch, GE's former chairman, was one of the most successful and respected CEOs in business history.

One hallmark of Welch's tenure as CEO was a series of big, important initiatives, or revolutions, at GE. First, Welch adopted a requirement that each GE business attain a number-one or number-two position in its market—or, alternatively, that the business be divested. He pushed hard to make the company more efficient. Later, Welch focused on quality, with major Six Sigma efforts. He greatly increased GE's emphasis on the services that could accompany its products. He pushed to incorporate modern information technology, including personal computers and the Internet, effectively throughout GE's processes.

Relatively late in his tenure, Welch focused on turning GE into an outside-in corporation. For over a hundred years, he commented, the company had been inside-out. Forcing the entire company around to the outside-in view would be a dramatic move; in Welch's words, it would "change the game."[1]

Jeffrey Immelt, who succeeded Welch as CEO of GE in September 2001, continued to emphasize outside in. For example, he required all GE employees to report upward in the organization just what they had done for customers lately. Immelt's first three-plus years on the job received highly favorable reviews. *BusinessWeek* began its list of the best managers of 2004 with Immelt, citing his two key accomplishments as repositioning GE's portfolio of businesses and creating a more diverse, global, and customer-driven culture.[2]

In 2005, explaining his vision of how to keep GE successful in times of slowed growth, Immelt spoke of being more focused on customers and of the importance of having a unique value proposition for customers. "You focus on solving customer problems," using technology and innovation in the global marketplace, he said.[3]

Welch and Immelt are clearly outstanding managers. Furthermore, GE has had many other extremely able and highly respected managers throughout its organization. Why then, we should wonder, did it take GE over 100 years to get to outside in? And why did it take Welch well into his second decade as CEO to decide that outside in changes the game?

Mind you, we can be happy for GE's sake that Welch reached the views about customers that he did. It's just that there is important information in the fact that even for such an outstanding manager, it took as long as it did.

Inside-out thinking shows up in many other places, too. As mentioned in the preceding chapter, I reviewed business and marketing plans and related strategy documents for existing businesses as well as plans for addressing new marketplace opportunities. I reviewed existing courses on marketing strategy and on entrepreneurship, to see what MBA students were being taught.

Plans for existing businesses, for the most part, did not contain thorough, in-depth discussions of customers. There were some exceptions, especially in the marketing-oriented world of consumer packaged goods, but these were clearly exceptions. Most of the plans lacked in-depth consideration of customer needs, of whether customers were actively looking to satisfy those needs, and of how customers would perceive benefits. They did not say how much customers knew and didn't know. They didn't explain the processes that customers would go through to evaluate and buy. They didn't consider the conversion costs customers might experience in adopting new products or processes. They didn't describe the types of communication customers needed if they were to evaluate, buy, and use the products. They didn't say where and how customers obtained needed information.

Frequently the plans did include market segmentations, generally using variables such as industry or company size in business-to-business situations and variables such as income or age for business-to-consumer ones. Usually, however, the plans did not present strong practical implications of these segmentations, such as differences in how customers would view benefits, differences in the conversion costs they would incur, and so on. I often wondered if different, less obvious segmentations wouldn't have provided more useful insights into customers.

In plans for addressing newer opportunities, there were often discussions of market size, arguments that a target market was large and/or growing rapidly. What was generally missing was a more careful look at the customers in that market—why they would care about the new product or service, what would motivate them to buy it, how they would go about buying it, and so on. There were glowing discussions of technology, descriptions of the previous experience of the innovators, and lots and lots of pro forma numbers. There were often discussions of competition, covering the technical and financial capabilities of other companies, but the discussions did not discuss how well the competitors did or did not appeal to customers.

Courses in business schools didn't focus from the outside in, either. They might emphasize concepts from business strategy (such as portfolio analysis or industry analysis), questions about financing new ventures, and related issues. None of the courses focused primarily on the identification and exploration of business opportunities, using the detailed analysis of potential customers as the key to understanding and then exploiting such opportunities. None made an outside-in approach the center of business.

People who write business and marketing plans are bright, highly committed, and experienced in the business world. They know that business success requires customers. Similarly, other people who evaluate business and marketing plans are also bright, committed, and experienced. Top managers, investors, and others know that customers are essential.

So, the questions about Welch and outside in become broader and more troubling. Why is it so easy to fall into the inside-out habit? Why is outside in so tough to achieve and maintain? This litany of the many faces of inside out does make it clear that inside out is widespread and outside in is really hard. That is the bad news.

But the bad news led me to opportunity. If I could understand the bad news well enough, perhaps I could figure out what was needed to help businesspeople break the inside-out habit or, even better, to avoid it altogether—a way to achieve outside-in and get a leg up in the marketplace.

NEEDED: A NEW DISCIPLINE AND A NEW HABIT

Here is my strong hypothesis about why the bad inside-out habit is so common and why outside-in is so difficult to achieve: First, businesspeople lack a clear discipline for creating and executing sound, explicit customer-based strategies. Second, they lack the habit of using such a discipline.

The idea of lack of discipline is relatively straightforward. It arises because businesspeople recognize that they don't know enough about customers. They know that they should consider customers carefully, thinking about the variety of issues that are missing from so many business and marketing plans. Who will the customers be? How will customers perceive benefits? How do customers go about deciding whether and what to buy? And so on.

Although businesspeople know that those questions are crucial, when they try to take an outside-in viewpoint, it turns out that they do not know nearly as much about their customers as they need to know. The problem is especially acute if a businessperson wants to develop products that are very different from what customers have experienced before.

In practice, there seemed to be two different variants of this problem. In some cases, businesspeople tried hard to take an outside-in perspective, to base their strategies and actions firmly on customers. However, they quickly realized that they didn't know enough about customers. Many tried, often very hard, to learn more. They found they couldn't learn nearly enough.

In other cases, businesspeople didn't focus as clearly on their lack of knowledge about customers. In the course of selecting and developing their strategies, they did gather whatever customer information they had. Having done so, many of them simply went on to the numerous other issues that required their attention, without expressly recognizing and confronting the paucity of their information about customers. It was as if they looked at the customer information, put a check mark next to that activity on their to-do list, and went on to the next item.

Regardless of which pattern occurs, the answer to this problem is *not* "just recognize your lack of knowledge and find out all you need to know about customers." Doing so is generally not possible. Customers often are not able to articulate their needs or to predict how they will go about evaluating and buying a product. Often, customers' predictions about what products they will buy and how they will buy them are not accurate. Often, customers aren't aware of or can't report accurately what communication sources they use and believe. Prospective customers for new or substantially changed products are particularly unlikely to realize that they will be customers. And so on.

This inability to learn enough is clearly the source of a good part of the difficulty with outside in. It's not possible to learn as much as you want (and need) to know about your customers, but you're still supposed to base your strategy and actions on those customers. It is (and should be) uncomfortable to base your entire marketplace strategy on something (customers) you don't know nearly enough about. It seems dangerous, even irresponsible. It seems so much more comfortable to focus on something else—like details of production, or a Six Sigma campaign, or any of a number of other things—about which you feel much less ignorant and perhaps even highly knowledgeable.

It's not at all surprising that businesspeople don't know quite how to base their strategies and their specific actions firmly on customers, given that they (accurately) believe that their detailed knowledge of customers is inadequate. Any effective alternative to the bad habit of inside-out has to work despite this reality of limited customer information. It has to provide a clear approach, a discipline for managing from the outside in within the constraints of the real world.

The second part of my hypothesis, concerning lack of habit, requires explanation. The basic idea is that repetition makes the discipline of outside-in thinking less uncomfortable. Because there is never enough customer information, doing solid outside-in thinking is not a comfortable process, even though I firmly believe that it is nevertheless a worthwhile process, one that substantially improves the chances of business success. The idea is to reduce the level of discomfort.

My experience with large numbers of my students (graduate students, average age about 29, each with several years of business experience) has convinced me that one can become relatively less uncomfortable with the outside-in process by using it enough to have it feel familiar—in other words, by making it almost a habit. In my courses, I was in a position to require my students to write numerous papers and to use the outside-in discipline repeatedly. After they had finished graduate school and resumed working in business, many of them told me that they almost automatically used the outside-in perspective. Their comments convinced me that the required repetition was a good idea and that, difficult as it is at first, explicit outside-in thinking can become a habit. And I firmly believe that it is good to develop such a habit.

The typical reader of this book will have substantially more real-world experience than those graduate students. (And I obviously can't require readers to write numerous papers using the outside-in discipline.) Even so, the students' experience in developing good outside-in habits is instructive. I strongly encourage readers to find appropriate ways to develop the habit of using the outside-in discipline, by thinking about the examples in this book and especially by carrying out the outside-in actions included at the end of each chapter to apply the discipline to their own businesses.

At this point, readers will find these arguments about the discomfort of explicit outside-in thinking easier or more difficult to understand depending on their individual experiences. Let's leave the topic for now, in the expectation that it will become more clear as the remainder of the book describes and then explores the outside-in approach.

THE ESSENCE OF THE OUTSIDE-IN DISCIPLINE

In essence, the outside-in discipline requires that you have an explicit customer-based reason for everything you do in the marketplace. True, you won't know nearly enough about customers, so your customer-based reasons may seem to be a distinctly shaky foundation. The discipline requires that you provide those explicit customer reasons anyway.

The discipline says that you should acknowledge your insufficient understanding of customers but you should still press ahead. The idea is to do the best you can—and to continue to do better and better over time. You start by wringing every bit of understanding you can from whatever information is available—from any hard data, from your experiences with customers and prospects, and from the experiences of others.

The discipline requires that you use your intuition explicitly, too. Because your solid customer information is usually badly insufficient, you supplement that firm information with hypotheses, intuition, and informed guesses. Combining these sources, you provide enough of a customer foundation to provide a reason for everything you do in the marketplace.

Doesn't this process mean that you are basing your strategy and actions on a highly shaky foundation of customer data, hypotheses, intuition, and guesses? Aren't there apt to be many erroneous assumptions in that foundation?

The answer to these uncomfortable questions is a resounding yes. My argument is that you are nevertheless better off—much better off—if you construct and use such a customer foundation.

For one thing, it's important to recognize that failing to make the assumptions underlying your actions explicit does *not* mean there are no shaky assumptions among them. Let's say you avoid building an explicit, shaky customer foundation and instead select and implement a strategy and a set of actions in the marketplace. Even though you haven't articulated customer assumptions, your strategy and actions will be consistent with some possible sets of (unstated) assumptions about your customers and inconsistent with other sets.

Deciding not to state your customer assumptions doesn't mean that your actions are assumption-free. It simply means that the assumptions are not visible; neither the assumptions that support your choices nor the ones that don't are visible.

The worst problem with this situation is that the assumptions cannot be examined and improved. It's difficult to analyze and correct them yourself. You can't run them by other people who might be able to help you improve or correct them.

In addition, even (or, actually, especially) when you start out with a really shaky customer foundation, you will quickly gain useful experience in the marketplace as you explore and eventually execute strategies and actions. Making your initial shaky assumptions explicit puts you in a much better position to recognize how new information does or does not fit with those initial assumptions. It therefore helps you to update and improve those assumptions over time and then to update and improve your strategy and actions accordingly.

This discussion should make it obvious that the outside-in discipline is not comfortable. After all, who wants to make explicit, and then continually confront, his or her lack of adequate knowledge, especially the lack of adequate knowledge about something as fundamentally important as customers?

The discipline is nevertheless important and worth while because, as the previous chapter discussed, it provides substantial benefits. It helps improve strategies and therefore increases the probabilities of success. It helps businesspeople communicate their strategies clearly enough for others to implement. It provides a sound basis for responding to changes in the marketplace and in a company's understanding of the marketplace. It helps businesspeople prepare adequately for the future. As Jack Welch said, the outside-in viewpoint changes the game. It makes customers the basis of the business in practice, not just in theory.

In a funny way, the difficulty and discomfort of outside in are almost good news because they create an opportunity. Many people find it difficult to achieve and maintain the outside-in perspective. Given that outside in provides all these benefits, you gain an advantage in the marketplace if you manage to make the outside-in discipline a habit while others fail to do so.

KEYS TO THE OUTSIDE-IN DISCIPLINE: CUSTOMERS, RIGOR, AND OPPORTUNITY

Thus, customers are the basis of the outside-in approach presented in this book, as they are the basis of business success. The key strategic questions concern customers (including prospective customers): Who are they, or who will they be? What are their needs? How will they buy? Most important, *why* will they buy? And so on.

The outside-in discipline requires you to have an explicit customer-based reason for everything you do in the marketplace. The first step is to organize your knowledge, hypotheses, and intuition regarding customers. You need to combine whatever hard data you have with your own insights, assumptions, and hypotheses and to construct descriptions of customers, which I call *customer pictures*.

The discipline calls for customer pictures, not lists. Lists don't make clear which aspects of customers' needs and behaviors are especially important. They don't make customers come alive. They are harder to understand, and they don't communicate well. Instead, as later chapters will explore at length, the outside-in discipline uses verbal descriptions that convey the essence of what matters about customers, descriptions that come alive. The idea is to use words to "paint" vivid pictures of customers.

The second fundamental concept for the outside-in discipline is *rigor*, the idea that sound strategic thinking should move logically and explicitly from analysis of the customer, based on a combination of data, intuition, and explicit assumptions, to practical, explicit actions in the marketplace.

The goal is to have each important part of your strategy follow logically from explicit statements in your customer pictures. When you say what capabilities you will build into your product, a careful listener should say, "Of course," because you have already explained enough about customers and their needs for the listener to see immediately how your proposed capabilities fit with those needs. When you describe how you plan to get the attention of prospective customers, the careful listener should say, "Of course," because you have already described how and where those prospects get their information, what sources they believe, and when they are receptive to new information. And so on.

The logic should be clear. If you have made your customer pictures clear enough, then when you reach each of your recommended actions, the response should be, "Of course."

As noted earlier and as the following chapters will demonstrate further, being explicit about the logic is what makes this approach so uncomfortable. However, being explicit is also what makes the discipline work. Businesspeople will always have to make decisions based on limited and sometimes incorrect understanding. The best way to deal with this situation is to address it directly, making your logic explicit and reviewing and revising it over time.

Before ending, this chapter highlights one more key concept for successful strategies in the marketplace. (Later chapters will introduce three more key concepts.) Success involves *opportunity*, a topic mentioned in the first section of the chapter. Marketplace opportunity begins with customers. Opportunities depend on customers' needs and on the choices the customers will make.

An opportunity may exist when there are problems with the current business approaches to satisfying those customer needs. First, of course, there could currently simply not be any way of addressing the needs. Alternatively, the current approaches might not satisfy the customers' current or future needs as well as they could. The products themselves might not match the needs. Or perhaps the products are sold in a way that customers find inconvenient or otherwise unsatisfactory. Customers may not receive the information and support they need to select and use the products effectively. Or, the current approaches could be awkward or even unprofitable for the companies employing them.

Thus, the whole key is first to describe customers and their needs. If there are existing products addressing those needs, the next step is to evaluate how well those products (and the strategies with which they are marketed) do or do not match customer needs and customer behavior. Then the task is to find feasible, profitable ways to minimize or eliminate the compromises or problems in any current approaches. Alternatively, the job is to find feasible, profitable ways to match customer needs and behavior that have not previously been addressed.

How can you accomplish these tasks of evaluating current and new approaches to satisfying customers' needs? With the outside-in discipline—customer pictures, rigorous analysis of how existing approaches do or do not fit with those pictures, and design of potential new approaches that do fit.

OVERVIEW OF THIS BOOK

The purpose of the remainder of this book is to explain and illustrate the outside-in approach to marketplace strategy. Actually, there are two joined objectives. One is to explain and illustrate. The second is to help overcome the discomfort that the discipline creates.

The following chapter continues to explore the reasons that outside-in thinking and action can be awfully frustrating. It describes common customer behaviors that prove especially frustrating for businesspeople. Because understanding customers has proven so difficult in the past, it is appropriate to confront and acknowledge the problems head-on and then to continue despite them. The chapter also revisits the concepts of customers and rigor, using examples to illustrate their application in spite of the frustration.

Chapters 4 and 5 focus on customer pictures. Chapter 4 explores customers' needs, emphasizing the aspects of customer pictures that are most directly related to product characteristics and capabilities.

Chapter 5 considers more complete (and more useful) customer pictures, expanding them to include more about customers' buying processes and their communication habits and choices.

Chapters 6 through 10 discuss outside-in strategies. Chapter 6 provides an overall discussion, with examples of outside-in statements of strategy. The following four chapters then consider the standard marketing topics of product, price, communication, and distribution. They definitely do not attempt complete discussions of those topics. Instead, they treat aspects of each topic that are especially important to the outside-in discipline and that often prove challenging in practice.

These middle chapters also have a second purpose. They offer readers more exposure to the outside-in discipline to try to help them overcome the natural discomfort with the explicitness of the approach sufficiently well to be able to use it effectively. In other words, they are intended to help readers build an outside-in habit.

Chapter 11 focuses on research about customers—learning more about customers as the basis for customer-based strategy. I have purposely left that topic until later in the book, in part as a signal that it is essentially never possible to learn nearly as much about customers as you would like to learn. At the same time, it is wise to work to increase your understanding of customers, and research in the marketplace can help. The objective of the chapter is not to provide a complete discussion of market research but rather to discuss selected topics that are most relevant to the approach presented in this book.

Chapter 12 considers topics that are of particular importance early in innovative ventures. It discusses the selection of initial target markets and initial customers within those markets. It treats questions of selecting and working with partner organizations.

Chapter 13 describes the outside-in corporation. It summarizes the book, with suggestions for the successful implementation of outside-in strategies. It emphasizes the ongoing use of customer-based thinking, with additional customer understanding being used to execute, update, and, sometimes, substantially modify marketplace strategy.

Throughout the book, I have tried to select examples that illustrate particular points as clearly and simply as possible. In using examples from my own experiences with companies, I have included company names only when I am using publicly available information.

Because innovators generally have especially scanty customer data, many examples involve marketplace innovations. My goal in using these examples is to demonstrate the application of the outside-in discipline even in such challenging circumstances.

Other examples concern established companies and strategies, especially when the products and situations are widely familiar and therefore easy to explain concisely. There is a deliberate mix of high-tech and lower-tech examples and of businesses that sell to end consumers and businesses that sell to other organizations.

The examples are also deliberately scattered over the past 60 years of business practice. The idea was to include some older examples, where we know a lot about the subsequent history, and also some current examples, where we do not.

I have tried to state principles as generally as possible and then have chosen examples for their clarity and simplicity. My assumption is that readers will apply the basic principles to their own situation, even if their level of technology, their type of customers, or other variables are very different from those in the chosen examples.

At a few points, such as this chapter's discussion of the need to develop an outside-in habit, I report my experience in teaching the outside-in discipline to my students. Although these are graduate students with appreciable business experience, the typical reader will have very much more business experience and very different demands on his or her time. Even so, I hope that some of the insights from my students can provide useful starting points for readers in fitting the outside-in discipline to their own experiences and situations.

This book's usage of a few key terms requires explanation. First, *marketing* covers a lot. I use the term very broadly, as do marketing academics and some marketing professionals. Marketing is *the identification and satisfaction of customer needs.*

This broad definition is neither new nor unusual. It is entirely consistent with Drucker's definition (discussed in the previous chapter) of marketing as the whole business seen from the customer's point of view. Thus, the assumption in this book is that marketing deals with a company's overall marketplace strategy and is a critical topic for the CEO and for the rest of the organization.[4]

Also, *customers* usually means customers or prospects. Marketers and marketing academics frequently use the term *customers* to mean both customers and prospective customers. In some cases they use *prospective customers* or *prospects* to make it clear that they are discussing potential rather than current customers. Often, however, they do not make the distinction.

This book follows that rather imprecise practice. For the most part, *customers* includes both current customers and prospects. In only a few instances does language such as *current customers* or *prospective customers* (or similar terms such as *existing customers* or *prospects*) make the distinction explicit in a specific context.

The book also uses the term *needs* in the broad sense typical in the marketing literature. Used in this way, *needs* covers what in everyday discourse would be called needs, interests, desires, whims, and other related names. True, there are important differences in meaning among those terms. Some marketing texts begin by classifying needs into a variety of categories on the basis of the strength of the need, the extent to which the customer is consciously aware of the need, and other variables.

In practice, however, those categories are rarely used and don't seem to be helpful, so this book follows standard marketing practice and uses the simple term *needs* instead. Readers who are not particularly familiar with the marketing literature may find themselves thinking, at some point in the book, "Wait a minute. The customer doesn't really need that." At such points, it should be helpful to remember that needs is being used in this very broad sense.

SUMMARY

The bad habit of inside-out thinking turns up all over the business world—in the careers of outstanding managers and in leading companies, in strategies and plans for existing businesses and for marketplace innovations, in courses in business schools. But the alternative outside-in perspective has the potential to provide real competitive advantage—to change the game.

Clearly there is something standing in the way, keeping businesspeople from abandoning or avoiding inside-out. That something is the difficulty and discomfort of outside in. The outside-in approach is difficult and uncomfortable because businesspeople essentially never know enough about customers.

The outside-in discipline provides a new discipline and habit to replace inside out. The essence of the outside-in discipline is to have an explicit customer reason for everything you do in the marketplace.

The discipline starts with customer pictures, built from data, intuition, and hypotheses. It then requires that every marketplace action be rigorously linked to those customer pictures. And, as your understanding of customers increases, the outside-in discipline tells you to improve your customer pictures and then the actions tied to them.

Because outside in is not easy, it's important to work to become more comfortable with the approach—to try to make it a habit.

OUTSIDE-IN ACTIONS

1. **Push yourself to write down whatever you think you know about customers.**

   Consider customer needs, stating just what is it that you believe customers need from your products or services. Also consider customer behavior, explaining as much as you can about how customers decide to buy products like yours, how they evaluate alternatives, where they get information to use in those evaluations, how they decide among alternatives, how they actually make the purchase, and how they use your products.

2. **Now, push yourself hard to add things that you believe are true of customers but that you aren't really sure about.**

   Again, consider what customers need from your products or services. Also consider customer behavior in deciding to buy products like yours, in evaluating alternatives, in getting information, in deciding among alternatives, in making the purchases, and in using your products.

3. **Don't try to combine the different statements into customer pictures at this point.**

   Just try to record as many different insights as you can. And don't worry if some or even many of your statements aren't true of all customers. You can say "some customers" or, even better, describe what type of customers a specific statement applies to.

4. **Get input from others in your organization.**

Ask others about what they think, especially about any insights they have into surprising or ignored aspects of customers' needs and behavior. Add to your list whatever you agree with, but also keep a separate list of customer assumptions that you think are wrong but that are held by others in your organization.

5. **Begin to check your statements of strategy for rigor.**

Start by listing, in reasonable detail, your overall strategy for succeeding in the marketplace and the various marketplace actions that you use to implement that strategy. Check whether the customer statements provide a clear, solid reason for each action. There should be an explicit, customer-based reason for every marketplace action. Note the actions that don't seem to be fully supported. They will deserve special attention later.

3

CUSTOMERS ARE FRUSTRATING

But the Outside-In Discipline Is Still Useful and Important

Consumers are unpredictable, varied, fickle, stupid, shortsighted, stubborn, and generally bothersome.
—Theodore Levitt

Businesses are not paid to reform customers. They are paid to satisfy customers.
—Peter Drucker

L EVITT DID NOT VOICE this opinion about consumers as his own. Instead, he attributed it to engineers, saying that they might not state the opinion openly but that, deep down, it was what they really believed. The clear tone of Levitt's argument is that this view of customers is unfortunate, harmful, and wrong.

I disagree. Although I would use less inflammatory adjectives, I think that customers often do, in fact, display such attributes. They are often hard to predict, especially for businesspeople who want to try radically new approaches. Customers certainly do vary—in their needs, in how they perceive and measure value, and in how they behave. Customers change their minds, either as their conditions change or as they become more knowledgeable.

Stupid doesn't seem the right term, but customers are often ignorant or uninformed—especially about what you and your product
might be able to do for them. They frequently focus on the job
facing them at the moment. They are often slow to change, and
that slowness could look rather like stubbornness.

Bothersome doesn't seem right. After all, customers are the ones
with the cash, or credit cards, or checkbooks in their pockets.
They're the ones who sign the purchase orders.

The challenge is to accept the reality of customers but then to
proceed despite their conservatism, slowness, ignorance, and so on.
As Drucker says, the task is to satisfy them, not to reform them.
And, those customers have an awful lot of power. As Sam Walton,
the founder of Wal-Mart, put it:

> There is only one boss. The customer. And he can fire
> everybody in the company from the chairman on down,
> simply by spending his money somewhere else.[1]

The preceding chapter argued that, although the customer-
based outside-in discipline is difficult and uncomfortable, it is
nevertheless worth while. The first objective in this chapter is to
probe the difficulty a bit more, to get the problem out on the
table, and to be clear about the ways in which customers can be
frustrating. The idea is to look realistically at the difficulty, not to
make it a roadblock but for precisely the opposite reason: to accept it and to move on anyway.

The second objective of this chapter is to provide a brief example of the usefulness of the rigorous outside-in discipline in
guiding marketplace strategy, despite the challenges. True, you
can never know as much as you would like about customers. Yes,
it's uncomfortable, to say the least, to acknowledge and confront
that relative ignorance. Of course it's uncomfortable to base a

marketplace strategy on what you know is flawed understanding of customers.

But you can't avoid assumptions about customers. The choice is whether to make them explicit, and therefore subject to examination and correction, or not. And customers are the basis of business success. So, after acknowledging and examining the difficulty in detail, the end of the chapter and the remainder of the book proceed anyway. They explain, explore, and share the outside-in discipline.

CUSTOMERS MAY SEE THINGS "INCORRECTLY"

Customers can be remarkably frustrating in the ways in which they view things—how they see both the world in general and your products and services in particular. Ultimately, marketplace opportunity and business success rest on customers' needs *as perceived by the customers*, not as perceived by the businesspeople who are trying to satisfy those needs. Businesspeople, especially innovators, frequently believe that customers see things incorrectly—that they do not view their situations, their needs, and the potential benefits of possible solutions as they should view them.

A product introduction by Rohm and Haas provides an example.[2] Rohm and Haas was already a leading player in the market for metalworking-fluid biocides. It sold a biocide product to companies that drilled, turned, milled, or otherwise worked metal. The Rohm and Haas product killed microorganisms in the fluid used to cool and lubricate a metal part as it was worked and to carry away chips, shavings, and other waste products of the operation.

Without biocides, owners of large systems had to clean their equipment and replace their metalworking fluid every few weeks. With regular additions of the Rohm and Haas product, they could avoid ever having to drain and refill their systems. These customers were generally knowledgeable about metalworking and the role of biocides, and, not surprisingly, they were very receptive to biocide products.

Biocides designed for large systems did not work in small ones. Lacking good biocide function, the operators of small-tank systems had to replace their fluid every few weeks.

Recognizing this customer problem, Rohm and Haas developed a new biocide product specifically for use in small systems. The new product could not extend the life of fluid in the smaller tanks indefinitely, but it could at least double or triple the useful life.

One obvious benefit, which would be readily apparent to customers, would be to reduce the total amount those customers would have to spend on purchases of metalworking fluid. An even bigger savings—(roughly six times the savings from reduced purchases of metalworking fluid) would come from avoiding some of the hefty fees the operators were incurring for disposal of used fluid.

Unfortunately for Rohm and Haas, the prospective small-system customers were generally not aware of how much they were spending for disposal. Most of them knew that they were having the liquid taken away, but the relevant decision makers did not know the cost of that disposal service.

In other words, from the perspective of Rohm and Haas's managers, the operators of small-tank systems saw things incorrectly, and, as a result, selling to them was extremely difficult. Rohm and Haas did not succeed with the product.

An interesting and frustrating wrinkle on the problem of customers viewing things "incorrectly" sometimes occurs precisely because customers view things the way suppliers in an industry have taught them to view things.

The history of Xerox provides an example.[3] Early Xerox

machines were intended to handle small and medium-size copying jobs. Often, the machines were placed in various locations throughout an organization to permit convenient use. In contrast, large jobs were handled by central reproduction departments on larger equipment using different technology, such as offset printing.

Xerox had introduced a tool called productivity matrices for comparing copying machines. Productivity matrices were tables with run lengths (numbers of copies to be made of a document) along one side and numbers of original pages in the job listed on the other side. In the cells of the table were the number of impressions per hour and/or the costs of the job if it was performed on a particular machine operating at full efficiency. In essence, Xerox had taught customers to view reproduction equipment using productivity matrices.

Xerox's problem occurred in the 1970s when it introduced a new machine, the 9200, which was designed for larger jobs and would compete more directly with offset equipment. Productivity matrices were a poor tool for comparing the 9200 with competitive offset machines.

Once it was completely set up and running at full efficiency, an offset duplicator could turn out a large number of copies per hour. It took a skilled operator and several steps to reach full efficiency, however. For example, the operator might begin a job with a trial run or two to adjust the ink balance of the offset machine and to make other adjustments needed to adapt to the specific type of paper chosen for the job. The operator would then start the actual production run. The equipment would first make a master of the first page and would then reproduce that page; however, each master could be used for only a specific number of copies, and so this step might not produce the number of copies of that first page needed for the entire job. The equipment would go through a cleaning step before making another master and printing the second page. If the run length was larger than could be made from one master per page, this process would have to be repeated with additional masters for each page until the entire run was complete.

Productivity matrices did not begin to capture what Xerox managers considered to be the benefits of the 9200 when compared with existing offset equipment. Instead, Xerox marketers and salespeople worked to get customers to think in terms of turnaround time—the time between the arrival of a job in a company's reproduction department and the departure of the job after completion. It was difficult and time-consuming to get customers to use the concept of turnaround time—in part because Xerox had been so successful in the past at getting them to use productivity matrices.

CUSTOMERS MAY NOT PAY PROPER ATTENTION

Customers can also be frustrating because they don't pay a lot of attention to some issues and because they are not willing to take the time to learn more about those issues.

My favorite example of this phenomenon concerns Quaker State, the company that markets motor oil.[4] A new CEO set out to make Quaker State more customer-oriented. As one step in that process, he wanted to convince the company's employees that customers found the labels on Quaker State products confusing. He invited some of the company's engineers to view a focus group of customers. The engineers were shocked that no one in the focus group could define synthetic oil. In a response that shows how lack of customer understanding is, unfortunately, sometimes received, one of the Quaker State engineers announced that they would have to find smarter customers for their focus groups.

The Merry Maids franchise organization provides an example of a far more constructive approach to customer inattention.[5] Merry Maids provided house-cleaning services. The organization did not assume that customers knew or cared enough to learn how to judge all of the details of a cleaning job. Instead, its operating assumption was that each individual cared about a few idiosyncratic aspects of cleaning, which the company called that customer's "hot buttons."

Merry Maids used several mechanisms to discover a customer's hot buttons and then to ensure that the hot-button jobs were executed well. Its managers believed that if they attended to hot buttons, customers would be forgiving if the cleaners occasionally missed other details.

Stew Leonard's Dairy in Connecticut dealt constructively with what might be considered customer ignorance or inattention.[6] Stew Leonard's was a highly successful food store (originally) in Norwalk, known for its customer focus and its business success. As part of the customer focus, the store's top managers ran focus groups of customers on Saturday afternoons.

One Saturday, a customer announced that she did not buy Stew Leonard's fish because it was not fresh enough. The outraged fish-department manager argued that the fish was bought fresh each morning at the Fulton Fish Market in New York. The customer insisted that the fish was obviously not fresh because it was wrapped in plastic.

One possible approach for Stew Leonard's would have been to try to reeducate customers—to try to teach them about fish, the Fulton Fish Market, and freshness. However, while it is sometimes necessary and effective, reeducating customers is frequently difficult, and it can be expensive and time-consuming. For Stew Leonard's, it was not at all clear that customers would pay attention to efforts to teach them about fish.

The happy ending of this story is that Stew Leonard's did not take on what proved in this case to be the unnecessary task of reeducating customers. Instead, the store installed, in addition to the chest of wrapped fish, an ice table with fish that customers could first select and then have wrapped specifically for them. Total fish sales for the store doubled.

CUSTOMERS MAY BE CAUTIOUS OR UNAPPRECIATIVE

Customers can also be frustrating in their reluctance to change, even when they are presented with products that would provide them with substantial benefits. Business-to-business customers are particularly likely to display such behavior. Managers in many businesses, especially established businesses, believe that they will be blamed considerably more for an unsuccessful change than they will be rewarded for a successful one. Often, they feel that there will be no penalty for choosing to do nothing. Their risk aversion creates inertia.

This phenomenon is familiar to many businesspeople. It is a particular problem for entrepreneurs, who are often asking prospects to do business with a new and relatively untried organization.

The problem has long plagued start-ups selling products in the general computer field. Established companies in that industry, particularly IBM, built parts of their past communication strategies around such risk aversion. For example, an IBM print ad from the 1980s had the headline: "What most people want from a computer company is a good night's sleep." The ad showed a pillow, with "IBM" embroidered on the pillow case.[7] (IBM has revived this same message in some more recent ads.)

Customers can be frustrating because they do not appreciate

the genius of our design. In his widely used textbook *Marketing Management*, Philip Kotler describes what he calls the product concept as the main guiding principle for some companies. According to the product concept, "consumers will favor those products that offer the most quality, performance or innovative features."[8]

Companies that are guided by the product concept often design their products with at best limited customer input. Instead, they proceed on the assumption that outstanding engineers will design outstanding products. The problem, of course, is that customers may have radically different views of what constitutes an outstanding product.

Product-oriented companies generally have complex products and highly trained specialists who develop those products. Such situations most commonly involve engineers. The perhaps unstated but nevertheless basic assumption in engineering-oriented companies is often that if the design is elegant and the design process was challenging, then the product is a good one. When a technology is new and it is extremely difficult to make a product work successfully, technical people are especially tempted to adopt this engineering-oriented product concept.

A similar orientation can occur in other situations where experts with very specialized knowledge design products. For example, in an insurance company, the actuaries had designed a product that was statistically elegant but that was also too complex for the customers to understand or for the salespeople to explain.

Like the Quaker State engineer discussed earlier in the chapter, developers of products that customers can't understand have a tendency to become frustrated with those customers. It would be so much simpler, they think, if the customers would appreciate the elegance and sophistication of the product designs.

CUSTOMERS MAY NOT BE ABLE TO ARTICULATE THEIR NEEDS

Even if they do not display the overtly frustrating behaviors just discussed, customers often cannot articulate their needs, especially when the proposed solutions to those needs will be radically new, involving highly innovative products and services.

To illustrate this point, let's look at Federal Express when it was an entrepreneurial venture, starting out in the 1970s.[9] Although Federal Express actually started by handling packages and then added documents soon after, for simplicity let's look only at documents.

It is clear now, and it would have been reasonably clear once Federal Express started operation in the mid-1970s, what were the major customer needs that Federal Express was designed to meet: reliable and predictable delivery, security, and so on. More challenging is the question of how Federal Express's founder could have determined those needs *before* starting operation and could have understood the needs well enough to design the details of the service. (And, given that the required $90 million in financing made Federal Express the largest single venture-backed start-up effort in U.S. business up to that time, it would certainly seem highly desirable for the founder and his investors to have felt confident that the needs were real and important.)

It was apparent that the document service would be aimed at businesses rather than consumers and that, within businesses, managers, professionals, and their support staffs would be the targets. So, imagine that, in the mid-1970s, some of these target customers are assembled and are willing to be interviewed. How should the discussions proceed?

Asking, "What are your needs regarding the delivery of documents" would surely not have elicited responses about absolutely-positively-overnight delivery, pickup at the desk of the support person rather than the mail room, purple-red-and-white envelopes, planes and vans, or other characteristics of the Federal Express service.

What the prospective customers could have provided was good information concerning what they disliked about their current solutions for getting documents from one place to another: either the less-than-fully-reliable mail service or very expensive human couriers for special cases. FedEx's founder had to translate those customer problems into a solution, with guaranteed delivery, with the consistent color scheme as a signal that the document was always in the safe hands of the same organization during its trip, and so on. (And, as will be discussed in Chapter 12, the prospective customers were even less able to predict how heavily they would come to use the new service. The entrepreneur had to find other ways of convincing himself of the eventual market size.)

Thus, especially when a planned product or service is unfamiliar, simply asking customers what their needs are won't provide the information needed for solid outside-in thinking. Customers frequently cannot articulate their needs, and they may find it very difficult or impossible to envision how they would actually use a radically new product.

Even with more familiar products, customers may have difficulty articulating their needs. They may understand how the product is used by others but still not envision just how they themselves would use it.

Furthermore, customers may say that they need something when what they really mean is that they believe they should need it. For example, consider the usage patterns of health clubs and gyms. It's an interesting experiment to visit the same health club at the same time on the same day of the week in early January and then again in early March and in early November. Many clubs are considerably busier in January.

True, many customers think that they need exercise and think that the clubs or gyms will help them get it. Their resolve tends to be especially high after the end-of-year holidays. For many, though certainly not all, people, that resolve soon decreases, and attendance drops. (And, as many readers will recognize, the managers of health clubs and gyms often design their procedures assuming such declines in resolve, regardless of what customers say about their plans for exercise in the future.)

THE OUTSIDE-IN DISCIPLINE IS STILL USEFUL AND IMPORTANT

Given this litany of problems, it is understandable that people find achieving and maintaining an outside-in perspective to be such a challenge. The outside-in discipline gives businesspeople a method for basing strategy firmly on customers and their needs despite the difficulty. The problems do not go away in this customer-based approach, but they do not create insurmountable roadblocks, either. The challenge is to proceed despite them.

The next two chapters look in more detail at customer pictures, the customer foundation for the outside-in discipline. The remainder of the book considers outside-in strategies based on customer pictures. First, however, this section pursues the Federal Express example a bit further, as an illustration of the power of the outside-in discipline. The discussion provides a reminder that it is in fact worth while to proceed with the discipline despite all the ways in which customers can be frustrating.

The preceding discussion emphasized how difficult it would have been to understand customer needs for document delivery in advance of the launching of Federal Express. This section continues the discussion to make the point that customer analysis would nevertheless have been extremely worth while, making clear some of the actions that the fledgling company should take in the marketplace.

To see this point, consider how, in 1975, the founders might have predicted that the new Federal Express service would be used, once it had been introduced. Assume that the company has already decided on and implemented its system of couriers in vans picking up documents and taking them to the airport, of planes flying each night to the hub in Memphis, of planes then flying to the destination cities, and of couriers in vans making the final deliveries. What would happen at a customer company to generate some individual's first use of the service?

The obvious answer is that there was an emergency involving a document in an office somewhere. Unfortunately, Federal Express could not predict exactly which office or exactly the time of the emergency.

The likely scenario was that a manager or professional was late in preparing a document. Having finally completed the document, that manager or professional then handed the problem to an assistant, stressing the importance of getting the document to another city fast.

Would the assistant have time to research possibilities? No. What would Federal Express want to have happen? Clearly, the key would be for the assistant, under stress, to think of Federal Express and then call for service.

At that point, the Federal Express system of couriers and vans and planes could kick in and save the day. And it would be extremely important that Federal Express did in fact save the day. If Federal Express failed to deliver the document as promised, that customer would be unlikely to use the service again and would be likely to tell others about the failure.

This description of customer behavior has not been proven, but it is plausible. It has come from a combination of knowledge and intuition about how offices operate. Most important, it is explicit, and therefore it could be run by other people who might help to improve or correct it. It could then be used to draw some important conclusions.

First, gaining awareness among potential customers was a critical early task for Federal Express. Because the company could predict neither exactly who its customers would be nor when those customers would first use the service, the communication campaign had to target a broad audience and encourage customers to contact Federal Express rather than vice versa.

The objectives of the communication campaign would be simple: to get the name "Federal Express" into the minds of people in business, especially support-staff members, so that the name would surface at times of document-related emergencies.

Second, operational excellence would also be critical. Customers would use Federal Express in stressful situations involving important documents; they would remember any failures and would not easily give the company a second chance. Thus, Federal Express's early emphasis on operational excellence and its classic early advertisements (stressing "absolutely positively overnight") were right on target.

FOCUSING ON RIGOROUS THINKING AND ON CUSTOMERS

The basic idea in this example, as in the entire outside-in discipline, is to create explicit pictures of customer needs and behavior and then, rigorously, to choose actions based on the explicit pictures. As noted in the previous chapter, the process is uncomfortable, largely because the pictures are essentially never as clear or as complete as one would like them to be.

The alternative, however, is worse. Not making assumptions explicit is in no way equivalent to making no assumptions. As noted earlier, there are always assumptions that make business decisions sensible; the question is whether you believe that those theoretical assumptions make sense in the real world. Similarly, there are always other theoretical assumptions that would make the same decisions foolish.

If you choose not to make your assumptions explicit, you simply make it enormously more difficult to make good initial decisions. You can't test possible decisions and actions by considering whether the supporting assumptions make sense. And it's much harder to get useful input from others. You also make it enormously more difficult to review the assumptions regularly, modify them on the basis of additional information, and use the revised assumptions to improve your business decisions.

There is an important distinction between what I call *rigor* and *precision*. The outside-in discipline provides a method for using rigor in designing and implementing strategies. It generally does not provide (and certainly does not promise) precision.

Rigor requires that you move logically from the explicit analysis of customers (as in customer pictures) based on data, intuition, and explicit hypotheses to practical, explicit actions. Precision, on the other hand, involves exactness, such as exact predictions of market size or of customer behavior.

Precision is rarely attainable in business situations, especially not in situations involving really good opportunities. If a situation is well enough understood for answers to be precise, that situation is most likely clear to many people, and the additional opportunity is likely to be small. Better opportunities are generally more murky; customer needs are not crystal clear, and the best ways to address those needs are also not clear. Thus, precision is generally least possible in situations involving substantial newness and uncertainty. Rigor is especially important in such situations, which include the types of situations that are most promising for successful marketplace innovation.

Unfortunately, customer needs also appear unclear in situations where there are not strong customer needs and, consequently, there are no interesting opportunities. One function of rigorous, customer-based analysis using the outside-in discipline is to help you distinguish murky situations that contain really promising opportunities from murky situations that do not. Rigor, not precision, provides that function.

Notice how strongly focused on customers all of the previous discussions have been. And there has been little consideration of competition. The remainder of this book also purposely spends very little time on competition. I believe that, first, in practice, competitive analysis gets relatively too much attention. Second, the common approach to competitive analysis is often not a particularly useful one.

The consideration of competitors frequently focuses on a competitor's technology, its balance sheet, or related dimensions. While such considerations are not totally irrelevant, they are not what matter most.

The more important questions concern how customers view the competitor's offerings in the marketplace or how they will view those offerings in the future. Competitors can be thought of as providing the context or the alternatives available to customers. The basic questions concern the relative attractiveness of your company's marketplace offerings and the offerings of other companies that customers will consider to be competitive. Thus, with the outside-in perspective, good analysis of competitors must begin with good analysis of customers.

The difference between a customer-based orientation and a competitor-based one is illustrated by an example from "Getting Back to Strategy," an excellent article by Kenichi Ohmae.[10] Ohmae described his work with a Japanese home-appliance company, helping its managers think through the design for a coffee percolator.

A competitive orientation, Ohmae explained, would have led his client to follow the competition's lead. If one competitor had just introduced a percolator that brewed coffee in ten minutes, then perhaps his client should aim for seven minutes. If a new model from another competitor used limited electricity, then perhaps his client should aim for even lower power consumption.

Instead, Ohmae urged his client to get back to strategy, by which he meant "getting back to a deep understanding of what a product is about." What did customers care about most in coffee? The clear answer was good taste.

Ohmae next set his client the task of determining what influenced the taste of a cup of coffee. The company's engineers learned that the most important factor was the quality of the water. They discovered that the grain distribution and the time interval between the grinding of the coffee beans and the addition of water were also crucial.

The result of this exercise was a coffeemaker with a built-in dechlorinating function and a built-in grinder. The customer put water and coffee beans into the machine, which then performed the steps automatically, producing consistently good-tasting coffee.

The key idea, as Ohmae described it, is to focus on what customers really care about, not on what competitors are doing. Similarly, I believe that useful competitive analysis also focuses on what customers care about, rather than on other, perhaps more easily obtainable, information about competitors.

SUMMARY

Customers can be remarkably frustrating. They may view the world and your product in ways you really wish they wouldn't. They may not know much about a topic that you consider important, and they may not be willing to devote time and effort to learning more. They may not pay attention the way you'd like them to. They may be highly risk averse and reluctant to change. They may not appreciate the great technology and insight you have incorporated into your products.

Customers may not be able to articulate their needs, especially in areas that would be addressed by highly innovative products and services. They may have difficulty envisioning just how they would use even more familiar products.

Despite all of these problems, the outside-in discipline is still useful and important. The key is to create explicit pictures of customer needs and customer behavior, basing the pictures on combinations of hard data, intuition, and hypotheses, and then to base your strategy and actions rigorously on that customer foundation. The idea is to have a clear, explicit, customer-based reason for everything you do in the marketplace.

OUTSIDE-IN ACTIONS

1. **Make a list of the ways in which your customers or prospective customers are frustrating or ignorant.**

   Answer the following questions:

   In what ways do your customers view things "incorrectly"?

   What don't they pay attention to that you consider important?

   Do they show overly cautious behavior, resisting or refusing changes that would provide them with large benefits?

   What do they fail to understand and appreciate about your products and services?

   What are they unable to articulate about what they need from products, about how they want to buy, about what they need in support and service, and so on?

2. **Push yourself to explore troublesome characteristics of customers and prospects.**

   Recall your least favorite experiences with customers and try to articulate what it was about those customers that contributed to making those experiences so bad. Ask your colleagues what they find most frustrating about your customers, too. Use their inputs to add to your list.

3. **Include these characteristics in your descriptions of customers.**

   Go back to the list of insights, assumptions, and hypotheses about customers that you constructed at the end of the preceding chapter. Incorporate important frustrating customer characteristics that you have identified.

4. **Resolve to achieve and maintain an outside-in perspective despite those frustrations.**

   As Drucker said, businesses are paid to satisfy customers, not to reform them.

5. **Continue to build comfort with the outside-in approach by applying it to other business examples.**

   Notice key needs and behaviors of customers—both consumers and businesses. Then ask yourself what actions would make sense in light of those needs and behaviors. And also work in the opposite direction. Observe the marketplace actions of some business. Ask yourself what assumptions about customers' needs and behaviors would make those actions sensible and what assumptions would make the actions ill-advised.

4

PICTURES OF CUSTOMERS
Begin with Customers'
Perceptions of Their Needs

What the customer thinks he is buying, what he considers
"value," is decisive—it determines what a business is, what it
produces and whether it will prosper.
—Peter Drucker

THE OUTSIDE-IN DISCIPLINE STARTS with customer pictures, capturing knowledge, intuition, and hypotheses about customers. The pictures should come alive, capturing the essence of the customers. As discussed in Chapter 2, lists of customer characteristics don't work nearly as well as pictures, and checklists are even worse. Lists don't make clear which characteristics matter most, how the characteristics interact, or other important information. Far preferable are verbal descriptions of customers that highlight their key characteristics and make the customers come alive—descriptions that I call customer pictures.

The purpose of these pictures is to provide a sound, explicit basis for decisions about what products or services to offer, to whom they should be offered, and how to offer them. The outside-in discipline requires that these pictures provide a customer-based reason for everything you do in the marketplace. The basic idea is to create pictures that will, with the some rigorous thinking, lead you to products or services (and strategies for marketing them) that give customers enough value to induce them to buy.

This chapter emphasizes the first parts of the customer pictures—the customer needs that are most clearly related to the products and services themselves. The following chapter then adds even more richness to the pictures.

One question that often arises in initial discussions of customer needs is whether a company can create needs. Although that question is in part a semantic one and readers should make their own decisions about it, I believe that one should not talk or think about creating needs (although companies do certainly create new markets).

It tends to be dangerous to think that one can create needs. Yes, one can satisfy needs that customers had never thought about. One can address needs that customers could not express. In all such cases, however, there must be something in the customer—some need—that responds to a product or service.

Too often, in practice, the assumption that companies can create needs leads to arrogance, the attitude that the company is smarter than the customers and will force its product or service on them. Such arrogance is akin to the product concept discussed in the preceding chapter. The approach generally does not work and is a trap to be avoided.

So far in this chapter, the language has carefully and explicitly included both physical products and less tangible services in the discussion. Constant use of the phrase "product or service" tends to become awkward, however, and, perhaps for that reason, it is common practice in the marketing literature to use "product" to cover both products and services. The remainder of this book will use that common convention and will distinguish products from services only when the distinction is central to a specific topic.

CUSTOMERS' PERCEPTIONS OF THEIR NEEDS

Businesspeople often have ideas about what customers should need and value. But customers will be the ones doing any eventual buying, and it is the customers' perceptions of their needs that matter. In some cases, customers don't perceive needs that product designers and marketers think they should have, or the customers may be unclear about just what they do need.

In other cases, however, customers have relatively clear perceptions of their needs, understanding them more clearly than do the businesspeople who are interested in satisfying those needs. For example, in the 1990s, managers at Inland Steel set out to provide value to customers rather than merely focusing on moving tons of steel.[1] Inland was unusual among U.S. steel companies because it retained its distribution business after its U.S. competitors had stopped running distribution centers. Inland's managers hoped to use the distribution centers to serve customers better than competitors could.

Inland initiated discussions with its 50 best U.S. customers in order to understand customers' needs. It was clear that the customers were increasingly operating globally. Inland asked them what they wanted from an overseas steel supplier. The customers said that they wanted the same quality of steel worldwide—not necessarily the highest possible quality, which would be hard to maintain consistently worldwide, but, instead, the same quality at each location.

In retrospect, the answer seems sensible. A picture emerges of customers trying to run integrated global operations, rather than having idiosyncratic processes at each location. Consistent quality would allow the customers to use the same procedures in all their plants and to transfer methods and personnel among locations more easily. In this case, the customers were able to provide clear information, and the resulting picture provided clear guidance for Inland's strategy for its distribution arm.

In another example, Dow Chemical adopted an approach to innovation that relied heavily on customers' abilities to articulate their needs.[2] Dow began by asking customers for a wish list of products or technical characteristics. Dow scientists and managers then considered whether it seemed possible to invent what customers were requesting. If the answer was yes, and if enough companies agreed to buy the product if it were in fact developed, Dow scientists began a project, essentially inventing to order.

In one instance in 1998 a consulting firm working with Dow assembled executives from more than two dozen customers that used fibers. The incentive for the customers to participate was the promise that they would be the first to be supplied with any resulting new products.

The process uncovered what Dow managers considered a critical insight. They had believed that customers wanted a low-cost imitation of the stretch fabric spandex. Instead, customers said that they wanted an improvement: a fiber that stretched but that also felt like cotton and was resistant to heat and chemicals. In response, Dow scientists developed a new fiber called XLA, which was launched in 2002. Some of Dow's customers began offering clothing made with XLA in 2004; initial market response was described as enthusiastic.

Even if customers are able to articulate their product needs, it's important to be clear about just what they mean, especially when they use some key words that can have a variety of significantly different meanings. A short initial list is *quality* and *service*. It is essential to explore what the terms mean to particular customers in specific situations.

For example, for a piece of industrial equipment, "quality" could refer to the precision of the parts produced by the equipment. Alternatively or in addition, it could mean the ability of the equipment to withstand hard use. Or it could have other meanings. As Peter Drucker has said:

> Customers pay only for what is of use to them and gives them value. Nothing else constitutes "quality."[3]

Similarly, a rapid response is sometimes the most important aspect of service. In other cases, getting a correct answer to a problem is much more important than the amount of time involved. There are numerous other variants. It is therefore a mistake for a businessperson to accept or use these terms without probing to understand just what each term means in the context of the particular business's customers and marketplace offerings. And, of course, different customers of a single company may use the same term to mean different things.

CHALLENGE FOR PICTURES: PREDICTING NEEDS

Unfortunately, customers frequently are not able to give clear information about their needs, especially about what their needs will be in the future. As stressed in the preceding chapters, the problem is particularly acute for products that are radically different from what customers have experienced to date. In such cases, the challenge is to create pictures that highlight how customers will respond in the future (and, perhaps needless to say, that challenge is a considerable one).

The early history of McDonald's, when it was still an entrepreneurial venture, provides an example.[4] In 1940, Dick and Mac McDonald opened a small drive-in restaurant in San Bernardino,

California. Drive-in in those days meant exactly that. Customers drove their cars into the restaurant's parking lot and then waited, in the car, for a carhop to arrive. The carhop took the customer's order, collected payment at that time, and delivered the order to the kitchen. When the kitchen had prepared the order, the carhop returned with it on a tray, placing the tray on a holder that was hung temporarily on the customer's partly-rolled-down car window. When the customer had finished eating, the carhop returned to remove the tray and the special holder, and the customer drove away.

The McDonalds' first restaurant in San Bernardino was highly successful, but the McDonald brothers began to worry anyway. The parking lot would become jammed with cars. On average customers waited 20 minutes for their orders, in part because there were many different items on the menu and in part because of the carhops.

Dick McDonald later explained:

> Customers weren't demanding it, but our intuition told us they would like speed. Everything was moving faster. The supermarkets and dime stores had already converted to self-service, and it was obvious the future of drive-ins was self-service.

In other words, the McDonalds had a customer picture that said that customers were increasingly valuing speed over personalized service.

Because they found that despite the variety of the menu 80 percent of their sales were hamburgers, they reasoned that most customers would be satisfied with hamburgers; their picture included an assumption that many customers liked hamburgers and would value speed over variety.

Further, the McDonalds believed that speed and low prices

would be especially attractive to young families, allowing them to eat out together for the first time. They considered children important in determining where those families went and whether they would return.

In the fall of 1948, the McDonalds closed the restaurant for several months to convert to a fast-food model with no carhops but with self-service, a limited menu, low prices, and speed. The kitchen was enclosed in glass because the McDonalds believed that children liked to watch burgers cooking, and employees were instructed to be especially nice to the children.

When the restaurant reopened, business fell at first. The brothers believed that many customers considered it safer to patronize popular restaurants; going to a restaurant with an empty parking lot seemed risky. Accordingly, the McDonalds resorted to telling employees to park in the restaurant's lot so that it would look as if there were customers. They found that they had to modify the menu a bit, adding milkshakes and French fries.

Over time, the new design caught on, especially with working-class families, and the restaurant became extremely successful. In 1952 the brothers began selling franchise rights.

The McDonald brothers thus used their understanding of customers, built on data, intuition, and explicit hypotheses, to drive their business decisions. Customers were not able to predict what they would want in the future, so customer requests could not be the main driver. The McDonalds didn't get everything right the first time. For example, they had to expand their original menu of hamburgers and beverages.

They did, however, have explicit customer-based reasons for what they did, and they revised their customer pictures and their actions as they learned more. They were, obviously, wildly successful. They designed their strategy for the market from the outside in, even though customers weren't clear enough about their future needs to say what outside-in actions would be appropriate for the McDonalds.

This process is clearly considerably easier in retrospect than it is in real time. This book's basic assumption is that the discipline of constructing strategy from the outside in is nevertheless important and valuable even (or, to be more accurate, especially) when the customer pictures are not entirely clear but must be based on combinations of a little data with a lot of intuition and explicit hypotheses.

CHALLENGE FOR PICTURES: "SHOULDS"

Other complications affect the process of ferreting out customers' needs. Customers often have ideas about what they should or should not need, and those ideas may not correspond to the customers' true needs as evidenced by their actual behavior.

The problem of what customers think they should need is especially acute in certain product areas. Innovators have discovered this fact when they tried to sell offerings aimed at health and lifestyle. Many customers apparently consider it virtuous and wise to consume a healthy diet. They believe that they should exercise. And so on. In practice, however, people eat considerably more of the familiar foods that they like, and many have great difficulty maintaining exercise programs over time.

The entrepreneurs who founded White Wave provide a clear example of the importance of understanding such attitudes and behaviors.[5] In 2001 founder and CEO Steven Demos wrote:

> I can honestly claim to be the head of the largest manufacturer of the most hated food in the United States. When you ask people what they think of soy foods, the first thing eight out of 10 say is "yuck."

The company was founded in 1977. The founders believed that soy was good for people and good for the world environment, and they set out to market soy food products. Two decades later, in 1996, their sales were just over $6 million.

The CEO observed that the company's biggest mistake had been selling what the founders thought customers should want. Of course, many customers might have agreed that they should eat healthy foods, including soy. They did not, however, buy much of White Wave's products.

Finally, after years of frustration and some experimentation, in 1996 White Wave introduced Silk, a liquid soy product that was sold in containers like milk cartons, located in the supermarket dairy case next to the milk, and made to taste like milk. White Wave's 2001 sales were $140 million. The CEO attributed the company's success to finally putting together what the consumer really wanted: familiarity, freshness, and a flavor that matched certain expectations.

The company finally reached a customer picture that said that consumers thought they should eat healthy foods but they actually wanted familiarity, freshness, and especially the flavor they expected. Many consumers would buy healthy products that offered those key attributes and would value the nice feeling that they really were doing something healthy, but they would not sacrifice familiarity, freshness, and expected flavor for the health benefits, regardless of what they thought or said they should do.

The strategy for Silk matched this picture. White Wave developers made the product's taste as close as possible to that of dairy milk. The product's package suggested using Silk on cereal because managers believed that Silk tasted and looked most like dairy milk when used in that way. They used a milk-carton-like container in the refrigerated section of grocery stores because they believed customers associated that kind of packaging with freshness.

Customers in other situations may be similarly reluctant to acknowledge some of their needs, both to others and to themselves. Consumers often think that their needs reflect on them— sometimes favorably and sometimes unfavorably. They are often reluctant to acknowledge needs that they think reflect poorly on themselves.

For example, it's remarkable how few people say they read tabloid newspapers sold in supermarkets, especially in light of the millions of copies of those tabloid newspapers sold each week. Similarly, business customers may be reluctant to admit how difficult it would be for them to learn to use new equipment effectively and how much education and support they would require in order to learn.

CHALLENGE FOR PICTURES: EMOTIONAL NEEDS

Especially in business-to-business marketing, customers have a tendency to discuss only the easily described needs related to a product's features and functions. Or, they may also talk about a product's effects on their own revenues and costs. Such needs and benefits are certainly important, but they are not the only relevant ones. There are almost always other important needs that are more emotional in nature.

Early in the personal-computer era, I liked to tease technical audiences by saying that I thought they needed a big, thick manual with their PCs—not to read (because they believed that only wimps actually read manuals) but to put on the shelves in their offices so that their colleagues would know that they had serious computers. There was enough truth in this picture for technical listeners to laugh a bit self-consciously and, often, to agree.

Similarly, in the example of Federal Express in the 1970s, one additional need was for importance—for the recipient to feel important for receiving a Federal Express shipment and for the sender to feel important for sending it.

In other situations, the emotional needs are more central. For example, Lifeline Systems was founded to provide monitoring and emergency response to elderly people who continued to live in their own homes.[6] The basic customer assumptions were that many older people very much wanted to continue to live in their homes but that they or their relatives worried about emergencies.

Lifeline gave the elderly customer easy ways to summon emergency help, such as speakerphones and wearable radio transmitters that communicated with the phones. The company maintained information about and contact with the customer's doctors, neighbors, and relatives. Its call center was staffed with people trained to respond to emergency calls and to deal well with elderly callers. In some cases, employees at the call center made regular calls to check on a customer.

All of these capabilities were obviously designed to detect and respond to emergencies, and Lifeline was successful in handling emergencies. In practice, however, the company found that the majority of the calls it received were not actual emergencies.

Some customers openly said that they did not have an emergency but wanted someone to talk to. Other customers said that they had hit the buttons on their communication device by accident, but when someone from the Lifeline call center then called them, the customers stayed on the phone to talk.

It was important for Lifeline to include this need for companionship in its customer pictures and then to decide what to do in response. The company's policy was that nonemergency calls were just fine. They brought considerable value to customers.

Costco Wholesale provides another example of a strategy based on a good understanding of more emotional needs.[7] The company established warehouse-club stores that carried many luxury goods, a concept that fit extremely well with its view of evolving customer needs.

A generation or two ago, for many middle- and high-income consumers, there was a stigma attached to shopping in discount stores. Many believed that such stores were for low-income customers. Over time, customer attitudes changed. Today customers at all income levels often take pride in their ability to save money on their purchases—and many are willing, even eager, to tell others about their shopping successes. The need to be a smart shopper has become important in customer pictures.

So has a willingness to shop in different types of stores. According to *BusinessWeek* in 2004, for the richest 10 percent of Americans, the store most visited by men was Home Depot, while the one most visited by women was Target. In fact, A.C. Nielsen reported that 54 percent of the customers at warehouse clubs such as Costco were affluent; this was the highest affluent percentage that Nielsen found for any type of retail store.

Costco's many upscale products were an excellent fit for these newer customer needs. Costco became the largest seller of fine wines in the United States. *Fortune* reported in 2003 that Julia Child bought meat there. The vice chairman of Berkshire Hathaway was another Costco customer; he asked, given that he looked for bargain securities for his company, why he shouldn't also like bargain golf balls at Costco.

Needs related to risk are often emotional ones. In essence, the question is, what are customers afraid of? Risk is especially important in business-to-business marketing, where customers often believe that purchase decisions that turn out badly can be career- (or at least job-) threatening. Such customers are understandably risk averse.

It is often very useful to ask what failure would look like to customers. Exploring the potential failures can uncover more emotional customer needs and views about risk.

As an example, consider the efforts of a company named VideoStar Connections to sell a private video network to Digital Equipment Corporation in the 1980s.[8] Digital needed the network for instantaneous communication with its sales and service centers throughout the United States.

What would failure look like for VideoStar? It's easy to imagine a senior manager, perhaps CEO Ken Olsen, on stage at Digital's Massachusetts headquarters while groups of sales and service people at Digital offices throughout the United States are staring at blank monitors. To put it mildly, the experience is clearly not career-enhancing for any manager who had been seen as the champion of the new video network. It's easy to see that customers would need strong assurance about VideoStar's abilities to provide products that would work, along with excellent service and support. It's easy to see why customers would be highly conservative in their purchase decisions.

Good insights into what makes consumers nervous or uncomfortable have been essential to some major successes in end-user marketplaces, too. An example from Japan is the wireless provider NTT DoCoMo, which introduced i-mode, a service providing Internet access over special i-mode cell phones.[9] DoCoMo carefully selected content providers, whose identifiers then appeared in lists on the screens of the i-mode phones.

Users could access the Web site of a partner by pushing a button on the phone. They were able to read the news, send and receive e-mail, check movie listings, buy tickets for travel, receive a different on-screen animated character each day, check the weather, or do many other things with their phones. Some of the content providers charged users for access, while others did not. Central to the i-mode service was its billing method. Users received a single bill each month from the cell-phone service, listing what they had spent with each content provider.

The i-mode service caught on quickly in Japan. In the 18 months ending in late 2000, DoCoMo signed up 10 million i-mode subscribers, and the service continued to grow. In part the success rested on a good understanding of the attitude of many Japanese consumers to technical terms. Takeshi Natsuno, one of i-mode's developers who went on to be director of the i-mode group, commented, "The fact that we are using the Internet isn't necessarily an attractive thing to subscribers." In fact, press coverage quoted an i-mode customer who did not have a regular phone or a computer, who spent over $150 per month on i-mode, and who believed that, although i-mode did have an Internet link, she wasn't interested in that capability.

Similarly, the innovators at a company named iRobot Inc. used insights into customers' fears effectively in developing and selling Roomba, a vacuum cleaner that was actually a robot.[10] Somewhat surprisingly, and very impressively for a group of high-powered engineers, the designers based central design decisions on the realization that many customers were afraid of complicated technology. They made Roomba extremely easy to use, and they did not promote it as a robot. Consequently, according to *Inc.* magazine, Roomba had strong sales and "the kind of product launch most entrepreneurs would sell their grandmother up the river for."

PICTURES SHOULD HIGHLIGHT WHAT CUSTOMERS VALUE

Thus, a key objective in constructing customer pictures is to understand the range of customer needs, whether or not customers can readily articulate and predict those needs. It is important to include both needs related to specific product features and other less obvious needs, including emotional ones.

The customer pictures become useful when they help to identify strategies and specific actions that are based firmly on the understanding captured in the pictures. The key is to provide customers with enough value that they decide to buy.

Fletcher Music Centers, a retailer of organs in Clearwater, Florida, provided that kind of value.[11] Organs are not usually considered a dynamic growth business, but Fletcher used understanding of customers to achieve considerable success.

The company's customer picture portrayed an elderly person who was retired. Often, the customers had recently moved to Florida. They might buy an organ because they had always wanted to learn to play or to continue music lessons that they had started long ago. Being elderly, many of them had some physical limitations. Fletcher's discussions with customers led to the conclusion that they were strongly interested in companionship, especially but not exclusively if they had recently moved to the area.

Using this customer understanding, the company made some product modifications, adding larger keys and knobs. It also began offering free weekly group lessons for the customer's lifetime with every organ purchase. Sales rose dramatically. In essence, Fletcher used its customer understanding to provide substantial value to its customers, offering things that the customers really cared about.

Identifying and delivering real value to customers is, of course, central to any business success. The outside-in discipline requires that the statement of value be explicit and customer-based. The following definition of value proposition provides a starting point.

VALUE PROPOSITION VERSION 1

An explicit statement of how and why our products, and every-thing that surrounds them, provide value (lots of value) to customers. For consumers, value might be performance of spe-cific tasks or it might be satisfaction of emotional needs. For businesses, value might be cost reduction or control or it might be competitive differentiation of the customer's products. It might include satisfaction of more emotional needs of man-agers in the businesses. Or, value might be many other things that matter substantially to a customer.

A BIG COMPLICATION IN PICTURES— THE DMU

The discussion so far has ignored some frequently important complications in understanding actual customers and providing value to them. It has used terms like "the customer" as if the customer were a simple single entity. But, especially in business-to-business marketing, the customer is not simple.

In almost all organizational purchases and in some consumer ones, there are several, and sometimes many, people involved. The different involved individuals have at least somewhat (and some-times very) different needs and fears. They have different roles in the purchase decisions. In business, they are likely to be measured or evaluated differently.

Marketing vocabulary labels the entire group of involved individuals the decision-making unit, or DMU. For instance, in the Lifeline Systems example discussed earlier, there were often several people involved in the decision to buy Lifeline's monitor-ing service. In addition to the elderly person who would use the system, his or her adult children were often involved, sometimes peripherally, but sometimes in key deciding roles. The elderly person's physicians might also be involved. Frequently the original suggestion to use such a service came from a doctor or from other personnel at a hospital where the elderly person had received care.

Similarly, consider a company that was selling software for use by engineers involved in product design. If the target engineers worked for a large organization, there were apt to be many people in the DMU. The engineers themselves were included; sometimes they were merely the end users of products bought primarily by others, but sometimes they had more central roles in product evaluation and purchase. Engineering managers were usually involved, especially for larger purchases and for decisions that affected company- or department-wide practice. Purchasing agents might participate. So might information technology managers, who were charged with making new purchases fit into the organization's technical infrastructure; sometimes the IT managers were heavily involved in product testing and evaluation. Someone from the finance or accounting department would often be involved, especially in large purchases. And so on.

We sometimes assign labels to the different roles of members of a DMU. Some participate as users, the people who will actually use any products that are purchased. Some participate as influencers, who do not buy or use the products, but who influence evaluations of products and decisions to purchase. Influencers can include people within the customer company (such as employee engineers who provide technical evaluations) or people in other organizations (such as architects or consulting engineers). A stronger version of an influencer is a specifier—someone, such as an architect in some circumstances, who can require the purchase of products that meet certain specifications.

DMUs often include gatekeepers, such as receptionists, assistants, or subordinates, who control access to the people who can actually purchase. They include the actual purchasers. They may include others who must approve purchases. And so on.

Thus, consideration of the DMU adds a lot of complexity. What makes matters even more complex is that often people from different departments have different roles and different levels of influence on purchases in the DMUs of different organizations. For example, some organizations give individual engineers considerable leeway in choosing products to use in their work, while others control software purchases tightly through their IT departments.

In addition, companies that sell to other businesses essentially always find that there are many people in a DMU who can say no to a purchase but few people who can actually decide to buy. Many members of the DMU can play the role labeled "vetoer."

For example, suppose that you are selling a new material for use in making wall tiles. Suppose the material will reduce the cost of making tiles and will also improve their appearance. Accordingly, your product might be of special interest to the customer organization's production manager (or someone else with responsibility to control costs). Alternatively, your product might be championed by the marketing manager because of its impact on product appearance. Either of these managers might have the authority and the motivation to buy from you.

A foreman within the factory is not likely to have either the authority or the motivation to purchase. Suppose, however, that the foreman has responsibility for the main tile-making machine, and suppose, in addition, that he announces that he will use the material if ordered to but that he can't guarantee that it won't gum up the whole machine and he thinks the change is a really bad idea. It will take a highly committed and powerful production or marketing manager to overcome the foreman's reaction. The foreman cannot say yes, but effectively he may well be able to veto the purchase.

These examples should make clear the importance of considering the entire DMU when more than one person will be involved in a purchase. Although the discussion will continue to talk of "the customer" or "customers," the assumption will be that these terms are understood to include the complexity of the customer's organization and DMU. Customer pictures should include all the important participants in the DMU. The value proposition should also incorporate consideration of the DMU. Thus, the following is an improved version of the definition of a value proposition.

VALUE PROPOSITION VERSION 2

An explicit statement of how and why our products, and everything that surrounds them, provide value (lots of value) to the customer overall and to the key players in the customer organization's DMU. The different members of the DMU will generally perceive value differently.

(Warning: additional versions of the definition of value proposition will be considered in the following chapter.)

ANOTHER BIG COMPLICATION: DIFFERENCES AMONG CUSTOMERS

Another serious complication in the process of understanding customers arises from the fact that there is usually substantial variation from one customer to another. Such variability occurs among end consumers and also among business customers. Different customers often have different needs. They may include different people in their DMUs or give different members of the DMU different roles and different amounts of influence. And so on.

Market segmentation focuses on differences among customers; most readers will be familiar with the term and will have seen the concept used. The next part of this chapter will nevertheless discuss segmentation because I believe that, in practice, the concept rarely provides as much value as it could.

Many business or marketing plans do include segmentations, often dividing customers into groups on the basis of age or income or industry or size. The segmentations are usually presented early in a marketing plan or early in the marketing section of a business plan, perhaps because the authors believe that there *should* be segmentation, but the segments often do not reappear later in the plans. They do not contribute real value to the plans or to the strategies presented in those plans. That's a shame, because the concept is a potentially very powerful tool.

Let's start with a definition. A *market segment* is a group of customers who would respond similarly to a particular marketing strategy. Note that this definition implies that a segmentation is specific to a particular situation.

An individual or a business is not in one set segment for all purposes. Most consumers and most businesses strongly emphasize low cost in some purchases but focus on other characteristics in others; they are not consistently price shoppers—or quality buyers or any other single type of customer.

In addition, the salient dimensions for segmentation differ from one business to another. For example, most businesses don't care about the height of customers, but for a few height is a key variable. Most businesses don't care how a customer business allocates the costs of the information that it purchases, but a few businesses find allocation methods extremely important.

Effective use of the concept of market segmentation involves first determining an appropriate segmentation of the customers in a specific business situation and then really using the result to improve marketplace strategy. Segmentation can help identify those customers to whom a business's value proposition will appeal most strongly. It can also help the business construct the value proposition in the first place so that it will appeal to specific groups of customers. Note that in either case, the segmentation is not just a required section of the business plan. Instead, it guides and improves actions in the marketplace.

Dell Computer provides a good example of effective segmentation.[12] Using ideas that I introduced in earlier work on industrial marketing, the company segmented its customers into transaction accounts and relationship accounts.

Transaction customers essentially consider one transaction at a time. They do not remain loyal to one supplier but instead look around the marketplace to consider various alternatives. In the computer marketplace, businesses with highly decentralized computer-purchasing processes and also most individuals were transaction customers. While they might appreciate additional services that Dell could provide, they often were not willing to pay extra for those services and were not made loyal by them. They often emphasized price.

Dell originally sold to transaction customers over the telephone; over time, it increasingly used the Internet. Transaction accounts were required to pay by credit card or on delivery. Dell might offer these customers some support, such as checking to see that a current purchase was compatible with previous ones, but it did not provide them with extensive services.

By contrast, relationship customers believe that it is worth while to be loyal to a particular supplier because of the benefits that come with that loyalty. In the computer marketplace, relationship customers cared about a great deal more than a particular computer and its price.

Various members of the DMUs of those accounts cared about enforcing adequate standardization on computer purchases across the organization in order to control maintenance and support costs. At the same time, managers wanted to have enough options available for employees to have computers that supported them well in their jobs. These customers cared about the costs of managing the company's computers, including the costs of mundane activities such as attaching physical-asset tags to new personal-computers and initializing the machines with the company's own software. They valued help in providing technical support to users within the organization. They cared about keeping their technology adequately up to date without suffering with new and untried technology. And so on.

Dell sold to its relationship customers through a combination of field salespeople, telephone salespeople, and the Internet. It would set up a special Web site for a customer to handle purchases from that organization and, at the same time, to show employees of that organization only approved products. It also helped relationship customers to set up customized versions of Dell's technical-support Web site. It offered them advice and education about advances in computers and computer applications. For a nominal fee, it would perform tasks such as attaching asset tags or installing customer-specific software, tasks that were previously carried out, at much higher expense, by the customer's organization.

To the initial surprise of many observers, Dell in fact earned higher margins from its larger customers. It did so by offering relationship customers bundles of services that they valued enough to pay for and that, in addition, kept the customers loyal.[13]

As this example shows, Dell really used its segmentation of customers to drive its marketplace strategies. In fact, the company even organized on the basis of the segmentation, with different parts of Dell focusing on the different segments. Notice in particular that Dell did in fact segment customers; it did not fall into the far-too-common trap of segmenting on the basis of product differences instead of differences among customers.

Such careful, thoughtful market segmentation (of customers, not of products) has the potential to contribute substantially to the effectiveness of many marketplace strategies. This tool is not used effectively nearly as frequently as it could be.

One particular problem crops up almost all the time in efforts to use segmentation effectively. I describe that problem by distinguishing between what I call meaningful segmentation and what I call actionable segmentation.

A *meaningful segmentation* divides customers into groups that are most directly meaningful for a specific business. For example, a meaningful segmentation for Federal Express's document-delivery service in the mid-1970s would have divided customers into two segments: one for those managers and professionals who had, or were likely to fall into the habit of having, lots of emergencies related to sending documents, and the other for everyone else. Surely the first segment was exactly the right target for the early Federal Express.

The problem was that Federal Express could not identify the members of that segment; unfortunately for the company, they did not walk around with signs on their foreheads or other clearly distinguishing characteristics. In my terminology, the segmentation was highly meaningful but not actionable.

An *actionable segmentation* is one that can readily be used in practice; in particular, it is often important that it be possible to find the members of the segment. There is almost always tension between highly meaningful segmentations and adequately actionable ones. The solution is to find a compromise—some practical, actionable way of dividing customers into groups that, although not identical with the groups in the most meaningful possible segmentation, are still useful because some have high concentrations of desirable target customers while others have low concentrations.

In the Federal Express example, in addition to using advertising as discussed in the preceding chapter, the company also sent salespeople to call on organizations in segments defined by type of business; examples were law firms or advertising agencies. Not all the managers and professionals in those organizations were good target customers for Federal Express, but the expectation was that there would be enough good targets to make calling on the organizations worth while.

A company called Rolm provides another example.[14] Rolm sold PBXs, telephone switches for use by businesses on their own premises. It was an early competitor to AT&T when deregulation first permitted the sale of non-AT&T equipment. At the time, in many organizations, the job of telecommunications manager was filled by an especially conservative person. Historically that manager had not had any choice of vendor; his or her job had been to deal with AT&T. The telecom manager was generally most strongly motivated to avoid problems, because other people in the organization tended to notice the telephones only when they did not work. Such managers were unlikely to want to experiment with a new vendor such as Rolm.

By contrast, the telecom-manager slots in a few organizations were beginning to be filled by a very different type of person. Some younger, more ambitious managers, often relatively recent MBAs, saw telecom as an area with relatively few employees that they might therefore be allowed to manage. They further believed that changes in the telecommunications marketplace made it possible for them to save their companies substantial amounts of money and, in the process, to advance their own careers. These new-style telecom managers were obviously the meaningful segment for Rolm to target.

It was not possible for Rolm to identify a group containing all of these promising targets and only these targets. Rolm could, however, find some good actionable substitutes. For example, many of the new-style managers attended seminars that were offered by industry experts to explore new developments in telecommunications. Although the seminars also attracted some of the older-style managers, they were sufficiently heavy with new-style managers that they were excellent places for Rolm to find targets.

The problem of meaningful versus actionable segmentation is almost always present. In many cases, however, it can be overcome sufficiently well for segmentation to contribute significantly to customer pictures and to effective marketplace strategies based on those pictures.

SUMMARY

Rich pictures of customer needs are the beginning of successful customer-based strategies. The pictures should emphasize customers' perceptions, especially their likely future perceptions, of their needs. They should include and explore emotional needs.

The concept of the decision-making unit, or DMU, is one complicating but important factor in understanding customers that should be incorporated into the pictures. Differences among customers create another complication. The concept of market segmentation can be used effectively to deal with such differences.

Good customer-based strategies include value propositions, stating clearly how the business will provide enough value to customers to convince them to buy. According to the definition at this point in the book, a value proposition is a clear, explicit statement of how and why a company's offerings will provide value to the customer organization overall and to the key players in the customer organization's DMU. (The next chapter will refine that definition.)

OUTSIDE-IN ACTIONS

1. **Review and improve the lists of characteristics of your customers that you compiled at the ends of the preceding two chapters.**

   Check that you have included all the important needs that are directly related to the features of relevant products or services. Be sure that you have stated the needs from the perspective of the customers, not from the viewpoint of people in your own organization. Include your best understanding of how customers use ambiguous words such as *quality* or *service*. Analyze more emotional needs, too. To uncover them, consider what risks customers fear. Explore what failure would look like. Note ways in which customer needs appear to be changing.

2. **Identify and explain the customer's DMU.**

   List the different types of participants in the DMU. As well as you can, specify the needs of each DMU participant. Note where those needs appear to differ or even conflict with one another.

3. **Select a good market segmentation for your customers.**

   Explore ways in which needs differ among customers. Then ask what would be a meaningful segmentation—a division of customers into groups that would clearly identify your best prospects, or that would separate customers with different needs relevant to your products, or that would serve other es-

pecially useful purposes. Next, try to find an actionable segmentation that helps you get close to the meaningful one. You
want a segmentation in which it is practical for you to identify
and reach specific segments but, at the same time, in which the
groups remain as meaningful as possible.

4. **Construct your initial customer pictures.**

You're finally ready to combine your insights into initial customer pictures. You should have considerably more detail than
you can incorporate into compelling word pictures, so identify
the customer characteristics that seem most important. Organize those important points into word pictures that capture the
essence of your customers, making them come alive. Don't dis-
card the customer insights that you chose not to use in your initial pictures. Keep them as backup. They may prove important
and useful in the future.

5

BETTER PICTURES OF CUSTOMERS

Add Insights into Customers' Behavior

The first step . . . is to raise the question: "Who is the customer?"—the actual customer and the potential customer? Where is he? How does he buy? How can he be reached?
—*Peter Drucker*

THE INITIAL CUSTOMER PICTURES discussed in the previous chapter can help businesspeople design more effective marketplace strategies, communicate the strategies to others, and respond to the inevitable changes that occur in the marketplace and in their levels of understanding of it. The pictures in that chapter were not complete, however. They focused strongly on customer needs and, in particular, on the needs that were most directly linked to the products or services themselves.

Those initial pictures did not explore the last two questions in Drucker's list: How does the customer buy? How can the customer be reached? Expanding the pictures to include these and other central considerations of customer behavior provides a substantially better foundation for formulating, communicating, and adapting marketplace strategies.

Customers' processes for buying and using a company's products involve several steps. First, customers must pay enough attention to think about buying. Then they must do whatever they think is appropriate prior to the actual purchase, exploring alternatives and making up their minds. They must then make the actual purchase. There may be additional steps, such as taking delivery of the product. Any of these steps can be important in a specific situation.

In fact, some of the examples in preceding chapters did consider aspects of the customers' behavior. For example, recall the discussion in Chapter 3 of a 1970s customer's initial purchase from Federal Express. That discussion painted a picture of the events in a business office that would lead to a purchase—the paper-related emergency caused by a manager's or professional's being late with some document, followed by a call to Federal Express by the assistant. Because Federal Express could not predict who would need the service when, and because the assistant did not have time to research alternatives once the emergency had occurred, it was critical for the company to get its name into the minds of the relevant people through a widely targeted communication campaign.

The preceding chapter's discussion of market segmentation briefly suggested that there were in fact some types of organizations in which there were enough high-potential prospects for it to be worth while to have Federal Express salespeople call. Further thinking about those organizations' processes for learning about, communicating about, and buying such services would have provided a good foundation for the sales calls.

The same chapter noted the McDonald brothers' theory that restaurant customers were significantly more likely to choose a restaurant that was popular with other customers. They believed that customers used the number of cars in a restaurant's parking lot as an indicator of its popularity. The McDonalds' strategy also rested on insights into additional aspects of customers' buying behavior, such as the role of children.

CUSTOMERS' BUYING BEHAVIOR: START WITH AWARENESS

In discussing customers' behavior in making purchases, the term *buyer* (or *buying*) *behavior* is used for both consumers and business customers. The term *decision-making process*, or *DMP* for short, is also used, especially in talking about businesses with multiple individuals in the relevant decision-making units (DMUs). A discussion of the people in a DMU almost invariably leads to some mention of the roles those individuals play in the DMP. The basic argument of this chapter is that explicit consideration of those roles, of other aspects of the DMP, and of the buying processes of even stand-alone individual consumers can significantly improve both customer pictures and the strategies designed from them.

The marketing literature is full of models of buying processes, some suggesting highly detailed generic steps for describing all buying processes. It's fine to use one of the more detailed models. I prefer instead at least to begin with a very simple model with only three major steps:

- *Awareness*. The crucial step in which customers begin to pay attention and to think of themselves as potential buyers of a product.
- *Evaluation*. The actions the customer takes to research, think about, try out, or otherwise evaluate a possible purchase.
- *Decision*. The customer's key determination that he or she will in fact proceed to buy something, the final choice of which alternative to buy, and the actual purchase.

Notice that the steps focus on customers' behavior up to and including the actual purchase. These early awareness/evaluation/decision steps are extremely important, and yet they are frequently ignored or treated very superficially. Subsequent steps in which the customer uses the product after purchasing it are considered later in the chapter.

The awareness step in the DMP is frequently a challenge. Customers are busy. Even if they are aware in a general way of the problems you could help them solve, they may not be focusing on those problems; they may instead assume that they have to live with their current situations. And, customers have learned to tune out a great deal of the marketing communication around them. To be successful, businesspeople must somehow break through all this inattention. Careful thought about the processes through which customers become aware can lead to strategies that are effective without incurring undue costs. An example can illustrate the point.

The founders of Nantucket Nectars identified young adults, especially active ones, as the most promising targets for the company's bottled juices.[1] The managers had a simple but clear view of how those target customers would become adequately aware of Nantucket Nectars' products to purchase them. They believed that customers bought primarily on the basis of taste. Further, they believed that the target customers would be quite willing to sample new beverages and would be receptive to products that they thought tasted good. The customers did not pay a great deal of attention to beverages, however. Although they would be inclined to buy products they had tried and liked, they might not think of those products when they were in the stores that carried them.

The key tasks for Nantucket Nectars (assuming that its products did in fact taste good) were therefore to get prospective customers first to try the products and then to remember to buy them. The company used distinctive labeling and, especially, the color purple for memorability. For trial, it sent its "mobile marketing squads," in purple Winnebagos, to hand out free samples in places that would have high concentrations of good target customers—marathons, baseball and football games, concerts. Squad members wore purple shirts, and the bottles all had purple caps.

Nantucket Nectars became highly successful, while devoting only 10 to 15 percent of the company's overall budget to its mobile marketing squads, public relations, and a bit of advertising on radio. By comparison, Coca-Cola spent 30 percent of its budget on marketing. Clearly, the smaller company used its insights into customer behavior to design a marketing strategy that was both efficient and effective.

Notice that the Nantucket Nectars founders did not assume that customers who had not tried the product would become aware just by seeing the bottles in stores—even with the distinctive labels and purple caps. By contrast, other entrepreneurs, lacking the money for extensive advertising and desperately wanting to communicate successfully with prospects, have acted as if consumers would in fact notice and read their packages on the shelves of supermarkets or other stores. Unfortunately for those entrepreneurs, most supermarket customers spend little, if any, time noticing, much less reading, the packaging of most products on the shelves.

With DMUs involving more than one person, it is common for one member of the DMU to assume, or at least to assist with, the task of making the others aware. For example, engineers who become aware of a product they think would be very useful to them not infrequently tell others in their organizations about the product. One of their objectives is to line up the other needed members of the DMU so that the organization actually does buy.

In essence, in such situations, one member of the DMU assumes the role of champion for the purchase. In effect, that person acts as the selling company's native tour guide to the customer–company's DMU and DMP. The selling company's task is to identify the tour guides and then to understand enough of the guides' behavior to help make them aware.

Consider, for example, a company that made and sold specialty chemicals for use in the construction industry. Architects often served as specifiers on projects that used the company's products; their specifications determined what products would be purchased. Managers for the manufacturer worked to understand the behavior of the architects and then used that understanding to focus the company's sales and advertising efforts on making the architects aware of its products.

Buying processes in the Lifeline Systems example described in the preceding chapter are another example of a complex DMU. As that chapter noted, the elderly person who would use the emergency-response system, that person's adult children, and the elderly person's physicians and other medical helpers might all be involved. These players could come together in several fundamentally different types of DMP.

In particular, different members of the DMU initiated the purchase in different cases. Sometimes the elderly person took the lead in finding a service that would allow him or her to continue to live at home. In other cases the adult children initiated a search process; they might include discussions with their parent's doctors in their search. In still other cases, the doctor initiated discussion with the adult children. In others, medical personnel broached the topic of a monitoring service directly with the elderly patient. And so on.

For Lifeline to be successful, its managers needed to understand the processes by which those potential initiators could become adequately aware of its services. As discussed further later in the chapter, they then needed to select marketplace actions that would produce the desired awareness in at least some of the potential initiators.

CUSTOMERS' BUYING BEHAVIOR: EVALUATION AND DECISION

Next in the list of the three major steps in buying behavior is evaluation, the processes through which customers examine and explore their choices. The evaluation step is very brief in some purchases but long and complex in others. Key insights into evaluation belong in many customer pictures.

Business customers often have explicit formal evaluation procedures for some of their most consequential purchases. They may use either standing or ad hoc committees, composed of a variety of members with a variety of different interests and perspectives. Other business DMPs include only informal evaluations. The less formal processes have the advantage of relative simplicity, but they may also be considerably less easy for an outsider to figure out.

Businesses may also use detailed processes for evaluating the financial implications of possible purchases. For example, those processes may require specific numerical data for assessing the performance of a product that is under evaluation.

For purchases that they consider both important and risky, business customers may want or require a trial or pilot use before they commit to a full purchase. For such companies, information about the selection and execution of such trials or pilots surely belongs in customer pictures.

Even without such formal processes, both businesses and consumers regularly include at least some evaluation in their buying processes. Again, the key details belong in customer pictures.

Consider a product called SpinBrush, developed in 1998 by four entrepreneurs.[2] Walking through Wal-Mart stores looking for inspiration, the founders had noticed that electric toothbrushes all cost more than $50. They decided that there would be a big market for a far less expensive product—that customers needed electric toothbrushes at affordable prices. They then spent 18 months developing a product that could sell for $5, including batteries; the price was only $1 more than the most expensive manual toothbrush.

In addition to thinking about these product-related needs, the founders also considered buyer behavior. Their first key assumption was that customers did pay some attention when selecting a toothbrush in the store, so that they would notice a distinctive new offering. As noted earlier, that assumption does not hold for many other consumer products. The second key assumption was that the customers would have to see the product operate before they would understand and believe in it enough to buy it. In other words, awareness could be achieved easily, assuming that the founders were able to place the product on the shelves, but evaluation required attention.

The entrepreneurs devised a battery-powered toothbrush packaged so that shoppers could make it operate while it was still fully packaged. A discount chain in the Midwest tried selling the product in late 1999, with great success. In 2000 the entrepreneurs expanded their distribution and sold 10 million units, compared with 3 million traditional (more expensive) electric toothbrushes sold in the United States that year. They achieved these sales without advertising, which they could not afford and which, fortunately for them, was not called for by their customer picture. In 2000 they also executed their planned exit strategy, selling the business to Procter & Gamble. Clearly, understanding the customers' processes for awareness and evaluation was central to the success.

With business customers, the third major step, decision, may involve formal procedures for final selection, approvals, and purchase. Frequently, even after considerable evaluation efforts, customers get stuck and don't move on to an actual purchase. Especially for that reason, key elements of the decision step, whether formal or not, often belong in customer pictures.

Insights into the decision step can also help bring success in consumer markets. The founders of Home Depot used such insights.[3] They believed that end consumers needed help in deciding what to buy. The customer's problem was not so much evaluating alternatives as it was figuring out what collection of parts and supplies was needed to carry out some task, usually a task of fixing or building something at home. The founders hired people who understood such tasks—carpenters, plumbers, and others—to work in the stores, wearing orange aprons so that customers could spot them easily. They told these employees that Home Depot was a service business, not a discount hardware store. As one of the founders put it:

> It's not what we [the founders] do, it's what happens in the stores. He who gives the best service wins.

This Home Depot example highlights another point. Notice that the founders were very clear about what service meant in their environment, and they used that understanding effectively in their strategy. As the previous chapter pointed out, service is a term that means very different things in different situations, and providing good service requires first figuring out what the term means to your customers.

CUSTOMERS' USAGE BEHAVIORS

Awareness, evaluation, and decision aren't the whole story. Customers go through other steps as they actually use your products. A careful exploration of the details of those usage steps can also contribute substantially to the design of marketplace strategy.

Customers who use a product regularly may have very definite ideas about how the product should and should not be used. Nestlé SA faced such strongly entrenched beliefs as it tried to sell more bottled water in Italy.[4] Research showed that Italians consumed especially large amounts of bottled water—the highest amount per capita in the world and more than $2\frac{1}{2}$ times the per capita rate in the United States.

The problem for Nestlé was that Italians had a combination of opinions and laws that discouraged the consumption of water on the go. Many of them apparently believed that eating or drinking on the street or elsewhere on the go was rude and unhealthy. In addition, strict Italian licensing laws made it extremely difficult for newsstands or similar convenient retail outlets to carry food or beverage items. Coca-Cola reported that on-the-go sales were only 5 percent of its total sales in Italy, in contrast with 50 percent of global sales.

Nestlé did not have to convince Italians that bottled water was good for them; the Italians were already convinced. The company did, however, face the dual challenges of changing the entrenched attitudes and of getting distribution. As of 2005, it was engaged in communication and sampling campaigns to try to convince consumers that small bottles of water were convenient, healthful, and acceptable. It was also engaged in a campaign to get bars to carry coolers with bottles of water. The jury is still out on the success of those campaigns.

In an article about understanding customer behavior in detail, Ian MacMillan and Rita Gunther McGrath gave a long list of questions concerning what happens after the customer has decided on and has ordered the product.[5] They suggested asking how the product is delivered, how it is installed, how it is paid for, how it is stored, and how it is moved around. They also asked what the customers are really using the product for and what help the customers need with those uses. They asked about returns and exchanges, repairs and service, and disposal of the product at the end of its useful life.

It's not a good idea to try to use this (or any other) list as a checklist, feeling that you have to provide a brief answer on each topic and that you are finished when you have done so. Instead, try using it as a starting point in a search for at most a few customer steps that are most important and that you can influence favorably (or unfavorably) with your actions. In other words, look for points of leverage.

It is also important not to be confined by such a list. There may be other important characteristics of the usage processes of your particular customers. The idea is to find any points in the customers' processes where you could do something to make a big difference and, therefore, increase your chances of getting a sale and getting repeat business.

Parts of the example of Dell Computer discussed in the preceding chapter showed effective use of Dell's understanding of some post-purchase-decision steps.[6] Without Dell's services, customer companies typically took physical delivery of new personal computers in their information technology departments. IT personnel unpacked the computers, attached physical-asset tags and entered the identification information into the company's inventory of assets, installed company software appropriate for the end user of each machine, and performed any other needed tasks. They then repacked the computers and sent them on to the end users.

Dell's managers estimated that performing these tasks might cost the customer $200 to $300 for each new computer. When Dell offered to assume the tasks for its relationship customers, it charged only a nominal fee of perhaps $15 or $20 per computer to perform them. The steps were not expensive for Dell to perform. The customers obviously would enjoy substantial benefits from having Dell's help, and they would therefore be considerably more likely to continue to concentrate their purchases with Dell.

For another example, consider Amazon.com.[7] True, the company competed using a wide selection and low prices, but it also did more. In 2004 the American Customer Satisfaction Index gave Amazon the highest rating ever scored by a retailer. Amazon's former vice president of global customer service attributed this success to the fact that the company's service was more friendly, more reliable, and easier to use than alternatives. The company designed and regularly updated its processes to fit with customers' processes. Many Amazon features addressed customers' buying processes, but others, such as the opportunity for customers to post their own reviews of books, concerned usage.

Customers for some products require post-purchase education to teach them how to use the products effectively. If the seller fails to provide the needed education, customers will generally be considerably less likely to continue to buy. The failure will also hurt the product's reputation.

As an example, recall the manufacturer of specialty products for use in construction. Earlier discussion noted the role of architects in specifying the company's products and, consequently, the company's emphasis on making those architects aware of those products. Specification wasn't enough, however. To obtain value from the products, customers had to use them properly. The products were actually applied by contractors at individual construction job sites. At some sites, the applications were tricky. In an effort to ensure that customers did in fact get value, the manufacturer sent technically able salespeople and sometimes technical specialists to job sites to help get the usage right.

Another example concerns the founders of a start-up company who had created an information service for use in the design and marketing of new products. They poured time and resources into developing their service, dealing with the numerous technical challenges involved. Their focus on the initial design almost led them to forget post-purchase needs.

The founders were neglecting questions about the education and support that customers would need in order to learn to use the service effectively. They had been focusing on how customers would use and benefit from the product once they were comfortable with it. But customers wouldn't become comfortable with the product instantaneously. The founders planned to sell the service on a subscription basis. Had they failed to recognize and satisfy the need for education, even if they had managed to attract some initial customers, they would have seen the impacts quickly enough in the marketplace—in the form of nonrenewals of subscriptions.

In other situations marketers find it important to remind customers of the product and to encourage them to use it. The preceding chapter discussed Silk, a liquid soy product that became successful in the 1990s after it was finally designed and marketed to fit customers' actual needs. In the 1990s, the company emphasized the task of getting customers to try the product.

By 2004, it faced a different marketing job.[8] The president and founder noted that thinking soy milk was "yucky" had become passé. Silk was carried by 97 percent of the supermarkets in the United States. The founder reported that 17 percent of the population had tried soy milk and that about 10 to 12 percent bought Silk, which was the category leader. His company's new communication job was to encourage consumers to use the product more often, promoting it as a healthy and now familiar food.

In other words, his customer pictures described buyers who needed to be reminded that they were doing something healthy when they bought and used soy milk. They didn't always think to use the product, but they might use it more frequently and in more situations if advertising reminded them about Silk.

Using insights into trade-offs among product features, prices, and convenience in buying and usage that its target customers (in numerous countries) would make, Sweden-based IKEA built a highly successful furniture-retailing business. IKEA's customer picture assumed that the often young customers would value stylish furniture, sized to fit in apartments and other relatively small living spaces, at affordable prices—and that they would willingly accept inconveniences in buying the furniture to obtain those benefits. IKEA built large self-service home-furnishing stores and sold furniture unassembled, requiring purchasers to perform the assembly themselves. The strategy has worked well.

CUSTOMERS' COMMUNICATION NEEDS AND COMMUNICATION BEHAVIORS

Customers' processes include using (or sometimes, to the frustration of businesspeople, ignoring or deliberately not using) information. Much but not all of this information is provided by companies through their use of the tools of communication (sales, advertising, and so on). To begin considering this aspect of buyer behavior, ask what customers need from communication.

For communication, the key customer questions are:

- When and where will customers be receptive to receiving communication?
- What messages do they need to hear?

Because a common mistake is to ignore the communication needs of customers after they have purchased, it may be helpful to distinguish customers from prospects and to state the key questions as:

- When and where will prospects be receptive to receiving information?
- What messages do they need to hear in order to become aware of, evaluate and purchase the product?

- What information do customers need after purchasing in order to appreciate and use the product?
- When and where would customers be receptive to receiving this information?

As the preceding discussion emphasized, analysis of customers normally identifies specific communication steps that are especially critical in individual situations—initial awareness in some cases and product trial in others, for example. Once the critical communication tasks have been at least tentatively identified, the customer analysis can then focus more strongly on the customers' communication behaviors that are most relevant for those tasks and on the ability of possible communication tools to do the required jobs.

Communication strategies must certainly contain the content that the target customers need. In addition, the strategies must recognize and fit with what I call the *communication habits* of the customers. By that I mean the sources that those customers would normally use to obtain information, especially information about the products and services under discussion.

The basic questions regarding communication habits are relatively clear. To what communication techniques are target customers regularly exposed? (Do they read specialized magazines? Do they attend particular trade shows? And so on.) How much attention do they pay? What do they think information from each of these sources is good for, and how credible do they find each source? How receptive are they to new ideas from that source? Where do they look when they set out to find something new? Can communication motivate them to decide to look for something new in the first place? And so on.

The difficulty, of course, is in answering these questions clearly enough for the answers to be useful in customer pictures and in strategies based on those pictures. This topic is best addressed through examples. Accordingly, the following two sections present examples of the use of customer behavior, including communication habits. First, however, this section covers a few additional points regarding customers' communication behavior.

Customers frequently influence other customers. In some situations, there are customers who are sufficiently influential to warrant the label *opinion leaders*. In the medical field, for example, well-known specialists and prestigious teaching hospitals are opinion leaders. Leading doctors write articles or give talks that influence their colleagues. Other doctors often seek information from the leaders, whose use of a technique or a specific product also often influences others. Not surprisingly, companies that sell medical products frequently target these opinion leaders.

Related to the concept of opinion leaders is that of *reference accounts*, early users of a product who will allow the marketer to use their names and sometimes to suggest that additional prospective customers contact them to discuss the product. Given the generally risk-averse behavior of most business customers, reference accounts can be extremely important in winning business sales.

Obviously, not all early customers will be willing to serve as reference accounts. Some will consider their use of a new product to be strategically important and will not want to share the details of that use with other customer companies that may be competitors or prospective competitors. Others may simply not want to take the time and trouble to talk with prospects. But when reference accounts are available, other customers often consider them an especially credible communication source.

A similar phenomenon operates in some consumer markets. Years ago, the executives at the advertising agency that handled the Kool Aid account explained that the product's main target was kids 6 and older. They said that advertising for the product was geared to 10- to 12-year-olds, however, because the advertisers believed that the older children served as opinion leaders for the younger ones.

In establishing its reputation with customers, the outdoor-clothing marketer North Face used what it called a "pyramid of influence" in analyzing prospective customers.[9] The pyramid placed mountaineers at the top, backpackers below them, secondary users next, and casual campers at the bottom. North Face managers believed that word of mouth flowed downward in the pyramid, from the most serious to the least serious users. Accordingly, the company focused its effort on meeting the product needs of the smallest customer group, the mountaineers.

USING A BETTER CUSTOMER PICTURE

Let's now return to Lifeline Systems for an example of the use of a more complete customer picture. First, consider the target elderly people themselves. Assume that they very much want to stay at home—to age in place, in the jargon of elderly services. Their adult children may be pushing them to move someplace where they will have more support. The elderly targets are strongly resistant to moving. At the same time, most of them have at least some awareness that they may face serious emergencies and need help. Most have some current medical problems. They do not move around as easily as they once did. Many are sometimes quite lonely.

Given that they spend a considerable amount of time at home, the elderly targets are likely to be heavy users of newspapers and some particular radio and TV programs, including news and weather. Many will be members of AARP and will receive AARP publications. A check in a good business library could uncover other publications to which the elderly population subscribes heavily. Some will be regular attendees at church services and activities. Some will frequent senior-citizen centers in their towns. Most will talk often on the telephone with friends and relatives. These target customers will see doctors regularly. For the most part, they will trust input from their doctors and rely on recommendations from them.

Next, consider a sketch of important points about the adult children. As just mentioned, the children may be pushing their parents to move to a place where they will receive more help. Assume that the children want their parents to be safe and happy. At the same time, the children will often be unwilling or unable to provide enough help and company for their parents, and they may very well feel guilty about not doing so.

Thus, the children need both good solutions for their parents and also reassurance that they themselves are doing what they should. In some but not all cases, this need to do what is right will motivate the children to become heavily involved in researching possible solutions for their parents. Some of the children will have regular contact with their parent's doctors, while others will not. The children will be representative of the middle-aged population as a whole, involved with their jobs, their own children, and their outside activities. Their communication habits will therefore be extremely varied.

The doctors will be a mix of geriatric specialists and general-practice physicians. They will have a mix of motivations. Assume that they do want their patients to receive good care. At the same time, most doctors are terribly pressed for time and under pressure to see many patients. They are also deeply interested in their professional reputations and do not want to do anything that would call their competence into question.

Doctors are part of a tightly knit professional community. They obtain information from medical publications. They attend conferences and brief courses to keep up to date. Doctors do spend time with salespeople from companies that sell pharmaceuticals and other products, but getting access to the doctors is difficult, and they tend to spend at most a few minutes with a sales representative. Many of them resent the amount of control that non-physicians from HMOs and other organizations have over the practice of medicine.

Some of the doctors will proactively suggest monitoring services to their patients (or to the patients' children) if they believe that the services are of sufficient quality. They may, in particular, require that any such service keep them informed while not wasting their time and that the service actively consult them in case of any serious problems. In other cases, doctors will not be the first to suggest a monitoring service but will be ready to discuss one with patients or their children.

Although managers at Lifeline Systems would want to go into even more detail in these pictures, there is enough here to suggest the basic outlines of some communication strategies. Doctors are involved in the DMP, sometimes as the initiators and sometimes as part of an evaluation process. Lifeline will find it important to give doctors information from sources they believe and must do so while using only small amounts of the doctors' time. If doctors have been convinced that the service is effective, they will value help in explaining it efficiently to patients and their children. Once they are receptive, the doctors would, for example, value being given printed explanatory material that they could give away.

The key task is gaining that receptivity, however, and that task is a difficult one, given the time pressures and the doctors' professional wariness. Getting the doctors' attention will be difficult, as will earning their trust. In fact, Lifeline solved the access problem by operating in partnership with hospitals. (The analysis would therefore have to incorporate consideration of the needs, DMUs, and DMPs of hospitals. To summarize briefly: Lifeline was able to offer the hospitals the ability to offer improved care, to provide a service that fostered relations between the hospitals and their communities, and to earn new revenues.)

In instances in which the doctor initiates the purchase process, the doctor's awareness is obviously the key. In cases in which the elderly person initiates it, Lifeline must reach doctors because they will be consulted, but it must also reach the elderly. The previous discussion of their communication habits suggests that the elderly can be reached. Lifeline would want to try to get news coverage both in general media, such as local newspapers and TV news, and in special publications aimed at or read heavily by the elderly. It might also be able to get exposure through senior centers, churches, or other organizations, although any analysis of those organizations would make it clear that they will be concerned about their reputations and will be very careful about allowing access to their member populations. Because elderly people are connected to other elderly people, word of mouth may be an effective tool. If it is respectful and not excessively commercial, a campaign of asking users of the service to give Lifeline the names of additional prospects might work.

In situations in which the adult children would begin the purchase process, communication is more difficult. The problem is that there does not appear to be an effective but economical way of reaching that diverse and dispersed group, some of whom will not even live in the same geographic area as their parents. Lifeline managers would certainly want to ensure that the company will be found easily by adult children who actively initiate a search for an emergency-response service (on the Internet, for example). It would be difficult, however, to use broad communication to make adult children aware in the first place and to convince them to begin searching. Unless it can find a cost-effective communication approach for those DMU members, Lifeline may simply have to concentrate on customers who will display the other buying patterns instead.

This discussion has focused on communication issues related to the initial purchase of the service. The customer pictures offer other insights, too, such as the desirability of Lifeline's including regular contact with adult children in the service definition in instances in which it will be welcomed, but avoiding it if the elderly person considers it inappropriately intrusive. For now, we can simply note that Lifeline could gain many other insights and ideas from these and from even more complete customer pictures.

USING OTHER CUSTOMER PICTURES

As another example of the potential power of understanding buying processes, recall the manufacturer of specialty products used in construction. A manager from the company estimated that the architect on a typical commercial or institutional building project has to make 25,000 individual decisions in the course of the design. The manager explained that it therefore made a great deal of sense for his company to offer help with the design of specific parts (or systems) of such buildings and, in particular, to offer full, integrated sets of products to address the design needs for the systems it targeted. The basic idea was to remove unwanted work and complexity from the architects and, by doing so, to increase the chances that the architects would specify the company's products.

Another example comes from the early history of America Online.[10] The company faced the key challenge of winning customers—lots of individual customers. Its managers believed that traditional advertising or related methods would not be effective with prospective customers. Instead, they thought that customers needed to experience AOL's service to know that they liked it.

The managers pictured customers as being reluctant to spend money for software that would allow them to use the service, especially before they had been convinced that they would in fact like the service. Still, the managers pictured prospects as sufficiently interested to be willing to try the service, if doing so was easy. And, the pictures said that prospects would be receptive to receiving information and tools for trial use from lots of sources.

Accordingly, in 1993 AOL began distributing free diskettes that provided the AOL software and offered a few hours of free service. The company mailed diskettes to millions of homes. It distributed them in magazines and at numerous locations, such as airplanes and football stadiums. AOL subscribers rose from 250,000 in July 1993 to a million in July 1994 to 5 million in February 1996.

As another example, consider MathSoft, a company that had developed a sophisticated PC-software package to help engineers and scientists with their work.[11] An example in the previous chapter noted that many different people may be involved in an organization's DMU for software—the end users, IT managers, engineering managers, purchasing agents, accountants or finance managers, and others. In addition, there can be very different DMPs in different organizations, with the processes driven from higher up in some organizations and decisions being made by individual end users in others.

For this example, focus on the customer companies in which the end users initiate the DMP, either because they can actually make the purchases themselves or because in practice they take products that interest them to their management or to IT for consideration. Regarding the design of the product, suffice it to say that the product won awards for its usefulness to engineers and scientists. Instead, consider the communication habits of the target customers.

Especially in the early 1990s, when this story occurred, many of the target customers at least occasionally read specialized publications about personal computers. They also read specialized publications in their fields. Many attended conferences, similar professional meetings, and some trade shows. They frequently talked about their work with colleagues and might be sufficiently interested to talk about new tools they had found. They paid attention to information sources that they found credible. They did not pay attention to what they considered junk mail. Many of them liked to experiment with new techniques and products. In addition, they often wanted to be able to try out a new product before purchasing it.

This brief picture clearly suggests some promising ideas about communication. Good product reviews in credible specialized publications would be useful. Display booths at trade shows and other meetings would be effective, especially if they were designed to let attendees try the product easily. Similarly, MathSoft might offer demonstration disks to interested potential buyers. (Internet demos were not yet possible in the early 1990s.)

Again, the complete design of a marketplace strategy would require more complete customer pictures and consideration of other possible DMPs. Analysis of organizations in which decisions were made by the head of engineering or a similar senior manager would lead to significantly different communication approaches. Analysis might therefore help the company decide to focus its early efforts on a particular segment defined not by industry or company size but instead by whether the DMP was centralized or decentralized. For now, however, the situation has provided another example of using the concepts of communication habits, awareness, and evaluation in customer pictures and in strategy design.

BETTER VALUE PROPOSITIONS

This chapter's discussion of the importance of understanding and addressing customers' buying processes suggests another improvement in the definition of a value proposition. For situations in which there is a single individual in the DMU, version 3a fits.

VALUE PROPOSITION VERSION 3A

An explicit statement of how and why our entire marketplace strategy (including not only the products themselves but also the ways we communicate with the customer, deliver the products, support the products, and so on) provides value—lots of value—to the customer.

For situations with more than one DMU participant, version 3b includes that complication.

VALUE PROPOSITION VERSION 3B

An explicit statement of how and why our entire marketplace strategy (including not only the products themselves but also the way we communicate with the customer, deliver the products, support the products, and so on) provides value—lots of value—to the customer overall and to the key players in the customer's DMU.

Finally, in most business-to-business strategies and in some business-to-consumer ones, one more improvement in the definition of the value proposition is appropriate. As noted in Chapter 3, business customers are frequently highly risk averse. The risk and reward systems of organizations, especially large organizations, often create lots of inertia.

Consequently, business buyers generally must have very strong reasons before they will make changes, including the changes involved in buying new products. Frequently, they must see solid, specific evidence that they will receive substantial benefits from potential purchases. As a result, it is frequently imperative for marketers to provide explicit, *quantified* statements of the value they will provide; vague general statements about high quality and great (or even amazing) benefits usually will not suffice.

Therefore, especially in business-to-business situations, it is frequently important to have a value proposition that meets the following definition.

VALUE PROPOSITION VERSION 4

An explicit quantified statement of how and why our entire marketplace offering (including not only the products themselves but also the way we communicate with the customer, deliver the products, support the products, and so on) provides value to the customer.

Again, the DMU should be included in some cases, so there would be a value proposition version 4a for single-person DMUs and a version 4b for multiperson ones.

SUMMARY

The initial customer pictures considered in the preceding chapter neglect the customer's buying behavior. Enriching the customer pictures by incorporating key aspects of customers' processes for buying and using products can significantly improve market-place strategies.

Frequently, it is especially useful to consider in detail the customers' processes of first becoming aware of the product, beginning to pay attention and to think of themselves as potential buyers, then evaluating possible purchases, deciding that they will in fact purchase, selecting what they will buy, and actually purchasing the product. It can also be important to consider customers' post-purchase processes for using the product. Consideration of the customers' communication habits is a central part of the analysis of buying behavior.

This chapter's richer analysis of customers leads to revised definitions of the value proposition. A value proposition is a clear and explicit statement of how and why a company's entire marketplace offering will provide value to customers, meeting customer needs and fitting with customer processes. For most business and some consumer situations, the value proposition should state how and why the company will provide value to the customer as a whole and to key members of the DMU; it should also quantify the benefits that will be provided.

OUTSIDE-IN ACTIONS

1. **Add information about customers' buying behavior to your lists of customer characteristics.**

   Describe explicitly how customers become aware, begin to pay attention, and begin to think of themselves as potential buyers of your products and services or those of your competitors. Add information about how customers evaluate possible purchases. Describe how customers decide that they will in fact proceed to a purchase, how they make their final selection, and how they purchase.

2. **Include information about the customers' communication habits.**

Describe the sources of information the customers use, the extent to which they find those sources credible, and so on.

3. **Also add key insights into customers' processes for using products or services like yours.**

Describe the customers' usage processes, identifying key steps that the customers take in actually using the products or services.

4. **Ask others in your organization what they know about customers' buying behavior, their communication habits, and their usage.**

Notice inconsistencies between your assumptions and those of other people. (You will probably find more contradictions and inconsistencies regarding behavior than regarding product-related needs simply because behavior often receives considerably less direct attention.)

Consider substituting some of these other assumptions for some of your own. At least, keep track of the areas where you and others have importantly different views about customers.

5. **Now improve your initial customer pictures.**

Decide which are the most important insights into customers' buying behavior, communication habits, and usage behavior. Incorporate those key insights into your pictures. Work to make the pictures come alive, capturing the essence of your customers. Save the insights that you don't put into the pictures now as backup for the future.

6

OUTSIDE-IN STRATEGY
An Explicit Customer Reason for Everything

[T]he heart of what strategy is about [is] creating value for customers.
—Kenichi Ohmae

H AVING CONSIDERED CUSTOMER PICTURES, we're now ready to explore outside-in strategies. The strategies (and the actions they contain) specify what to do for customers in order to satisfy their needs and match their behavior in some area and to earn profits in the process.

To repeat the essence of the outside-in discipline: have an explicit customer-based reason for everything you do in the marketplace. If you have good customer pictures expressing your view of customers, your strategic choices should seem obvious. If you have said clearly what you believe customers need from your product, then, among other things, your choices of product features should seem very clear and reasonable. If you have said that customers are especially interested in reliability, then it would be entirely understandable for you to build redundancy into your product. If you have explained the customers' communication habits, then it should be easy to accept your decision to advertise in a particular professional journal or to hire salespeople with particular types of skills. And so on.

The customer pictures are the foundation for the strategy. The pictures are based on what hard facts you have, together with your intuitions, hypotheses, and even guesses. To be sure, it's uncomfortable to have a foundation that, in many cases, feels very shaky. Making the customer pictures explicit creates a good deal of discomfort. For that reason, this chapter returns to the topic of explicitness, explaining why being explicit is so essential.

The major part of the chapter then discusses outside-in strategy, first giving a simple framework and then exploring examples of strategies. The end of the chapter returns to the assertion made at the beginning of the book: if you achieve and maintain an outside-in perspective while others do not, you get a leg up in the competitive marketplace.

EXPLICITNESS IS ESSENTIAL

With the outside-in discipline, strategy rests on a foundation of explicit customer pictures. The explicitness is essential, but it is also what makes the discipline so uncomfortable. Let's look a bit more at why it is so essential to overcome the discomfort and be explicit about your view of customers.

By this time most readers will have become at least somewhat uncomfortable with at least some of my customer pictures. Any particular reader is likely to have special knowledge relating to one or another of the examples and, as a result, will find my pictures incomplete and perhaps seriously wrong in some particulars. I am sure that some of those readers will be completely correct in their assessments.

Some readers may then conclude that the errors or lacunae in my pictures cast doubt on the approach of rigorous analysis with the outside-in discipline. I strongly disagree.

Suppose that instead of laying out my logic, I had instead simply announced that I am an expert in marketing and had then advanced an action plan for each of my examples—in other words, that I had leapt directly to recommendations, delivered as forcefully as I could. Assume that someone else with particularly impressive credentials had strongly advocated a different set of actions, without laying out the logic underlying them. Surely my recommendations would not have been 100 percent correct, especially for marketplace strategies that are substantially new and different. Certainly the other expert would also make some mistakes, especially in situations involving a lot of newness.

If we do not explain the logic, how are you to have any hope of identifying and correcting our wrong assumptions? How are we to have any hope of doing so, either? Granted, you or we are not likely to find all the mistakes, but surely it is better to find and correct some of them and then to continue evaluating the assumptions, correcting more mistakes as more information becomes available over time.

It may be useful to remember that respected business managers have been spectacularly wrong in some of their individual assumptions, too. The reaction of Kenneth Olsen, founder and long-time CEO of Digital Equipment Corporation, to the arrival of personal computers in the marketplace was, "The personal computer will fall flat on its face in business."[1]

Or consider Albert Pope, an early entrant into the automobile industry. Pope had a good sense of the potential of the automobile; in 1900 he predicted that within a decade there would be more cars in American cities than there were horses in those cities in 1900. Pope's customer picture led him to bet on the wrong technology, however. He favored electric rather than internal-combustion engines because he believed, "You can't get people to sit over an explosion."[2]

In working with people who are trying to use the outside-in

discipline, I say that I will follow them to any conclusion (within broad limits of reasonability), provided that they lead me each step of the way—in other words, provided that their customer pictures are rich and that there is a clear customer reason for every recommendation. I am pretty sure that some of their explicit assumptions will be wrong, but I don't think that trying to get people to guess what assumptions I happen to consider correct would provide much value—even if in fact I had opinions on that subject. Instead, I want to help people develop the challenging skill of being explicit and rigorous.

The key to understanding this approach is my belief that *making those customer assumptions explicit and linking them clearly to strategy is perhaps 80 percent of the battle.* Once the assumptions are on the table, they can be considered, reviewed, and corrected by other people. If they are not explicit, they are far less likely to be challenged, and, especially in situations involving a lot of newness, they need to be challenged repeatedly.

To get the most value from this outside-in discipline, businesspeople need colleagues and advisors with whom they can talk and even argue a lot about flawed but explicit customer pictures leading to marketplace strategies. The process does not guarantee success, but it does increase the chances that the strategies will be sound. Repeated discussions and revisions over time provide the basis for improvements in initial, certainly-less-than-perfect strategies and also increase the probabilities of business success.

One example that can help make the point about explicitness involves a relatively simple consumer product: rice.[3] In the mid-1990s, a company named RiceTec was working to increase sales of its Texmati and Jasmati products; both were aromatic specialty rices. The specialty-rice market in the United States was very small. Most Americans knew very little about different rices and did not pay much attention when they added rice to their supermarket carts. RiceTec had limited resources and needed to devise inexpensive communication strategies to attract more consumers to high-quality aromatic rices and to Texmati and Jasmati in particular.

In considering this example, some people suggest that RiceTec should use its packaging to attract typical U.S. grocery customers. The outside-in discipline says that we should accept the logic of that recommendation if (and only if) they have previously stated explicitly that typical U.S. grocery consumers would actually stop and read packages in the rice aisle in an attempt to identify interesting new products. (Although we could, of course, challenge that part of their customer pictures, the logic linking the picture and the action would be clear.)

Once those necessary assumptions are clearly articulated and are out on the table for examination, most people themselves reject them. At least, they conclude that consumers wouldn't start examining rice packages without some additional motivation.

At that point, people's attention turns to ways in which they might generate the needed motivation. Some decide that in-store sampling would work; again, the outside-in discipline says that we should be prepared to accept their logic if it is explicitly tied to customer pictures. Others decide that the more typical consumer is not the right target after all. They might focus instead on serious cooks and people who are seriously interested in food, exploring the behavior of those customers and then identifying other appropriate communication and distribution choices to reach them.

Thus, the outside-in discipline emphasizes sound explicit logic rather than good insights per se. Good insights are wonderful, of course. I hope you have lots of them. I hope you can work with other people who also have lots of them. The outside-in discipline of rigorous thinking will help improve both mediocre and good insights, however. And, to repeat, in situations in which the answers aren't clear (which include situations with lots of opportunity), no one's insights will be complete.

Another story, this one about my students, explains one more reason that I've come to believe so strongly in this rigorous outside-in discipline. To encourage the kind of examination and discussion I've mentioned here, I had my students write their papers in small groups. I provided extensive feedback on all the papers, commenting especially on whether the students had presented rich customer pictures and whether the pictures provided a customer reason for every recommendation that followed.

Each semester I found at least one or two students who were very strong and convincing in class discussions but who were highly disappointed with the feedback their groups received on the first paper. I eventually formed a hypothesis that those students' strong presentation skills had, in the past, shielded them from thorough scrutiny of their underlying logic. They weren't used to having someone examine their thinking in as detailed (even nitpicking) a way as I did, checking each step.

Fortunately, the students were adults (average age about 29) and decided, at least for the course, to play the game my way. By the end, I am delighted to report, they had mastered the rigorous approach, and they left the course with a combination of presentation skills and the outside-in discipline. And those presentation skills are, I believe, more valuable in the service of good thinking than they are in masking weaker logic.

I don't know how to make the outside-in discipline comfortable. As one very strong student explained after her group had written its first paper, making all her assumptions that visible made her feel as if she were out on a limb. But the alumni who return after spending time in business report that the effort and the discomfort of learning the approach were worth while. I do know that practice helps; people become used to the discomfort and are increasingly able to use the approach effectively. That's the reason my premise is that businesspeople lack both a discipline and the habit of using that discipline. The discipline does in fact work. The habit makes the use of the discipline practical.

OUTSIDE-IN STRATEGY

Having emphasized customer pictures to this point, we can now turn to discussions that emphasize marketplace strategies based on those pictures. The remainder of this chapter presents and considers a definition of outside-in strategy. The following four chapters consider components of strategy, emphasizing the aspects that are most important in customer-based outside-in thinking. They also contain examples and discussion of outside-in thinking that are intended to help make readers sufficiently comfortable with the approach to use it.

An outside-in strategy is *a consistent, coordinated set of choices for the components of strategy, meant to address the needs of one or more segments of customers.* The strategy components are shown in the following diamond:

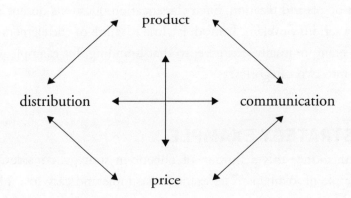

(Many readers will recognize the four listed elements of strategy. In the marketing literature, they are often called the marketing mix. They are sometimes called the "4 Ps" and given names that all start with the letter p: product, price, place, and promotion. Although it is common to see these four components of the mix, they are not universal. In fact, Neil Borden, who first introduced the concept of the marketing mix, gave a longer list of components and specifically said that he expected other people to use different elements from those he did.)[4]

The most important thing about this definition is that it requires that the strategic tools be chosen to address the needs of one or more market segments. There must be a clear customer foundation, based on customer needs and behavior.

In addition, the components of the strategy must fit with one another and work together; they must be consistent and coordinated. The diamond shows all the pairwise connections between strategy elements, emphasizing this need for consistency and coordination.

Although these four elements—product, price, communication, and distribution—are used extremely widely in marketing and strategy, it is not always clear exactly where a specific marketing tool fits into the picture. For example, branding is sometimes considered to be part of product policy. At other times, it is treated as part of communication. Such classification questions do not create a serious problem. Instead, it's fine to think of the elements as not being mutually exclusive, so that branding, for example, can fall into two categories.

A STRATEGY EXAMPLE

To introduce this definition of outside-in strategy, consider the example of Bic pens. The example is simple and easy to explain and is therefore a good place to start. In addition, my experiences in places ranging from Boston to Singapore to Beijing and with people from all over the world suggest that people have very similar pictures of customers for Bic or similar pens.

So, think about customers for Bic pens—typical adult customers who buy their own pens. (For now, ignore the common situation in which an individual gets a pen from the supply closet at work. Also ignore bulk back-to-school purchases for kids.) What needs does Bic satisfy?

Most people start by saying they need something to write with. Many add other needs. The pen should be inexpensive, so that they can chew on it and otherwise abuse it and so that they don't feel too bad when they lose it. They need a pen that is of sufficient quality that it won't leak all over their pockets and will write for a reasonable time before running out of ink.

Next, consider the awareness step in buyer behavior. Why and when do people decide that they are customers for Bic pens—that they are in the market? People say that they might have lost their last pen, or that they might be having trouble finding pens at home when they need them, or some similar reason. Do they go to the store specially to buy a Bic pen? The answers are that occasionally they do, if, for example, they are on their way to a meeting and haven't found a working pen to take with them. Usually, however, they do not. Why, then, do they think to buy? The overwhelming answer is that they buy because they notice the pens in a store. What kind of store? Drugstore, convenience store, discount store, newsstand, supermarket. . . . Why do customers notice the pens? Because the pens are placed near the checkout counter and the customers notice them while waiting in line.

What about the evaluation and decision steps in the buying process? Those steps are unusually simple for this purchase. If the store has another brand instead of Bic, do they go to another store to look for Bic? The virtually universal answer is no, they buy whatever brand the store stocks.

Now consider the elements of Bic's strategy for this individual user (not for the bulk business buyer or for the back-to-school purchaser, who would require different approaches). The product is a high-quality though inexpensive writing instrument that writes reliably and does not leak. The company has very efficient (high fixed cost and low variable cost) plants and is expert at manufacturing small plastic products.

The price is low. Actually, the situation is more complicated than that. True, the price to the end customer must be low. At the same time, Bic must entice retailers to place its products in some highly desirable retail real estate—the places next to the registers. Retailers give those places to products that will earn the most profit for the store. So, the combination of the sales velocity and the margin per pen must make retailers decide to put Bic at the checkout. And, the requirement for high margins but low consumer price makes it even more clear that there is no room for sloppiness in the Bic strategy.

Bic distributes its products extremely widely—and it must, because customers won't go looking for Bic. As for communication, Bic does not use broadcast, print, or similar advertising for its pens. Its general policy is to advertise new products to make customers aware of them, but then not to advertise. That policy is sensible, given that customers do not exhibit brand loyalty but buy whatever brand they see at the store. At the same time, Bic's packaging and display are important point-of-purchase advertising; their job is to get the attention of the customer who is waiting in line at the checkout.

Notice how clearly the basic elements of Bic's strategy are linked to customer needs and behavior. Notice also how the elements fit together to form a consistent, coordinated whole. Any good strategy should similarly consist of marketing tools that are clearly linked to customers and that fit together to form a consistent whole. Almost needless to say, achieving good customer foundation, consistency, and coordination is not easy, especially with complicated products or with products that offer customers fundamentally new ways of doing things.

STRATEGIC LESSONS FROM MORE EXAMPLES

For comparison with this example of Bic, let's turn to Cross pens and, again, consider purchases by individuals. When asked what needs are served by Cross, people talk about fashion and status, often even before they mention the need to write. Many people say that they buy Cross because they need a gift to give to someone else. (I like to suggest that Cross is what they buy when they need a gift that is nice but not too personal and they have no other ideas!)

The awareness step in buying is often straightforward. The customers need to buy a gift for some occasion, such as a graduation. The rest of the buying process is also relatively simple. People say they do make special trips to the store in this situation—to a stationery store, a jeweler, or some other store that they expect to carry Cross.

Asked what they would do if the store turned out not to have Cross pens, a few people say they would try to select something else, but many disagree. They say that in situations in which they want to buy a Cross pen, they don't have other ideas, they do think Cross is an especially appropriate gift item, and they would go to another store.

Now consider how Cross's strategy appears to fit this very simple description of customer behavior. The pen is high quality and comes in a box suitable for gift wrapping. It also comes with a lifetime warranty, a nice touch for occasions such as graduations.

The price is in the range that people expect to pay for such gifts. The margin to retailers must be high enough for Cross to get adequate display and attention in stationery stores, jewelry stores, and its other retail outlets. Cross does not have to be as widely available as Bic because customers will shop for Cross pens. The pens must be reasonably convenient to find, but they need not be everywhere. And Cross does advertise, generally using print advertising in publications such as airline magazines and often positioning the product as a status gift.

Again, notice how the parts of Cross's strategy fit together, as did the parts of Bic's. They show the consistency and coordination required for an outside-in strategy.

Notice also that mixing some parts of the Cross strategy and other parts of the Bic strategy would lead to a mess. An outside-in strategy needs to be designed as a consistent whole, not one part at a time. This point is important. Neglecting it can lead to serious problems, both for start-ups and for existing businesses.

First, consider start-ups. Frequently in practice, especially for complex products that are difficult to design and to make, entrepreneurs try to do the product part of strategy (or occasionally the product and price parts) first. Unfortunately, they may then wind up with products that cannot be serviced adequately by the available distribution channels, or that require more technical knowledge from salespeople than is realistic, or that create some other extremely serious problem.

Earlier consideration of all aspects of strategy can help to avoid such problems. It can help to ensure that product designs are not so expensive that customers will be unwilling to pay enough to provide profits for the company. It can lead to product designs that include helpful diagnostics or designs that use disposable modules to get around the limited technical expertise of the people who will have to service the products. And so on.

Next, as an example involving an existing business, consider IBM.[5] In particular, consider IBM's introduction of personal computers in the 1980s. At the time, IBM's strategy was to provide all IBM sales and service to a customer, especially a large customer, through a single salesperson or sales team. Highly competent (and expensive) salespeople were an important part of IBM's approach for satisfying customer needs.

At first, IBM treated the PCs like any other product. Customers could order them and obtain service for them through their normal sales team. In other words, IBM used a strategy that changed the product (and price) but left the remaining elements intact. Soon, however, IBM found it necessary to change the strategy. Under the revised policy, customers could buy PCs direct from IBM only in quantities of 20 or more. For smaller orders, the customers had to go through other channels, such as computer stores.

The problem was not the size of the purchase; customers were still able to buy electric typewriters (which IBM still made at that time), even one electric typewriter, direct from IBM. The problem was the amount of support a novice PC user often required. I believe that IBM's change was intended to shield its expensive field sales force from having to spend time holding the hands of new PC users. (And IBM could allow sales of 20 units or more because a customer company buying that many PCs at a time was expected to have its own PC-support staff.)

Thus, IBM could not simply apply its traditional mainframe-oriented strategy to personal computers. It had to change all the major elements of strategy for PCs: product, price, communication, and distribution. The strategy for PCs had to be consistent and coordinated—and based on customer needs and behavior.

An understanding of customers and the outside-in discipline can lead a company to a strategy that is markedly different from the strategies of others in its industry, as illustrated by Zara, the major portion of the Spanish company Inditex.[6] Zara's founder, Amancio Ortega, built his company on a few key insights into his target customers: primarily young women, initially in Europe.

The customers wanted absolutely current fashions at moderate prices. They didn't want to wear exactly the same thing as everyone else was wearing, however. Although they wouldn't pay extremely high prices, they would definitely pay slightly more for fashion and timeliness. They would make frequent visits to a store that carried things they liked and that changed its merchandise often. Advertising was not a major motivator for them, but they were influenced by fashionable displays in clothing-store windows.

These and similar insights led to Zara's outside-in strategy. The company emphasized time to market as the most important thing in fashion retailing. A large number of designers, along with the store managers, worked constantly to uncover the latest fashion trends. Zara manufactured more than half of its own clothing, in sharp contrast with the cost-oriented outsourced manufacturing of its competitors, and it also operated its own distribution system. It could therefore get new items from concept stage into the stores in a few weeks, as compared with nine months for Gap. Zara introduced over 10,000 items each year. It made deliveries to each of its stores twice a week, with new styles arriving all the time and none lasting more than four weeks; in contrast, competitors introduced new items only once or twice each season. Unlike competitors, Zara used very little advertising, although managers used displays in the store windows as important communication tools.

Founded in 1975, Zara became a large, successful company,

especially in Europe and South America, but on other continents as well. A 2000 article (headlined "The Most Devastating Retailer in the World") emphasized the importance for Zara of having a strategy that was entirely consistent and that rested firmly on customers' needs and behaviors:

> Zara is an integrated system, not just a collection of parts. . . . Even in an age of perpetual turmoil, the truly successful companies are still those whose structure feels organic, and whose business is rooted in a strategy that governs everything they do.[7]

THREE MORE OUTSIDE-IN CONCEPTS: FOCUS, INERTIA, AND SCALE

Chapter 2 introduced three concepts for the outside-in discipline: customers, rigor, and opportunity. This section introduces the remaining three foundation concepts: focus, inertia, and scale.

People cannot *focus* on too many things at once. Managers may have to be aware of many things, but successful businesspeople and business academics alike report the importance of identifying a few key action areas and focusing strongly on those areas.

One purpose of customer pictures is to help with focus. A major problem with checklists or other long lists of customer characteristics is that they don't convey a sense of what is most important about customers. If customer pictures are to make the customers come alive, they need to emphasize those customers' essential characteristics. The pictures, in turn, make it easier to determine which customer-related tasks are most critical to a strategy.

A good outside-in strategy focuses on a few clear areas that are most important for success. In the stunning improvements at

Tesco described in Chapter 1, the company used the idea of simplicity to help achieve and maintain focus. The efforts emphasized three guiding principles: better (for customers), simpler (for staff), and cheaper (for Tesco). The principles were highlighted in "The Tesco Way," which made clear to employees that they should be using their talents to simplify rather than to complicate, that Tesco should focus on simple solutions to serve customers better.[8]

One more example involving my students may suggest ideas for achieving focus. I strictly limited the length of my students' papers to three pages (space and a half). It is much harder to write a good short paper, where you must select and present the key points, than it is to write a longer paper, where you can throw in all kinds of things and hope that readers will find what they need. By the end of the courses, the students were able to describe customer pictures, a basic strategy to address the pictures, and some implications for implementing the strategy—all within the page limitation. As they gained that efficiency, they became better and better able to identify the key action areas on which the managers should focus when executing a specific strategy.

Obviously, readers of this book will not use required paper writing as the means of achieving focus. But focus is extremely important for success, so you will want to find some way to make yourself select the appropriate areas for focus. You may find it helpful to put limits on the lengths of your customer pictures and especially of your strategy while, at the same time, checking that you have managed to include the key elements of your strategy and that there is a customer reason for each one. The rigor and explicitness of the outside-in discipline can help with that task.

The next concept is *inertia*. Some marketplace tools take considerably more time to deploy and to change than others. For example, building relationships with distributors takes time and effort and, as Chapter 10 will discuss, changing distribution strategy can be extremely difficult. Similarly, brand image takes time to build, and—in situations in which brand does in fact matter to customers—changes in brand image, especially improvements, are difficult.

The concept of inertia facilitates discussion of the relative ease or difficulty of deploying or of making changes in different marketing tools. As noted in Chapter 2, many businesspeople told me about regrets that they had not spent a bit more time early enough thinking about high-inertia tools such as brand image. They talked about such problems frequently enough to suggest that considerations of inertia are important for strategic success.

The idea is to devote a bit of special attention to high-inertia tools, laying the groundwork now so that those tools will work well when they are needed in the future. It's sometimes hard to take time from the press of immediate issues you face, but having the discipline to spend a little time preparing for the longer term seems to pay off handsomely.

The final fundamental concept is *scale*. The basic idea is that some business actions can be taken a bit at a time, whereas others are larger and not divisible.

For example, consider Toupargel, a French company that provided home delivery of frozen foods.[9] Every few weeks, customers could order from an extensive catalog of items stocked in Toupargel's two warehouses. Orders were delivered in refrigerated trucks that were based at Toupargel's branches, located in several regions of France.

The company's managers took some relatively small, though still important, actions, such as efforts to improve the utilization of one of the trucks or decisions to include a specific new item in the catalog. The decision to buy a new truck was a bit larger. The decision to add a branch was considerably bigger. And the decision to establish an additional central warehouse was bigger still.

It obviously makes sense to devote special care and research to the larger decisions. In addition, it is frequently important to begin thinking about and gathering information for the larger decisions well in advance. Thus, the idea of scale is related to the idea of inertia.

Scale is also related to the idea of experimentation. When you're doing something new and it isn't clear what strategy makes sense, it can be extremely helpful to find ways to experiment—in other words, to use small-scale actions to try out options and to learn, rather than to make larger decisions without being sure that they make sense. Incorporating smaller-scale actions into a strategy can reduce the risks by allowing you to learn from experience and get the strategy right. You may be able to use experiments to improve your understanding of customers, update your customer pictures, and then choose even better experiments.

One of the founders of a company called dollarDEX.com provided a good description of the experimental, small-scale approach. His company, which will be discussed at more length in Chapter 12, started an Internet business in Singapore to help consumers purchase financial products such as home mortgages. Unlike the majority of Internet start-ups, dollarDEX.com has been successful.

The founder and CEO explained that he and his partners understood that the Internet was new and that businesspeople had not yet figured out what types of communication would work well with consumers, especially for high-risk products like home mortgages. He emphasized that in such circumstances, it was "not good to bet the farm on one particular marketing approach."

Instead, the dollarDEX.com founders tried many different smaller experiments—everything from putting fliers on the windshields of cars, to placing printed marketing materials at new condominium projects, to joint efforts with Internet-service providers.

Significantly, they tried many different things in parallel, at the same time. They were careful to have explicit, quantitative ways to measure the results of each experiment. Many of the techniques did not turn out to be profitable and were dropped. Others worked well and were continued. The result of the experimentation was efficient and effective communication without large, expensive mistakes.

OUTSIDE-IN STRATEGY GIVES YOU A COMPETITIVE LEG UP

After numerous discussions pointing out that the outside-in discipline is difficult and uncomfortable, let's now return to the more positive message that started this book. Yes, there is bad news. Businesspeople have fallen into a bad habit of inside-out thinking. Attaining the good outside-in habit is difficult. But there is also good news. If you succeed in achieving and maintaining the outside-in habit, you gain a competitive leg up in the marketplace.

Looking back at the dot-com mania at the end of the twentieth century provides illustrations. First, consider the bad news: the strategies that many dot-com companies presented to the world were definitely not outside in. They seemed to assume that customers were easily manipulated, an assumption that is usually wrong. What was especially distressing about many of those strategies was their emphasis on what economists and business-strategy experts call first-mover advantage: the importance of being first.

The strategies frequently made it their overriding objective to be the first company with which a customer did business in some area (such as the online retailing of products for pets). Entrepreneurs found the need to attract initial customers to be so critical that many started with prices of zero, giving their products or services away for free.

For example, Netpulse was a company that made devices that attached to exercise machines and allowed users to surf the Web while they worked out.[10] Netpulse had trouble selling its devices, which it originally priced at $2,500 each. When the company instead started giving away the devices, adoptions rose sharply. The company's CEO said that the audience of users in health clubs was worth more to Netpulse in attracting advertisers than the cost of providing the devices gratis. He told *Fortune*:

> People in health clubs are totally bored, actively seeking distraction. Their minds are up for grabs.

Entrepreneurs, investors, and the business press began to speak about the importance of attracting eyeballs, by which they meant attracting people who saw (visited) a Web site. With help from Credit Suisse First Boston, *Fortune* magazine calculated the market capitalization per pair of eyeballs (market cap per customer) for a collection of Internet stocks. Toward the high end, though not the highest, was Chemdex, an online business-to-business exchange for laboratory chemicals. Its market cap per pair of eyeballs was $104,903. Yet at the time, according to *Fortune*, Chemdex was losing $1,299.76 on each customer.

Think for a minute of what customer assumptions could possibly make this emphasis on eyeballs (regardless of immediate profit) make sense. The companies would have to have some reason to expect sizable future profits in order to justify the short-term losses and the high market caps. If customers were forced to stay at the same Web site and make lots of profitable purchases in the future, that might be a reason. And, in fact, entrepreneurs and investors at the time talked about what they called "stickiness," the idea that customers would stick to a particular site.

Unfortunately for the dot-com entrepreneurs, most of these expectations of stickiness were wishful thinking. The very things that people (businesspeople, business writers, and, most important, customers) said were most attractive about the Internet directly contradicted such a possible reaction. The Internet was supposed to provide customers with the information and the flexibility that would allow them to find the product and price that were best for them. It was supposed to allow them to shop around, not to leave them stuck at one Web site.

Thus, many dot-com strategies lacked sensible customer foundations. People seemed to ignore what customers were in fact saying and doing about Internet usage. There was a lot of bad news in the prevalent strategic thinking.

For an example of good news, consider eBay.[11] Even in 2000, at the time of the *Fortune* analysis of eyeballs, eBay was making a profit on each customer. In the roughly seven years from the time Meg Whitman became CEO until the end of 2004, eBay's revenues grew from just under $6 million to just over $3 billion. Those numbers made eBay the fastest-growing company in business history.

The success of eBay rested firmly on an understanding of how customers did, wanted to, and would behave. Scott Cook, the founder of Intuit and an eBay board member, reportedly joked that Whitman (and eBay) "found a parade and ran in front of it." But that's what I would call (granted, in language that's less colorful than Cook's) getting the outside-in perspective right.

Whitman and eBay got it right while so many other people were building dot-com companies without good outside-in strategies. As a result, eBay prospered while those companies failed. And eBay has continued to prosper, with strong emphasis on customers and on outside-in strategy.

It has turned out that it was in fact important for eBay to be first—first into a country. There really is a first-mover advantage in its business. Customers prefer an auction site with more (quality) buyers and sellers in their areas of interest to a site with fewer participants. The company's managers learned that lesson in Japan, where eBay was second and soon withdrew from the market.

By contrast, in Germany, eBay became the leading auction site by buying a small local online-auction company in 1999 and then growing it. German laws strictly limited the hours of operation of bricks-and-mortar retailers, so German customers' needs were an especially good fit for eBay's shopping alternative. By 2004, eBay was highly successful in Germany; its trading volume in that country amounted to more than $100 for every German man, woman, and child. And by 2004, eBay was applying the lessons it had learned in earlier markets to China, investing aggressively to build critical mass.

The eBay success story is an illustration of the power of achieving an outside-in perspective when others don't. The company and its managers focused on real understanding of customers, even in the midst of the dot-com mania, with its emphasis on eyeballs and IPOs. What a wonderful thing it is to find a customer parade you can run in front of! The company learned more and more about its customers from its experiences in the marketplace, including from what turned out to be mistakes, such as the entry into Japan. Its managers continued to improve their understanding of customers and then to improve their strategies. Their outside-in thinking gave them a big leg up in the marketplace, and, to date, their success has been phenomenal.

The outside-in perspective can also bring competitive success in other marketplaces, ones that lack the strong first-mover advantages that eBay found. In competitive markets where you will continue to face strong competition over time, the key to success can be to identify a segment of customers and then design and execute an outside-in strategy to meet those customers' needs and match their behavior better than competitors do.

The athletic-shoe company New Balance provides an example.[12] In 1998 the *Wall Street Journal* described the company's strategy as a "flashless formula," but a formula that, if without flash, was successful. Wearers of the company's shoes included Bill Clinton, Steve Jobs, and Dustin Hoffman. Its sales were growing briskly, while those of other manufacturers of athletic shoes were sluggish.

New Balance emphasized the needs of the baby-boomer generation. Its managers believed that many such people did need athletic shoes. They were especially interested in the 20 to 30 percent of the market whose feet were not fit by the two standard widths offered by other marketers of athletic shoes. Some customers had feet that were narrower than the standard, but, especially because of being overweight, many others had wide feet.

The target customers wanted shoes that fit well, functioned well, and were comfortable. New Balance managers believed that their targets did not view athletic shoes as fashion items to be updated frequently. Instead, when customers wore out one pair of shoes, many preferred the convenience of being able to buy the same model again. The customers were willing to pay moderate but not high prices for the shoes.

New Balance's CEO noted that the target customers would not have posters of sports superstars hanging in their bedrooms, as some younger customers would. He believed the New Balance customers would not be influenced by celebrity endorsements and would much prefer that the company not spend money on such endorsements but offer lower prices instead. Such customers might be influenced by podiatrists, who provided some of them with orthotics, special devices that fit into shoes to correct the wearer's stance.

The New Balance strategy fit the managers' customer picture. The company offered its shoes in five widths, from narrow to extra-wide. Its prices were moderate. It did not use celebrity endorsements in its advertising. It did, however, hire serious athletes to help with product research, in order to have shoes that functioned the way customers wanted. To provide more stability in its product line, New Balance changed models much less frequently than its competitors did. It communicated with podiatrists, who could influence shoe purchasers.

New Balance's strategy differed substantially from the strategies of other leading manufacturers of athletic shoes, such as Nike and Reebok, because New Balance managers believed that their target customers differed significantly from the customers of the competitors. They believed that Nike and Reebok customers were much younger and that they were more fashion-conscious, more willing to pay high prices, and more influenced by celebrity endorsements. Those customers were not likely to be attracted by the New Balance strategy, but New Balance's own targets were.

New Balance was using a strong outside-in perspective to gain a competitive leg up in a large and attractive segment of the market. Rather than go head-to-head with its large competitors over the same customers, it identified an attractive segment that was underserved by those competitors and designed its own outside-in strategy to succeed with that promising segment.

SUMMARY

The outside-in discipline is generally not easy or comfortable, but it is an effective approach for designing and communicating successful strategies. And the approach is even more important when businesspeople are unsure about customers' needs and behavior. The good news is that if you succeed in achieving and maintaining an outside-in perspective, you improve your chances of success in the marketplace. If your competitors are not outside in while you are, you have an additional competitive advantage.

An outside-in strategy is a consistent, coordinated set of choices for the marketing tools (product, price, communication, and distribution), meant to address the needs of one or more segments of customers. The elements of strategy should form a consistent whole, and they should be clearly linked to customers' needs and behavior.

Basic ideas that help in thinking about and designing successful strategies are customers, opportunity, rigor, focus, inertia, and scale. *Customers* are the basis of marketplace strategy. An *opportunity* may exist when current approaches are not satisfactory for satisfying customer needs. The *rigor* of the outside-in discipline leads logically from customer pictures (based on data, intuition, and explicit hypotheses) to specific strategies and actions. Because people can truly concentrate on only a few things at a time, it is important for a strategy to identify the few key areas on which to *focus*. Despite the pressures of day-to-day management, there is substantial payoff from devoting a bit of attention to high-*inertia* tools that will become important in the future. Most strategies combine larger- and smaller-*scale* decisions. It's important to pay enough attention to and do enough advance planning for the larger decisions. It is also sometimes possible to design a strategy to include more smaller-scale decisions, thereby facilitating learning and adjustment.

OUTSIDE-IN ACTIONS

1. **Create a clear, explicit strategy statement of your approach to customers and your marketplace.**

   Return to the description of your strategy and supporting actions that you began constructing at the end of Chapter 2. Expand or revise that description if appropriate.

2. **Combine your customer pictures with this statement of your strategy and check for rigor and consistency.**

   Verify that each element of your strategy is supported by explicit information in the customer pictures. If not, it may be that the customer reason for a strategic element was simply omitted from the customer pictures; if so, include the needed reason. Alternatively, the strategic element may not fit with your beliefs about customers; if so, select a different strategic action that fits with your understanding of customers. Also, check that the elements of your strategy fit clearly with one another. If not, explore changes to your strategy to achieve consistency and coordination among its parts.

3. **Cycle through the steps as necessary.**

   You may have to cycle several times through these steps, describing the customer pictures and strategy and then checking for focus and consistency, to arrive at clear customer pictures that support every part of a clearly articulated, coordinated, and consistent strategy for the marketplace.

4. **Choose the few strategic actions on which you should focus.**

   Identify the actions that are essential to the strategy and that require special attention if they are to be executed well.

5. **Look for smaller-scale experiments that can help you improve your customer understanding and your strategy.**

   There will be some parts of your customer pictures or of your strategy about which you are particularly uncertain or with which you are uncomfortable. Look especially for experiments that could help you learn about those areas.

6. **Identify and address the high-inertia elements of your strategy.**

   Find the action areas that require a long time to execute and that are difficult to change. Resolve to devote at least a bit of attention to those areas well ahead of the time when you will need to have them in place.

7

OUTSIDE-IN PRODUCT DECISIONS

Customers' Needs and Perceptions Are What Count

IBM is a solutions company. We start with a customer's business problem, and work back to the right combination of technologies and expertise.
—Louis Gerstner, IBM's former CEO

THIS CHAPTER DISCUSSES PRODUCT—the first of the four major tools of marketplace strategy. It focuses on those aspects of product policy that are especially important for and especially influenced by the outside-in discipline. It does not attempt to cover the entire very large topic of product, as whole books have been written on this subject and it is covered at length in major chapters of texts on marketing or product development.

Although they are often made in relative isolation, as the previous chapter stressed, to be effective, product decisions must fit into a complete marketplace strategy that is a consistent and coordinated response to the needs and behavior of one or more segments of customers.

The fundamental questions to understand about a product are what benefits the product offers and to whom. Actually, to be more precise, the fundamental question is what benefits customers believe the product offers.

CUSTOMER PERCEPTIONS
ARE WHAT COUNT

Customers often perceive product benefits differently from the way businesspeople perceive them. Especially with technically complex and advanced products, businesspeople tend to focus strongly on the product's attributes and capabilities. This phenomenon is so common that some industries have their own shorthand terms for referring to a strong orientation toward product capabilities per se. In the information technology (IT) industry at one stage, the common term was "bits and bytes." Somewhat later, the same general phenomenon was evoked by the term "speeds and feeds."

Customers, of course, instead care about the benefits that the product offers them. There are numerous examples of products that have failed because of overly technical product-oriented approaches that neglected to provide benefits to customers or to communicate those benefits clearly. Rather than talk about failures, let's instead look at a company that at first was extremely successful but that eventually got into trouble. I believe the company had a product focus rather than a customer focus in thinking about its products. That focus eventually interfered with its continued success.

The example is Digital Equipment Corporation, or DEC (which in the 1990s became part of Compaq, which in turn later became part of Hewlett-Packard). DEC was a tremendous entrepreneurial success and is thought of as having started the minicomputer industry. For a long time, the company was considered a—or perhaps the—minicomputer company, able to sell minicomputers to anyone who needed them.

That characterization of DEC may well not have been the most useful one, however. Yes, DEC did make minicomputers. The early minis served the needs of departments or individuals who wanted to have their own computing power, under their own control, rather than using their organization's centralized computer facilities. Those early customers worked primarily in laboratories, engineering groups, and similar technically oriented departments.

It was absolutely key that the early customers were technically sophisticated. DEC's products fit their needs well. For example, DEC's bus architecture was well suited for hooking up instruments. The early users had the technical knowledge (and the tools, such as oscilloscopes) necessary to establish the needed connections. Other aspects of DEC's early strategy, such as its approaches to maintenance and support, also fit the needs of these users.

The problems occurred later, when DEC tried to sell minicomputers to more general business customers with substantially less technical knowledge (to say nothing of their lack of oscilloscopes). Essentially the same physical product was perceived very differently by those newer customers; the requirements for sales, support, and service were very different, and DEC struggled.

DEC would have had a much easier time understanding the new types of customers, I believe, if it had defined itself at the outset as a sophisticated-users computer company rather than as a minicomputer company. The changes necessary to serve business users would still not have been easy, but at least it would have been a lot clearer that those changes were necessary. And perhaps DEC would have decided not to try to serve business users but instead to offer additional products to its existing customers or to other sophisticated users.

Overemphasis on product capabilities rather than customer benefits leads many people to act as if only highly technical products are worth offering. Good new technical products can be wonderful, of course, but there are also other good opportunities.

One rather fun example is a small company named Lansdale Semiconductor that was in the business of producing "trailing-edge chips."[1] Semiconductor manufacturers eventually discontinue chip designs. Intel's long-lived 8080 lasted from 1974 until 1987, when Intel stopped making it. More recent chips have had considerably shorter lives. Officially discontinued chips continue to function in some customer equipment, however. For example, the U.S. military often builds systems to last 20 to 25 years or more. Lansdale bought manufacturing rights and, when it could, even tooling and customer lists from semiconductor manufacturers and then served the customers' needs for old-design chips. Provided that Lansdale did a good job, its approach also benefited the chip manufacturers by satisfying their customers.

A common refrain when customers don't seem to appreciate some exciting new product is, "We'll change the customers' perceptions." True, informing and, to some extent, educating customers are parts of successful marketing. Sales calls, printed advertisements, public relations, presentations at professional meetings, and a variety of other tools can help. At the same time, it is awfully difficult and usually extremely expensive to make fundamental changes in customers' perceptions. Sometimes the effort is feasible and worth while. Often it is not.

One example of a situation in which the company decided it did have to change perceptions was Xerox's introduction of its 9200, discussed in Chapter 3. Although Xerox had previously taught its customers to use productivity matrices to compare machines, the benefits of the 9200 as compared with its competition, offset duplicators, seemed to require consideration of the reproduction department's turnaround time for actual jobs. Xerox's managers and its highly respected sales force set out to perform the needed education. They created models to demonstrate the total flow of jobs and tasks in a reproduction department. For important customers and prospects, they went through the highly laborious task of clocking the customer's actual job flow and then using models to show what the turn-around times would have been with the 9200 and with an offset competitor. This campaign obviously required very substantial resources.

Although it can be hard to reconcile oneself to doing so, especially if customers are failing to understand the true beauty and elegance of a wonderful technical design, it is important at least to have realistically limited ambitions about changing customer perceptions—and it is sometimes best simply to accept the flawed customer view as a given.

As an example, consider Frank Perdue's early efforts to brand chicken.[2] Perdue discussed chicken with a variety of consumers and found that many thought that chicken with yellowish flesh was of higher quality than chicken with whiter flesh. Rather than argue with that perception, Perdue set out to use the insight. He began including marigold petals in his chickens' feed. The chickens' flesh became more yellow, and Perdue got the added benefit that marigold petals were inexpensive and his feed costs actually decreased. Nice golden flesh was one of the ways in which Perdue differentiated his product and, as a result, obtained higher prices.

CUSTOMERS SEE AUGMENTED PRODUCTS

When customers make a purchase, they are buying more than the basic product or service, no matter how technically sophisticated that product or service may be. They may care about documentation, training, delivery, installation, maintenance, brand name, warranties, or a host of other things that are related to the product and the company that sells it. The marketing term *augmented product* refers to the product as viewed by the customer—the basic product plus the support, brand name, documentation, and all the other attributes that customers think matter. The following schematic shows the concept.

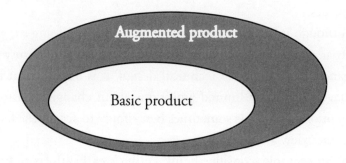

The augmented product is the entire larger oval, which contains the basic product plus all the attributes that augment it. The line between what is basic and what is augmented is frequently not clear and often changes over time. That lack of precise definition generally does not create a problem. The key idea is to consider what the customer buys and cares about—the entire larger oval.

There are situations in which the augmentation is extremely important in customer perceptions, as at the left in the diagram below, and situations in which the basic product dominates, as at the right. Again, the key is to consider the entire larger oval, no matter what its exact relation to the smaller one.

The discussion in Chapter 4 of Dell Computer's success with its relationship customers showed a highly effective use of augmentation. Dell helped those customers control the number of different types of computer products being used by their employees while still providing adequate access to powerful technologies.

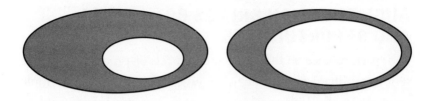

It helped customers order and support technical products. It helped with initial setup and inventory of the customer organizations' personal computers. And so on.

A Japanese retailer named Daiichi used augmentation effectively to earn considerably greater profits than its competitors did.[3] Daiichi was a retailer in the Akihabara district of Tokyo, an area full of consumer-electronics retailers that offered extremely wide product assortments and competed on price.

Daiichi managers understood that most Japanese homes were small and that as a result customers could not buy additional appliances. The company therefore augmented its products by offering to store seasonal items such as humidifiers or floor fans when they were not needed. Daiichi also offered three-year rather than the standard one-year warranties. At the beginning of the third year of each warranty, it offered a free inspection of the appliance so that problems could be fixed before the warranty ran out. The company kept information about specific customers and the appliances they owned so that it could tailor its direct-mail advertising to individuals.

Daiichi's strategy paid off handsomely. In the early 1990s, the company obtained 70 percent of its sales from repeat customers (as opposed to 20 percent for competitors). Its response rate to direct mail was four times that of its competitors; its return on assets was five times the competitors' rates.

AUGMENTATION BRINGS BOTH RISKS AND OPPORTUNITIES

Poor performance on the augmented aspects of product can create serious problems for a strategy. An especially well-known example concerns Intel's Pentium chip in 1994.[4] Customers discovered an error in the floating-point arithmetic on the chip. Intel managers reasoned that the problem would make a difference for only a small number of users. They offered to replace the chips of any customers who could demonstrate that they needed the fix.

Customers were outraged, and the publicity was extremely negative. The situation was even the basis for *Dilbert* cartoons for an entire week. (And surely it is very bad news when your product problem becomes the topic of an entire week of *Dilbert*.) Intel backed down and offered to correct the problem for anyone who asked. Andrew Grove, the company's founder, commented, "The past few weeks have been deeply troubling. What we view as an extremely minor technical problem has taken on a life of its own." A telling *New York Times* headline at the time read, "Intel's Crash Course on Consumers."[5]

Customers obviously did not think that they were dealing with an extremely minor technical problem. Instead, they emphasized Intel's apparent attitude toward its customers and the company's policies regarding product problems—two aspects of augmentation that they found important.

During the 1990s, augmentation, often in the form of services, became fashionable. Some companies used such augmentation to change the basic nature of their offering in the marketplace. Johnson Controls had been a manufacturer of thermostats and energy systems. The company expanded its capabilities and began instead to sell the entire management of heating and cooling in other companies' buildings, using the physical products it manufactured as just one part of a much broader offering.

Key aspects of CEO Louis Gerstner's turnaround of IBM were increased listening to and contact with customers and a major expansion of IBM's services business to provide more of what customers needed. Gerstner noted that services were the fastest-growing part of the information technology industry. The services business was already twice as large as the hardware business, and there was not yet a dominant competitor in services. Gerstner therefore considered services an excellent opportunity.[6]

CEO Jack Welch made services a key part of GE's strategies in the 1990s.[7] For example, rather than selling just aircraft engines, GE pursued contracts with customers to provide the engines plus all required maintenance for them. Welch commented in the mid-1990s, "Our job is to sell more than just the box. . . . We're in the services business to expand our pie." By 1996, almost 60 percent of GE's profits came from services, as compared with just over 16 percent in 1980. Welch said he wished the percentage were already 80 percent.

Another GE manager commented at the end of the decade that services had given the company a way "to bury ourselves so far into the customer that they cannot survive without us."[8] (We'll return to the somewhat troublesome tone of this comment later in the chapter.)

Part of the reason that augmentation has become so fashionable of late is that managers believe they are facing increasingly tough competition. It often seems that no sooner do they get a new product to market than there is a competitor ready to enter. Product life cycles seem to keep getting shorter. Competing in part on product augmentation is a possible way out.

The good news is that customers frequently do care a lot about some types of augmentation, so that successful augmentation can be effective. Moreover, especially when it involves people, such as service people or support people, augmentation can be difficult for a competitor to copy. Perhaps unfortunately, the reason augmentation is difficult to copy is that executing augmentation with consistently high quality is a challenge.

There is another potential trap with augmentation. As described well in an article by James Anderson and James Narus, in trying to win or keep customers, many companies simply add one type of augmentation after another to their offerings.[9] They let salespeople offer all the available options at no extra charge. As a result, they provide a specific customer with many things that the particular customer does not value, as well as a few that really do matter. The process reduces or eliminates profits.

The authors observed that the problem is especially acute in companies with high fixed costs, where managers are under great pressure to avoid idle capacity. Their article suggested ways for companies to try to dig themselves out of such a mess and to capture more of the value from the supplementary services they provide to customers.

In this instance, entrepreneurs appear to have a real advantage over managers in existing businesses. Careful, explicit planning about augmentation from the outset can allow them to avoid the problem, and it is far easier to avoid it than to solve it after it appears. The basic idea is to understand what types of augmentation matter to specific customers and then to control the use of free add-on services that are expensive to provide. Companies may decide to offer some supplementary services without charge to each customer but to limit the number or the amount. Or, they may charge for services, especially for customers who purchase less or who are expensive to serve. There are a variety of options. In all cases the key is to make these decisions on a firm foundation of understanding about what customers will and will not value.

FOCUS ON AUGMENTATION THAT CUSTOMERS WILL VALUE

There are many other potential ways to augment products. Guarantees are a form of augmentation that was extremely fashionable in the United States a decade ago. They are still popular, although not quite the fashion item that they were then.

A well-known example is "Bugs" Burger Bug Killers, a pest-extermination company that was based in Miami.[10] In serving restaurant and hotel customers, the company offered an extremely strong guarantee. A dissatisfied customer could request a refund of the price of up to a year of "Bugs" Burger's services plus fees for another extermination service, chosen by the customer, for up to a year. If a customer's business location were ever closed because of the presence of roaches or rodents, "Bugs" Burger would pay any fines, all lost profits, and an additional $5,000.

The underlying customer logic was that pests are an extremely serious problem for operators of restaurants and hotels, who are therefore willing to pay a great deal for outstanding extermination service and a guarantee. "Bugs" Burger charged as much as 10 times what its competitors did, yet it had high market shares in the geographic areas in which it operated.

The company's augmentation went beyond the guarantee. To be able to offer the service and guarantee profitably, it had to make sure that its customers followed acceptable practices for cleaning and storage. Thus, the exterminator also advised and educated its customers about sound practices and then required that those customers follow approved procedures. The augmented product included education and advice, extermination services, inspections, and a guarantee.

General Stair Corp., a Florida company that made prefabricated stairs, also used guarantees effectively, but it found that to do so it had to make other changes in its business approach.[11] The president of the company believed that "all prefab stairs are pretty much the same; they go up, and they go down." He set out to differentiate his company's offerings.

His customer analysis revealed that having the stairs delivered on time was important to customers, particularly to builders who had many houses under construction at once. The stairs were required to pass a framing inspection, a milestone that triggered a payment from the bank. The president decided that his company would offer a guarantee of on-time delivery. The payout would be $50 for every day late; analysis suggested that a builder would lose about $50 in interest for each day's delay.

When General Stair implemented the new guarantees, an unforeseen problem arose. It turned out that many builders did not have good enough information to be able to tell the company just when the stairs would be needed in each of the houses they had under construction. General Stair kept the guarantee but changed the job definition of its salespeople; they became responsible for monitoring progress at the customers' construction sites so that stairs could be delivered when needed. Thus, the company went from offering a largely undifferentiated product, prefab stairs, to offering stairs augmented by a guarantee and by a service that determined when the stairs were needed.

Several types of augmentation are really tools for educating customers. Documentation and training are obvious examples. As discussed in Chapter 5, for some products, postsale education to teach customers how to use the product effectively is critically important. Postsale communication can also augment the product by reassuring customers that their purchase decisions were wise, helping them to feel good about their choices.

Customizing a product for customers is another possible form of augmentation. In particular, mass customization involves tailoring the product for each individual customer. For a while in the 1990s, one read about mass customization everywhere. I believe the concept was overhyped, with the result that many people eventually concluded that it was not really interesting. That's unfortunate, because there have been highly successful applications of mass customization and it is likely that continuing technical and manufacturing developments will allow other useful applications in the future. The concept obviously requires excellent customer understanding and an outside-in product policy, however.

One company that succeeded with mass customization was ChemStation, a manufacturer of industrial detergents.[12] The company's strategy rested on the assumptions that at least some industrial customers would place high value on obtaining detergents that were specifically designed for their cleaning tasks, that they would also value not having to worry about being sure to order detergent before they ran out, and that they would value those benefits enough to remain loyal to a company that provided them.

ChemStation's chemists custom-designed detergent for each customer. Salespeople helped in that process, communicating necessary information about the customer's operation to the ChemStation labs. Special equipment was installed at the customer location to store and dispense the detergent. Once ChemStation had developed a product that fit the specific customer's cleaning job, it began a delivery program in which its salespeople, supported by information technology, monitored the customer's usage and saw to it that a new batch of the custom detergent was made and delivered before the customer ran out.

ChemStation used a form of market segmentation that helped make its strategy successful. The process of custom-designing a detergent was time-consuming and expensive, and the company therefore wanted to be selective about the customers for which it did the customization work. It targeted those customers who had been seriously dissatisfied with standard solutions, on the theory that such customers would remain with a satisfactory supplier for a considerable period of time. The approach was successful.

ChemStation's strategy was made possible in part by relatively new technology that allowed the company to make its specialized formulations efficiently. Continuing technical advances in both manufacturing and information handling will almost certainly make it feasible for increasing numbers of companies to offer successful customized approaches, provided, of course, that the customized products are a good fit with customer needs and buying and usage processes.

In another example, General Electric Plastics used technology to help customers customize their choices of plastics while, at the same time, reducing GE's own costs.[13] In 2000, GE Plastics began to use its Web site to allow industrial customers to custom-design plastics for their own applications. GE also provided a virtual lab so that the customer could, for example, check how a possible choice of plastic would flow in molding without actually having to buy the plastic or build an expensive mold for the test. The customization tools substantially reduced the time required for customers to obtain plastics that fit their needs well, thereby reducing the customers' product-development times—and many of those customers cared a great deal about development time. In addition, the tools shifted some of the work from GE employees to the customers; as a result, GE was able to reduce the number of engineers assigned to customer support.

CUSTOMERS MAY ALSO NEED FOLLOW-ON PRODUCTS

Up to this point, the discussion in this chapter has sounded as if what is being sold is a single product. In many situations, however, an initial sale of some piece of equipment is followed by sales of supplies, parts, and service for that equipment. I use the term *cascaded demand* to refer to the phenomenon in which demand for the basic product is followed by demand for follow-ons.

The follow-ons can be critical to the profitability of the company selling a product. For example, consider Hewlett-Packard's ink-jet-printer business.[14] In the late 1990s, analysts estimated that ink-jet supplies accounted for only 5 percent of Hewlett-Packard's revenues but contributed 25 percent of the company's profits. A few years later, when several sectors of Hewlett-Packard were struggling, ink-jet supplies contributed 100 percent of the company's profits.

The follow-on products in a cascade can also have an important impact on customers' perceptions of a vendor and on their willingness to buy from that vendor again. The early history of Xerox provides an example.[15] Xerox sold a complete cascade of products: copiers, maintenance, parts, paper, and toner. The Xerox strategies did an excellent job of considering and addressing customer behavior regarding maintenance, but they were considerably less successful with regard to toner.

The story requires an important product insight: when a Xerox machine began to malfunction, the failure was often not abrupt. Instead, the machine made copies of increasingly poor quality. The key customer insights relate to that product insight. Customers often did not think to request preventive maintenance. And, when copy quality decreased, customers often did not call for service. Instead, they might decide that Xerox really didn't make very good machines and that they should buy some other brand next time. Similarly, poor toner quality led to reduced copy quality, which many customers blamed on the machine rather than the toner.

Xerox's strategy for maintenance seems to have fit the customer situation extremely well. The strategy for toner did not. Xerox allowed customers either to buy maintenance as needed or to buy a service agreement under which Xerox handled all the service for a fixed price. Xerox set prices so that the maintenance agreements were substantially less expensive for customers. Many customers signed up for the agreements; Xerox made sure that these customers' machines received regular preventive maintenance, and copy quality was therefore considerably more likely to remain high. In contrast, Xerox set toner prices high and competitors entered the market, sometimes with seriously inferior products. Copy quality suffered.

Although this story could be told as one of good pricing strategy, it is also about the importance of understanding the roles of follow-on products in the eyes of customers—and then of making other choices, such as pricing decisions, in light of that understanding. It appears that Xerox had a far better understanding of the role of maintenance than it did of the role of toner.

Manufacturers of products such as heavy construction equipment have also faced competition in the often-lucrative business in parts for their products. The competitive parts are sometimes called pirate parts or will-fitter parts. Because many businesses expect to earn much, if not most, of their profits from follow-ons, the pirate parts have a serious impact on the manufacturers' financial results. In addition, if the pirate parts have any quality problems, they may also damage the manufacturers' reputations and their relationships with customers.

This issue has arisen recently in the market for cartridges for ink-jet printers. When the price for machines that refilled used cartridges fell sharply at the beginning of the century, several companies began selling franchises for cartridge-refilling businesses. A subhead in a 2004 *Wall Street Journal* article about those businesses told the story: "Ink-Jet Cartridge Refillers Spread to Malls, Main Streets; Going After H-P's Lifeblood."[16]

The story stressed the large profit impacts on Hewlett-Packard (H-P), Lexmark, Canon, and Seiko Epson. It also quoted the H-P vice president of supplies marketing and sales, who said that H-P's name-brand cartridges provided better value; he cited a 2004 article in *Consumer Reports* magazine that found that the refilled cartridges were lower in quality and messier than name-brand ones. If the refilled cartridges did indeed have quality problems, they posed a double threat to the printer manufacturers.

FOCUS ON CUSTOMERS' PERCEPTIONS OF PRODUCT STANDARDS

The final topic in this chapter's outside-in look at product decisions is standards. This topic is covered extensively in the literature on management of technology and in parts of economics. This discussion does not present those approaches to standards but instead considers how customers often view standards. To do so, it uses the framework of transaction buyers and relationship buyers that was illustrated by the example of Dell Computer's market segmentation in Chapter 4.[17]

Transaction buyers view their purchase decisions as discrete events. They think about one transaction at a time, and they do not believe that their past purchases dictate their current ones. They are able to base their decisions on specific product features, on price, or on other immediate inducements to buy. Transaction buyers can purchase as they do because they have low switching costs; it is easy for them to change suppliers.

In contrast, relationship buyers have high switching costs. Changing suppliers is difficult for them. They may have to modify existing plant equipment or existing computer software to integrate the products of a new supplier. Individuals within the relationship buyer's organization may have spent years learning to get the most from the existing suppliers' products; they would have to go through an analogous learning process with a new supplier. The customer's business procedures may have been designed in part to work with those of an existing supplier.

Thus, switching costs can take a variety of forms. Because they face high switching costs, relationship buyers change only reluctantly and infrequently. They generally have lasting relationships with their suppliers.

An earlier section of this chapter reported the comment of a GE manager that services had given GE a way to bury itself so deep in the customers that they required GE for their very survival. The tone of this comment suggests the different attitudes of customers and suppliers toward relationship buying. Many suppliers love the idea of having customers who are relationship buyers; being critical to the survival of your customers sounds terrific. Suppliers happily describe such customers as loyal. The customers often use other, far less happy, descriptions, such as captive or locked in. They understand how dependent they are on their current suppliers, and that dependence usually makes them uncomfortable.

True, customers do accept relationship buying. They do so because they believe the benefits outweigh the costs. For the most part, however, they see their lack of real choices as a definite cost.

In reality, this dichotomy between relationship buyers and transaction buyers is too simple. It is more realistic to think of customers as occupying positions along a spectrum between relationship buying and transaction buying:

Relationship
buyer

Transaction
buyer

Most real customers occupy intermediate points along this spectrum. And, creating even more challenge, every company that I have looked at closely has customers occupying a broad range of positions along the spectrum, with some closer to the relationship-buying end and some closer to transaction buying.

This diversity substantially increases the complexity of the job of understanding customers, but it does not alter the usual differences in attitude between buyers and sellers. In the majority of cases, sellers are considerably happier about having customers toward the relationship-buying (left) end of the spectrum. Customers tend to value the freedom of choice they have farther toward the transaction-buying (right) end if they can get it.

THE IMPORTANCE OF STANDARDS TO CUSTOMERS VARIES

In the case of Dell Computer, the augmented services that the company provided to some customers did indeed move those customers toward the left, making it more difficult for them to change suppliers. I find that customers are normally quite aware of how much choice they do or do not have, and therefore I assume that the Dell customers knew that they were giving up some of their ability to switch when they became relationship customers. We can assume that the relevant decision makers believed that the benefits they got from Dell more than offset that loss.

In comparison, consider IBM in the heyday of mainframe computers—say 20 or 25 years ago. Many customers, especially sophisticated ones, knew that they were locked in. Computers from different vendors were not compatible. Changes required modifications in software and substantial new learning.

Some of these customers decided to do something about the situation. They pushed for what they called network architecture—for standards that would allow products from different suppliers to work together and would therefore allow customers to buy from alternative sources. In interviews about the histories of their organizations' purchase and use of computers, participants in those efforts said that they had been very clear about what they were doing. One explained that he had expected that network architecture would "keep IBM honest."

In the terminology of my spectrum of buying behavior, standards allow the customers to move toward the right and behave more transactionally. The customers would still be locked in to the technology embedded in a specific standard, but they would be able to purchase products from any of the various vendors that adhered to the standard.

There are additional examples of customers pushing for standards.[18] In the past, customers finally resorted to a two-week buying moratorium to induce DEC to offer products that were compliant with the MAP (Manufacturing Automation Protocol) standard for computer products for manufacturing environments. Similarly, a customer group called the Aerospace Industry Association announced that its members would require that products conform with standards critical for early e-mail; soon afterward, IBM changed its policy and announced that it would follow that standard in the United States after all. Currently, customers, including governments outside the United States, are one of the forces pushing the open-source Linux operating system.

The history of EMC Corporation, a manufacturer and marketer of data-storage equipment, provides another recent example.[19] In 2000, the company dominated the high end of the market for storage devices. It sold extremely reliable and sophisticated storage hardware, along with the software to operate it.

Customers apparently needed the power and reliability of EMC's products, because they paid at least twice what they would have paid for products from EMC's competitors. EMC had 71 percent of the high-end storage market, with reported profit margins of 57 percent. The company had been one of the top-performing stocks of the 1990s.

EMC sold proprietary software that did not work with products from other storage companies. *BusinessWeek* described EMC's customers as locked in. In late 2000, EMC's CEO described his company as recession-proof. His explanation: "We make the highest-performing stuff." He categorically refused to make EMC software work on hardware from other vendors.

In 2001, two forces hit EMC. As the Internet bubble burst, overall demand for storage and other IT products dropped. At the same time, other IT companies, both large and small, were increasingly competing with EMC. IBM developed software that would work with collections of storage devices from different vendors, including EMC.

Customers had been unhappy with the lack of standards in the storage market; they believed that that lack made managing storage too difficult. They welcomed open software from credible sources like IBM. They also resented the past behavior of EMC and its salespeople—behavior that both *Fortune* and *BusinessWeek* characterized as arrogant.

In 2001, EMC's margins on hardware dropped from 57 percent to 32 percent. Its share of the high-end storage market dropped from 71 percent to 57 percent. By the end of that year, the company's new CEO essentially split it into two parts. One would continue to sell storage hardware. The other would sell open software—software that was supposed to work equally well with storage hardware from EMC or from its competitors.

In all these examples, the customers viewed open standards as giving them more freedom of choice, allowing them to avoid being captive to a single suppler. In other situations, however, customers don't care as much about standards because they don't believe those standards offer them clear benefits.

In residential water meters, for example, it was not customers but the largest manufacturer that pushed the effort for standards.[20] In the United States, towns and cities generally have their own water departments. Those departments run the systems for delivering water to customers. They install and then read the meters that measure customers' usage of water, and they bill customers on the basis of that measured usage. Towns and cities purchase the water meters, with decision-making units (DMUs) that generally include several types of employees.

Without standards, engineers in different municipalities tended to choose their own unique designs for water meters, and manufacturers would find themselves having to make small quantities of a large number of different meters. With standards, there were fewer models, and the largest manufacturer enjoyed economies of scale. It could translate those economies into lower prices, which might not appeal to the engineers in the customer organizations but did appeal to other municipal officials in the DMUs.

Thus, customers for water meters did not directly perceive a need for standards. However, they did value the lower prices that standards enabled. The outside-in view of standards was very different in this marketplace from what it was in information technology.

As noted at the outset, this discussion is certainly not intended as a complete consideration of standards. Instead, it should make the point that customers sometimes (but not always) care about standards. When they do, their views may be significantly different from the views of those who emphasize the technology issues involved. Instead, customers may view standards as a way to move to the right on the behavior spectrum, obtaining more freedom of choice and more leverage with their suppliers.

SUMMARY

The key questions about products are what benefits customers believe the products offer and to whom. It can occasionally be sensible to try to make big changes in customers' perceptions, but doing so is usually difficult and expensive.

Customers buy not just basic products but augmented products—the basic product plus other important attributes, such as service, installation, brand name, and guarantees. Many companies today try to use augmentation to differentiate their offerings in increasingly competitive marketplaces. Good augmentation can be highly effective for that purpose, in part because augmentation is often difficult to execute well. At the same time, augmentation can be risky. Companies have a tendency to give customers more and more augmentation, regardless of whether customers actually value the additions. In the process, the companies incur high costs.

In some situations companies sell a cascade of products—equipment, parts, service, and supplies. With such cascaded demand, good outside-in analysis includes consideration of the roles of follow-on products in the eyes of customers and the impact of follow-ons on customers' perceptions.

The outside-in perspective also helps with other product-related issues such as standards. Customers often emphasize not the technical issues involved in standards but instead the promise that standards can allow them to avoid being locked in to a single supplier.

OUTSIDE-IN ACTIONS

1. **Be sure that you are using customers' perceptions of your product rather than your own views.**

   Revisit your customer pictures and outside-in strategies from the previous chapter. Make sure that the pictures contain the customers' perceptions of your products. Compare customers' perceptions with your perceptions. If the two views are significantly different, explore those differences. Consider whether they should lead to changes in your product strategies.

2. **Explore how your current product augmentation contributes to your strategy.**

   Begin by describing what customers value beyond the basic product. Identify the types of augmentation you currently include in your strategy. Check whether or not those forms of augmentation are the ones that are of most value to customers. Ask whether each type of augmentation in your strategy provides enough customer value to be worth the expense and effort it entails. If not, explore ways to reduce and control the amount of augmentation you provide.

3. **Consider whether to implement additional types of augmentation.**

   Looking at what you found in the previous step, identify what, beyond the basic product, customers value highly but you don't currently provide. Explore adding augmentation to your offering to give customers that value.

4. **If you sell follow-ons for your products, take the outside-in perspective on each part of your product cascade.**

   Explain customer needs and behavior relative to each part, saying how each influences the customers' satisfaction with your products and their views of you as a vendor. Examine whether your strategy for each part of the cascade is consistent with this analysis of customers. If not, explore ways to modify your strategy.

5. **Take the outside-in perspective on every other important part of your product policy, such as your approach to standards.**

Identify customer needs and behavior relative to this area of product policy. Explore how this area contributes to customers' satisfaction and to their views of you. Ask whether your strategy in this product area fits with your analysis of customers. If it does not, explore ways to improve the strategy.

8

OUTSIDE-IN PRICING
Customer Benefits Are the Key

Customers pay only for what is of use to them and gives them value. Nothing else constitutes "quality."
—*Peter Drucker*

AT FIRST GLANCE, TAKING a customer-oriented approach to pricing may seem relatively straightforward. Customers are frequently more than willing to talk about prices. In many situations, if you ask customers what they want, they will tell you loudly and clearly that they want lower prices.

The problem is that such customer responses can reflect two very different things. First, price may in fact be extremely important to at least some customers. But second, most customers find it easier to think and talk about price than to think about and articulate other potentially important improvements to your marketplace strategy: new product capabilities, or valuable product augmentation, or better ways of communicating with customers. When they are asked what they need, many customers find that price comes easily to mind.

In many (probably most) situations, however, when you examine customers' actual behavior, you find that price is not nearly as important in determining purchases as customers' statements might suggest. The challenge is to base your strategy on customers' real attitudes toward price, not on the fact that they find it easy to talk about prices. The challenge is to view price within the overall outside-in strategy, giving it appropriate but not undue attention.

PRICING APPROACHES: SELLER'S COST OR CUSTOMER'S BENEFIT

The first key question is how to approach pricing—how to think about and choose prices. In practice, the selection and use of an approach to pricing turns out to be deceptively tricky, especially because it's so important to maintain an outside-in orientation. For that reason, let's begin by examining possible approaches.

The most common approaches to pricing are cost-based pricing and benefit or value pricing. Most businesspeople know that one isn't "supposed" to use cost-based pricing, but many people do in fact use it. It seems that the people I speak with know that they shouldn't use the approach and report that they don't use it themselves, but they always know someone down the hall who does. This observation suggests that this discussion should define cost-based and benefit pricing and review the argument about the superiority of the benefit approach, but that it should also try to explain why cost-based pricing remains so widespread.

The basic idea in *cost-based pricing* is to take your costs, add a profit, and use the total as your price in the marketplace. A simple version is:

> Variable cost of making one unit of the product
> + all other variable costs of one unit (variable selling cost, variable distribution cost, and so on)
> + a share of the fixed costs directly tied to the product
> + a share of other fixed costs (overhead)
> + a fair profit
> _____
> = PRICE

People can and do argue about some of the details in this calculation, especially about what constitutes a fair profit. People can also introduce more realistic complexity, such as experience-curve effects that reduce the variable costs with increased volume. However, this simple version captures the essence of the approach.

Benefit or *value pricing* emphasizes the value that customers receive from a product. (The terms are equivalent. *Value pricing* was widely used in marketing, but then fast-food chains began using the term to refer to low-cost items on their menus. Some confusion resulted in marketing discussions. It doesn't seem necessary to try to wrest the term back from the fast-food industry; it's easier simply to use *benefit pricing*.)

The basic idea of benefit pricing is summarized as follows:

Benefits to the customer from the product
– costs (for the customer) associated with the product, other than price
_____
= maximum price the customer would pay

A benefit price below this maximum is chosen, leaving the customer with an excess of total benefits over total costs. Companies may choose to make that excess smaller or larger, depending on their specific circumstances. It must, however, be large enough for the customer to decide to buy.

An imaginary balance scale can help explain this definition. On one side of the scale goes everything good—all the benefits the customer would obtain from the product. On the other side goes everything bad—the price the customer must pay plus any other costs associated with the product. Customers will buy only if the balance is sufficiently attractive.

Note that the costs on the balance scale are not costs to the manufacturer of the product, as in the definition of cost-based pricing. They are additional costs incurred by the customer. Those other costs can be considerable. For example, a report from the Gartner Group estimated that companies spent approximately $6,000 each year for hardware and software upkeep on a $2,000 PC running Windows 95.[1] In other cases, the additional costs could include the trouble of learning to use a new product, the inconvenience of the way the product is delivered, or numerous other considerations.

Most people find that the benefit approach fits well conceptually with how customers make decisions about what they will buy. We can envision customers looking at a product, learning enough about the product to feel that they can evaluate it, and seeing how that product affects their balance scales. They might then go on to make a similar evaluation of another product and perhaps another, or they might not. At some point they will decide that continued shopping is itself a big negative, and they will buy the alternative that has felt best on the scale thus far.

WHY BENEFIT PRICING—OR MAYBE MARKET PRICING

Most people respond to this idea of benefit pricing by saying that, yes, it does describe conceptually the way they evaluate and purchase products. The problem is that the model may be right in concept but using it in practice is extraordinarily difficult. I believe it describes my behavior, but I certainly couldn't attach numbers to the benefits and costs that I associate with the alternatives I consider. Moreover, surely other customers, who also could not quantify the benefits and costs they perceive, would make different assessments of benefits and costs from mine.

How, then, is a company to base its price on customers' benefits and costs? The answer is that many companies do not do so.

Instead, managers base prices on their own costs, which they believe they know.

The problem is that for almost all products cost-based pricing does not work. (It obviously does work for cost-plus contracts, and it might work for products that have no fixed costs and are made by companies that have no overhead. We'll exclude those situations from the rest of this discussion.)

Reexamination of the definition of cost-based pricing reveals the problem. Determination of the variable costs (manufacturing and other) may not be easy, but it is certainly possible in principle. The problem comes with the phrase "a share of." What share? The share of fixed costs to be borne by one unit of a product depends on the number of units that will be made and sold. And what determines the number of units that will be sold? All those customers with their idiosyncratic balance scales.

In summary, cost-based pricing does not work in practice, as much as businesspeople might wish that it did. Customers do not make their decisions on the basis of the seller's costs; they use their own evaluations of their own benefits and their own costs. As the president of Boeing said in 1995, "An airline boss said to me the other day, 'You don't seem to understand that your cost to build the airplane has no bearing on the price we are willing to pay for it.' "[2]

So, we are back to benefit pricing. A later section talks about some ideas for making benefit pricing a bit less difficult. (It is rarely easy.) First, though, let's turn to a third pricing approach that often does make sense.

The discussions in preceding chapters mentioned competition only as the source of alternatives that customers may choose to evaluate and may decide to buy. That is also the proper role for competition in pricing discussions. The key question is how your benefits and costs to the customer compare, in the customer's eyes, with those of competitors.

In situations in which businesspeople offer products that are quite similar to competitive offerings, the prices of alternatives in the marketplace will strongly influence what those business-people can and should charge. I call this pricing approach *market pricing*.

This approach often involves using competitive prices as a starting point and then adjusting them a bit. For example, one person might decide that her product was in fact superior to the competition's because it offered somewhat higher quality and was easier to use. Suppose she believed that customers would value those advantages. She might decide to price the product at a 10 percent premium over the competition. Another person might admit that his product was not quite as attractive as competitive offerings, perhaps because delivery was slow and the product was a little more difficult to repair. He might price the product at a 5 percent discount from the competition.

This approach still involves assessment of customers' perceptions in order to select appropriate premiums or discounts. Even so, it feels much more rooted in real data than does a pure benefit-pricing approach.

The problem is that market pricing is appropriate in situations that are inherently less attractive. The approach fits when your offering is very close to competitive offerings. Really attractive market opportunities instead involve offering something that provides customers a significant advantage over alternatives. Hard-to-implement benefit pricing is a requirement in high-opportunity situations because there are no really close competitive comparisons.

In reality, there are not simply two sensible pricing alternatives. There is a spectrum that runs from pure benefit pricing at one end to pure market pricing at the other. Most real situations lie somewhere between the extremes. The difficult conclusion of the preceding discussion remains, however. The more new and different and exciting to customers your offering is, the more you have to do benefit pricing.

THE POWER OF BENEFIT PRICING

Benefit pricing can be very profitable. The key, of course, is to provide lots and lots of benefits to customers—enough benefits so that customers can pay substantial prices and still have lots of net benefits remaining. Thus, the first and most difficult challenge is to find a way to provide customers with exceptionally high benefits.

A disguised case study telling the story of a company it calls Cumberland Metal Industries provides a good example of the power of extremely high benefits and benefit pricing.[3] Long ago, when the U.S. Congress began to impose limits on the emission of pollutants from automobiles, the auto manufacturers scrambled to find technologies that would allow them to meet the new requirements. As the deadline for the new limits approached, the big three U.S. automakers faced increasing pressure. Cumberland Metal Industries (CMI) used its technical expertise to create a crucial seal for the exhaust-gas-recirculation (EGR) systems of two of the big three U.S. automakers.

CMI's managers understood that their company's expertise and its slip-seal product were critical for the customers. In fact, it would not be an exaggeration to say that with its initial product, CMI was selling not a metal seal but the ability to sell automobiles, because the customers could not sell cars that did not meet the new emission standards. Perhaps needless to say, the ability to sell automobiles was an extraordinarily valuable product in Detroit.

Traditional wisdom would have predicted that a small supplier like CMI would be beaten up and generally abused by Detroit's famously fierce purchasing departments and would have earned only small profits on the slip seals. Conventional wisdom would have been seriously wrong. In fact, CMI's margins were high, exceeding 70 percent on some items. Benefit pricing proved very profitable indeed, because the benefits to customers were so high.

Readers may be thinking that CMI's high initial prices probably just led to the entry of competitors. Competitors did enter the market, but I believe that that fact does not argue against the initial high prices. CMI's customers believed very strongly in having second sources for all of their purchases. It was inevitable that there would eventually be competition for slip seals. Eventual competition therefore is not a convincing argument for CMI's charging low initial prices.

Competition does provide an argument that CMI should have brought its prices down over time, but that argument can also be made in terms of benefits to the customer. As discussed, at the outset, CMI was selling the ability to sell cars, and its customers were happy to get the product they needed, even at high prices. Within a few years, however, after the customers had met the emission limits and competitors had begun to manufacture similar products, customers saw the CMI product less as a critical business saver and more as a routine part.

Truly disciplined ongoing outside-in thinking could have alerted CMI's managers to the change and motivated them to lower their prices. (And they could sensibly have explained that the early development had entailed substantial learning, expensive technical talent, and risk. As the manufacturing process became more settled and less costly, it would have been credible for them to share the savings with customers.)

At the same time, CMI's technical expertise continued to be valued, especially by the engineering departments of the auto manufacturers, and CMI could have continued to command some price premium because of the value of this augmentation to some members of the customers' decision-making units (DMUs). In fact, CMI's managers did not anticipate the speed with which their high-tech, esoteric product would begin to look routine to customers, and, as a result, their eventual price cuts were more forced and more awkward than they need have been.

Another recent example illustrates an application of benefit pricing close to the market end of the spectrum.[4] Apparently, many consumers believed that FedEx provided quicker and more reliable delivery than UPS. The two delivery companies charged their company customers pretty much the same prices. Some of those customer companies, however, charged consumers more for FedEx shipments. "We love it when customers ask us to ship on Federal Express," commented one customer. "We can charge more, even though our cost is about the same."

Some people have the impression that benefit pricing necessarily implies high prices. That impression is not correct. Sometimes it leads to high prices, but sometimes it does not. Notice, for example, that in the case of CMI, thorough understanding of customers' views of benefits would have led to relatively high initial prices but substantially lower prices over time.

In other cases, a realistic look at the benefits that customers would receive from some potential new product shows that those benefits are less than the manufacturer's cost of making and selling the product. In such cases, the answer is not simply to raise the price. The manufacturer might be able to redesign the product so that it provided sufficiently more benefits that prospective customers would be willing to pay enough to cover the new costs. Or, the manufacturer might redesign to reduce its costs for making and selling the product; if the benefits to customers remained high enough, that strategy could make sense. If neither option is possible, except under very special and very unusual circumstances, the product should not be introduced.

Up to this point, the discussion has ignored the complication that price is often not just one number. Terms and conditions, discounts, and add-on fees are among the other parts of price. And they can be important in influencing customer benefits and perceptions and in determining the seller's profits.

In the early twenty-first century, fees became a popular pricing tool. Increasingly, consumers saw fees on their telephone bills and their credit-card bills. They saw more and higher fees for government services, for bank services, and for many other purchases. Businesspeople apparently believed that customers either would not notice or, at least, would accept the fees; they considered higher fees preferable to increased base prices.

Eventually, however, customers did begin to notice—and a significant number of them were unhappy with what they saw.[5] A 2003 *BusinessWeek* cover story on the topic said that there was a popular backlash against the fees. It suggested that people could accept higher fees for customers who actually required special service, but that they resented having fees imposed or raised without justification.

This last example highlights another point about outside-in pricing: customers are often willing to pay substantial prices for what they consider substantial benefits. At the same time, they don't like being taken advantage of. Businesspeople who are providing lots of benefits to their customers thus walk a fine line between charging appropriately high prices and seeming to be gouging. One effective tool in doing this successfully is to communicate with customers about the benefits, clearly and repeatedly. The following chapter returns to this topic.

ACTUALLY DOING BENEFIT PRICING

The preceding discussion argued that benefit pricing is essential, especially in the situations with the most opportunity. That argument does not mean that benefit pricing is easy or that benefits can be determined with precision. Benefit pricing is always challenging, and the results are not precise. There are, however, techniques that provide some help with the challenge.

The key to benefit pricing is understanding customer value. Chapters 4 and 5 argued that an explicit value proposition for customers, often a quantified value proposition, is a key part of outside-in strategy. Benefit pricing and constructing a quantified value proposition involve the same difficult job of attaching numbers to the value customers receive.

Discussions with customers are central. Although customers may not be able to attach numbers to benefits and costs, they can give useful information. They will almost always be able to provide insights into what they do not like about the products and approaches they currently use. They can sometimes respond usefully to descriptions of potential new products, saying whether they think they would like the new products (although with some new products customers will have difficulty envisioning how they would use the product and what it would mean to them).

Observation is another useful technique. Watching customers perform relevant current activities can help uncover the ways in which those activities would be improved by a new product. Observing the time-consuming and troublesome aspects of a manufacturing process, for example, facilitates insights into the value that would be provided by products for improving that process.

Wherever possible, would-be benefit pricers can collect measurements in these discussions and observations. For example, they can ask customers how long it takes to recover from the breakdown of a piece of equipment or how much time it takes to integrate data from noncommunicating computer programs. Such estimates then provide inputs to simple calculations of value.

Consider the example of pricing a service that gave product designers access to a library of computerized 3-D drawings of parts, suitable for inclusion in product designs. The pricing process might have started with questions to product designers. Suppose the designers indicated that they currently had to create the computerized representations of parts themselves, a laborious process that they did not enjoy and that required perhaps two hours per design. Suppose, in addition, that designers reported creating 10 designs per month on average.

Value calculations could start with the amount of time saved and then attach a dollar value to that time, perhaps based on the compensation rates for designers. The reduction in drudgery could also be considered, although the number to attach to that benefit would be less precise.

Further exploration might find that senior managers in companies doing product design were strongly concerned with reducing time to market. Again, the benefit of getting products to market more rapidly would not be readily available, but some simple calculations involving margins earned before and after competition arrived could provide estimates of the value of extra time before competition. The estimates would provide information to use in pricing—and to discuss with prospects during the selling process.

When possible, experimentation can be extremely helpful in gathering information to use in benefit pricing. For example, the manufacturer of a product for use in the construction industry found two interested customers willing, even anxious, to try out a new product on representative jobs. The manufacturer and customers carefully monitored those trials, collecting data about the performance of the new product compared with that of the products previously available. Such information was obviously extremely useful for pricing, although it did not remove all the problems. Jobs vary, and the benefits obtained on one job would differ from those on another. Even more important, customers often vary widely in their levels of awareness of benefits and costs, and, therefore, in the ways they will view and evaluate new products.

In another example, someone who had been involved with the first digital watches described experiments that were used to set the initial prices. Market researchers worried that since the product category was entirely new, customers would not be able to predict how much they would be willing to pay. So, the pricing process included experiments in which customers were shown an assortment of more familiar products, along with digital watches. They were given a product and then allowed to exchange it for other items from the assortment. The resulting data provided useful information about what they might pay for the new watches.

Other sources of information can also help. Sometimes there are analogous products. For example, a marketer of toys, after deciding that a new product should be positioned as a highly educational toy, might investigate the range of prices that customers were accustomed to paying for educational toys.

In other situations, experts can provide information that is useful in calculating value. A company that was developing a product that could reduce theft from retail stores used information from a well-known expert on retail theft in estimating the value of the new product to retailers.

Information from annual reports and other public documents and statements from customer companies can also contribute. A company whose new product will help retailers improve inventory management can find information about amounts of inventory from such documents; assumptions about the inventory reductions the new product will provide, combined with estimates of the cost of working capital, can then be used to give estimates of value.

Some types of benefits are obviously more difficult to estimate. For example, a product that is sold to businesses may promise to increase the revenues of those businesses. It will not be possible to predict the revenue increases at all precisely. Similarly, the estimates of the value of reduced time to market in one of the previous examples will not be at all precise.

It is important, nonetheless, to try to consider and to quantify those benefits if they will be important to customers. When the numbers are especially imprecise, it can be especially useful to try several approaches to estimating them and to plug several different numbers into value calculations in order to understand the range of values and what really drives them before settling on a price. It often makes sense to discuss a range of benefit numbers with customers in the selling process, too.

This discussion certainly does not make benefit pricing sound easy, and it is not. Nevertheless, there are companies that do succeed in taking a customer-based approach to pricing. Business-to-business situations are a bit easier because, even though the products and usage processes are generally complex, customers are accustomed to thinking in terms of quantified benefits and costs.

Let's therefore consider an example of a company that takes a customer-oriented approach to pricing in a challenging consumer market. A past CEO of Gillette explained the basis of the company's approach:[6]

> In each of our product categories we keep a market basket. For the blade business it includes the daily newspaper, a candy bar, a bottle of Coke and 15 to 20 other items. People don't remember what they spent two years

ago for something, but they remember if it's now more expensive than a Coke and wasn't before.

On top of this foundation of consumers' general price expectations, Gillette then added consideration of the benefits consumers seemed to derive from its products. For existing products, the company kept its price increases below the average for the relevant market basket. For a new product, it might set prices sharply above the prices of old products and the basket, provided that the new product offered customers substantial improvements on dimensions that mattered to them. Reactions of customers trying the products in the Gillette "shaving labs" provided input for the required judgments about customers' reactions to shaving products, for example.

One final approach that can contribute is experimentation in the marketplace. The basic idea is to introduce a product at some price and then, if necessary, change the price later. There is one important caveat with this approach: it is much, much easier to cut prices than to raise them. Therefore, it is far better to introduce a product at a price that may be too high than to enter the market at too low a price. (This caveat was ignored by many companies during the dot-com craze. Companies started with low prices or even gave their products away without charging for them. Few of these companies ever succeeded in raising their prices.)

ROLES OF PRICE IN MARKETPLACE STRATEGY

Price plays more than one role in a business's strategy. Of course, one function of price is to provide revenues and profits for the business. There are additional roles that are tightly linked to customer needs and customer behavior, however.

Customers frequently interpret prices as reflecting the quality or value of products. Thus, price itself communicates something about the value of a product. It is possible to price a product too low, making customers believe that the product is not a good one. In one example, a manager explained that his company had substantially raised the prices of some of its low-volume products. The intention was to eliminate sales of those products without refusing to offer the products to the few businesses that had actually been buying them. The company's managers were shocked to find that after the price increases unit sales of the products went up rather than down.

Pricing can also encourage specific types of customer behavior. The preceding chapter described how Xerox used the pricing of its maintenance services to encourage regular rather than sporadic use of maintenance. Companies frequently offer price discounts or even zero prices on customers' initial purchase of a product; the objective is obviously to encourage trial. This approach does not violate the caveat at the end of the preceding section. Customers readily understand that clearly identified trial prices, especially trial prices of zero for one purchase only, will be followed by higher prices.

Pricing choices are sometimes made to fit with the customers' decision-making process (DMP). For example, hospitals frequently require formal approval from the hospital's board of directors for purchases of pieces of equipment costing more than some limit. It is interesting to see how many vendors choose to price hospital equipment just below the limit.

Outside-in pricing may also reflect details of the customer's processes for budgeting and for evaluating individual employees. Consider a company that sold an information service to other businesses. In some customer companies, project managers kept (and were evaluated on) budgets for individual projects. They strongly preferred to pay for the information service on a per-usage basis so that they could easily charge usage that was tied to specific projects directly to those projects.

Other customer companies managed information services as resources for the entire organization, rather like libraries. The managers in charge of acquiring and managing information had fixed budgets for each year and were evaluated in part on staying within their budgets. Such managers strongly preferred fixed pricing—either outright purchases or set annual fees—for information sources.

The company selling the information service could have adopted usage-based pricing and targeted the first type of customer, could have used fixed pricing and targeted the second type, or could have found it necessary to manage the complexity of multiple types of pricing to accommodate different types of customers.

On occasion, simply having prices and pricing policies that are clear and understandable can become a way to provide benefits to customers. Sun Microsystems took that approach of simplification in 2003, announcing that its new prices would be determined by multiplying a customer company's number of employees by a clearly stated price per head for the Sun products it purchased.[7] The number of employees would be taken from the customer company's required annual filings with the government. In what a Sun vice president called the "happy meal" approach, although Sun would continue to sell individual products, it would offer substantially lower total prices to customers who bought packages of products that worked together.

Sun's new pricing procedure was part of a total marketplace strategy, so it could not alone be credited with Sun's subsequent success or blamed for its subsequent failure. However, initial reactions to the new approach, as reported in the press, were favorable.

One article noted that the usual practice in the IT industry was to price high-end enterprise software on the basis of many complex factors describing a customer company's usage environment. It described Sun's openness about its prices as revolutionary. The Sun vice president noted that Sun's new policy was intended in part to give customers more ability to predict the prices they would actually have to pay.

THE MOST DANGEROUS PRICING STRATEGY

In practice, people make a variety of pricing mistakes. They may communicate far too much about price and far too little about benefits. They may fail to integrate their pricing decisions with the other elements of their marketplace strategies. They may compensate their salespeople in ways that encourage price cutting. There are many other types of mistakes in pricing.

My candidate for the most dangerous pricing mistake of all is contained in the following statement:

We'll price low and gain market share.

Yes, it can occasionally make sense to price low in order to gain market share. Before I agree that the strategy makes sense, however, I want to see a clear, explicit assumption that it is in fact high price that is either keeping more customers from buying or keeping existing customers from buying more.

Most often, it is not. Customers may not be buying because they aren't aware of the product. They may not understand the product and may not be adequately aware of the benefits it offers. They may make false assumptions about how difficult it would be to incorporate the product into their existing processes. And so on.

Only occasionally is low price the magic answer to the difficulties of marketing a product successfully. And too low a price creates several problems. It may communicate low quality, as noted earlier. It may leave the marketer with too little money to pay for education, installation, or other activities that are what customers really need in order to buy more. And, as discussed earlier, prices that are too low are usually very difficult to correct.

This point suggests considering the concept of inertia (introduced in Chapter 6) in relation to price. In one sense, pricing has low inertia. Price changes can be announced quickly and easily. In reality, however, there is much more inertia in pricing. Price increases are tough. Experience shows that customers remember low prices for a long time.

For example, when asked what it costs to fly from New York to Los Angeles, respondents frequently give the lowest price they remember seeing—and they can remember sale prices from years earlier.[8] Inflation provides some cover for price increases, because customers expect increases in response to inflation. They do not expect increases in excess of inflation, however, and in times of low inflation price increases are especially hard to implement.

This problem is exacerbated by the need of many customers to believe they have been good shoppers. Chapter 4's discussion of Costco mentioned that company's emphasis on the insight that many consumers view saving money as a badge of honor. Many business buyers are evaluated and compensated on the basis of how much money they have saved their organizations. Such customers are hardly likely to welcome price increases.

A FEW MORE INSIGHTS ABOUT COSTS

Lest this chapter seem to advocate not considering costs at all, it should end with a bit of clarification. The preceding discussion argued that a seller's costs are not the relevant basis for pricing. I should now add that I also believe that most companies would benefit from understanding their own costs far better than they currently do. The idea is not to price on the basis of costs, but to use costs to make other good decisions.

As mentioned earlier, costs provide a floor for pricing. If customers do not receive enough benefits from a product to be willing to pay prices higher than the seller's costs of making and marketing the product, then the seller needs to either fix or abandon the strategy.

A good understanding of costs can also help managers understand which market segments, which customers, and which specific orders are in fact profitable. It can help them change the ways they do business with some customers, to make those customers profitable. It can guide them to turn down orders on which they would lose money. It can make them decide that a specific customer is not worth serving.

Some companies have in fact developed measures of the attractiveness of individual customers and then have acted on the basis of those measures. Some of those measures are relatively sophisticated ones, based on activity-based costing. Other simple measures have also been effective.

In the late 1990s, FedEx analyzed its business with roughly 30 customers that together accounted for 10 percent of its total volume.[9] FedEx had discounted its prices for those customers in anticipation of the future revenues the customers had promised they would generate for FedEx; FedEx managers found that some of the customers were not providing the volumes of business they had promised. Especially troublesome were customers that not only fell short of promised revenues but also required many residential deliveries, on which FedEx's costs were relatively high.

FedEx imposed higher prices for some of these customers; some of the increases were over 10 percent. A few customers refused to pay more, and FedEx consequently refused their business. A spokesman said that FedEx had been willing to risk a percentage or two of market share to correct the situation.

The managers of a Swedish company named Kanthal used activity-based costing to analyze the profitability of individual customers.[10] (Kanthal made and sold electrical-resistance heating elements.) An analysis of Kanthal's Swedish customers found that only 40 percent were profitable. Those profitable customers generated 250 percent of the company's profits; the remaining 60 percent of the customers lost 150 percent of the profits, leaving a net 100 percent. The analysis uncovered the fact that frequent small orders (even from large customers) and orders for nonstandard products were largely responsible for the lack of profit in that 60 percent of accounts.

Kanthal managers then worked to improve the situation. For example, Kanthal personnel worked with customers to achieve better communication and planning. With more advance information about what parts a customer would need and when, Kanthal reduced the number of small last-minute orders it received. Similarly, Kanthal salespeople could sometimes help a customer use standard rather than special-order parts; the customer received lower prices, and Kanthal earned higher profits.

The tool of activity-based costing can provide estimates of the profitability of individual segments, customers, products, or orders. If it is used as an aid to making sound decisions and not as an elaborate accounting exercise, activity-based costing can be a powerful new tool for successful marketing. The insights into costs that it can provide are terrific. Costs are important. They just shouldn't be the basis of prices.

SUMMARY

Prices are only one element of marketplace strategy. It's important to avoid the potential trap of overemphasizing price.

Although people know that they "shouldn't" use cost-based pricing, many in fact do. The problem is that cost-based pricing doesn't work without assumptions about how much customers will buy. And, customers base their purchase decisions on the benefits they perceive, not on the manufacturer's costs.

Either benefit pricing or market pricing can be the appropriate approach. There is a spectrum between the two. The more a product differs from any other products that customers perceive to be alternatives, the closer the pricing approach should be to the benefit end of that spectrum.

Unfortunately, benefit pricing is extremely challenging. Discussions with customers, information from experts and public sources, observation, measurement, and experimentation can all help. They cannot, however, make benefit pricing easy.

Customer analysis suggests several roles for prices: to communicate value, to fit with the customers' DMP, to fit with customers' budgeting and evaluation processes, to encourage specific types of customer behavior. Good customer analysis also provides the basis for identifying the (minority of) situations in which price is the main deterrent to increased sales, so that lower-price strategies make sense. More commonly, pricing low to gain market share is a highly questionable approach.

Although a manufacturer's costs are not the proper basis for pricing (because customers care about their own benefits and costs, not the manufacturer's), a good understanding of costs can help the seller in other powerful ways. Used sensibly, simple measures of profitability or even activity-based costing can provide information about costs and profits that can contribute significantly to profitable marketplace strategies.

OUTSIDE-IN ACTIONS

1. **State explicitly the benefits and costs that customers see in your offering.**

   An explicit statement of benefits (or value) is the core of your value proposition and of outside-in prices. Remember that it is customers' perceptions of value that matter. If you decide that it is really worth while to try to change those perceptions, be sure that you have included the required actions in your strategy. In most cases, it will be essential to work to quantify the value that customers receive. Also identify and quantify as well as you can the negatives on the customers' balance scales, the costs other than your price that customers face when they buy and use your product. Try to find multiple sources of information about the benefits and about the negatives.

2. **Consider differences among customers.**

   Don't be surprised if you find that different customers receive significantly different value. Try to segment the customers into groups that respond similarly to your products. Quantify the benefits and costs for representative customers in each major segment.

3. **Decide on the roles that you want price to play in your marketplace strategy.**

   Ask whether, beyond giving you a profit, price should communicate something about your product, such as its quality. Consider whether price should be selected to fit with the customer's DMP. Explore whether the price structure could usefully encourage or discourage specific behavior by customers. And so on.

4. **Decide where your pricing should be on the spectrum between pure benefit and pure market.**

   If market pricing will be involved, identify competitors' prices. Analyze, state explicitly, and then work to quantify the relative benefits that customers perceive from your products and from competitors' products. Decide whether you should price at a premium or at a discount compared with competitors, and decide how large the difference should be.

5. **Finally, review (or, for a new product, select) your price.**

   Choose both the basic price and the pricing details, such as terms and conditions or discounts. Check that all the pricing decisions fit with your preceding analysis of customer benefits and costs and with the desired role for price in your marketplace strategy. Also check that price fits with the other elements of the strategy in a consistent and coordinated whole. If either of these conditions is not met, adjust the pricing, other elements of your strategy, or both.

6. **At least consider using measures of attractiveness of customers to improve your marketplace strategy.**

   If the idea of measures seems to be a good one, start by considering simple measures that could help. Be sure to include plans to use these measures to guide specific actions—perhaps for selecting customers or for determining how you interact with customers. If the idea of measures seems especially promising, consider using activity-based costing. (And start by consulting the business literature on that subject.)

9

OUTSIDE-IN COMMUNICATION
Fit Customers' Communication Needs and Habits

The great quest of marketing management is to understand the
behavior of humans in response to stimuli to which they
are subjected.
—Neil Borden

THE RECORD OF OUTSIDE-IN thinking and communication is a
mixed one. On the one hand, there are excellent examples of
outside-in thinking in the broad area of communication strategy
and especially in advertising. On the other hand, when businesspeople fall into the bad inside-out habit, they are even more likely
to neglect customers' communication needs and communication
habits than they are to neglect the needs that translate more directly into product features.

Some account executives at more strategy-oriented advertising
agencies give impressive outside-in explanations, particularly in
discussions of some of the consumer products they have supported. They may make clear, explicit statements about who were
the target customers, how those customers purchased, and what
information would be most important to those customers; those
explanations then lead to explicit statements of the objectives for

advertising, the messages the advertising should convey, and the best media choices for delivering the messages to the target customers. In other words, some advertising executives present clear outside-in explanations of advertising campaigns.

Although they are considerably less common, I've found a few clearly stated outside-in sales strategies, too. Individual salespeople are, of course, focused on customers. In addition, in some organizations, senior managers (including but not limited to sales managers) have given the salespeople a clear, explicit statement of their understanding of customers: what customers need, how they evaluate products, how they actually buy, and so on.

In one impressive example, the head of a business had created a document describing several types of customers. Those customers were segmented not by size or industry or how much they purchased; they were segmented instead by their approaches to their own marketplaces and by how the company's products fit into their strategies. For each type of customer, the document went on to suggest specific approaches that salespeople could use to serve the customers' needs and sell to them successfully.

The bad news is that this type of behavior is by no means typical. There are lots of situations in which the customer-based logic behind communication decisions is simply not clear. Many descriptions of customers completely ignore their communication needs and habits. And in many situations, decisions about communication in a marketplace strategy are made more or less as an afterthought, after and separate from decisions about product and price.

It's less common for the basic communication strategy to be designed along with the other aspects of strategy so that the result is a consistent, coordinated whole, firmly rooted in outside-in thinking. The flip side of this problem is opportunity; having a sound outside-in communication strategy as part of a complete outside-in strategy can give you a competitive leg up. This chapter covers aspects of communication that are most central for achieving such outside-in discipline.

START WITH CUSTOMERS' COMMUNICATION NEEDS AND HABITS

Chapter 5 suggested thinking of three major steps in purchase processes: awareness, evaluation, and decision. Following those purchase processes, customers' usage processes can also have numerous steps.

The basic outside-in communication questions are deceptively simple. What information do customers need at each step of their buying and usage processes? When and where would customers be receptive to receiving that information?

These basic question then lead to more detailed questions. Can communication motivate prospective customers to decide to look for something new in the first place? If so, what does it take to get their attention? How does formal communication fit with the customers' evaluation processes? What information do they need for evaluating alternatives? What information do they need in the actual purchase step? And how does or could communication fit into customers' usage processes, to help them obtain and recognize value from what they have purchased?

Customers typically have habits about where they get information and about the extent to which they find different information sources credible. The questions for analyzing such communication habits are also deceptively simple. To what communication techniques are the customers regularly exposed? (Examples include specialized or general magazines, trade shows, particular types of television shows, and so on.) How much attention do they pay to each source? How credible do they find each source?

For what do they consider information from each source useful?

Customer pictures help identify specific communication steps that are especially critical in individual situations—initial awareness in some cases and product trial in others, for example. Once the critical communication tasks have been at least tentatively identified, outside-in thinking can then focus more strongly on the communication habits relevant for those tasks and on the ability of possible communication tools to do the required jobs.

The following sections will consider examples of this outside-in approach to communication. First, though, let's look at what can happen without the outside-in discipline. Failure to base communication choices firmly on an understanding of customers frequently leads to communication problems, sometimes rather spectacular ones.

Cabot Corporation sold a variety of industrial products, including industrial earplugs, for which it held a 50 percent global market share.[1] Cabot managers wanted to find new markets for E-A-R®, the material used in the industrial earplugs; one obvious possibility was the consumer earplug market.

Because it lacked experience in consumer markets, Cabot hired a well-known market-research and consulting firm to help it develop and execute a strategy for entering the consumer market. The research firm had extensive experience with consumer packaged goods. It designed, sold to Cabot, and executed a program of research and test marketing that was typical of the work it conducted for consumer packaged goods clients.

The research firm first conducted focus groups with consumers who either had trouble sleeping or had other problems resulting from noise. The focus groups were shown and asked to react to 11 subtly different advertising-concept boards (pages that presented rough versions of potential ads).

The second stage of research consisted of a concept test and an in-home congruence test. Hundreds of target consumers in five geographically dispersed markets were exposed to simulated radio ads for the product and were then asked how interested they would be in buying it. After the interviews, the respondents were asked to take four pairs of the product home to try for two weeks, after which they were interviewed again to explore their reactions to the earplugs.

Next were two waves of advertising/promotion study. The first wave measured awareness of the product in four cities prior to test marketing. Test marketing was done in the four cities for three months, placing the product in retail stores and using advertising and sampling to try to generate sales. Finally, the researchers measured awareness and usage of the product at the end of the test marketing.

The end results of this extensive market research were lackluster awareness and low sales. Cabot did not succeed in the consumer market.

Needless to say this program of market research was extremely expensive. Unfortunately, its unstated assumptions about consumer behavior were wrong. For typical frequently purchased consumer packaged goods, which the research firm normally studied, consumers often paid attention to TV, radio, or print ads or to coupons; some then noticed the product on store shelves and decided to try it.

Consumer behavior in buying earplugs differed in several important ways. Most people did not purchase earplugs frequently. More important, earplugs were more what is called a push product than a pull product. In other words, advertising did not induce consumers to take the product off retail shelves, thereby pulling it through the retail distribution channel. Instead, consumers needed a push—at the right time—to buy. The recommendation of a doctor or a pharmacist might provide that push, as might an informative retail display. Frequently, the right time was when the consumer became so frustrated with not sleeping or being otherwise bothered by noise that he or she was motivated to ask for advice. Broadcast advertising was not the appropriate choice for this product—and it was expensive.

The basic problem in this example is that by selecting this particular research firm, Cabot made an implicit choice of communication strategy. Explicit analysis of customer buying processes and communication habits could have avoided very large but ineffective expenditures for packaged-goods-oriented research and for advertising. An effective strategy for consumer earplugs would have used a very different communication approach.

DETERMINE COMMUNICATION'S ROLE WITHIN STRATEGY

The basic rule for using any communication tool effectively in a specific situation is:

- First determine the role that tool should play in the overall marketplace strategy.
- Only then proceed to make specific decisions about how to deploy the tool.

The entire marketplace strategy should, of course, be based on rigorous, explicit outside-in thinking.

Thus, for example, in using advertising, the first job is to determine how advertising should fit into the overall strategy. In the example of early Federal Express, the discussion in Chapter 3 demonstrated that the central role of advertising was to get into the mind of prospective customers the name Federal Express, the idea that the company could provide guaranteed, safe, overnight delivery, and the invitation to call for service. This strategic role translated into highly memorable and effective ads in which a character who spoke extremely rapidly described a problem that Federal Express could solve and then said that the company would get the document where it was supposed to go "absolutely positively overnight."

The president of one of the largest advertising agencies provided other examples. Asked whether advertising agencies could be held accountable for results, he said he was happy to have the results of his agency's work measured provided that objectives that reflected the advertising's strategic role had been made clear at the outset. For example, he said that it was appropriate to judge advertising for a consumer packaged good by the sales of the product, because advertising could convince or remind customers to purchase the good. In contrast, he said that advertising for automobiles could not actually make the sale. Instead, he believed that advertising could be asked to bring potential purchasers to the automobile showroom—and he was happy to have results of the advertising evaluated using showroom visits.

The strategic-role-first rule applies equally to other communication tools. In the late 1980s and 1990s, Nestlé's baby-food business in France executed a successful outside-in communication approach.[2] Sensibly, Nestlé managers wanted to concentrate their communication on parents of infants. They believed that parents would purchase a product that their babies had tried and liked, so trial use was a central objective. They also believed that new parents would welcome information about nutrition for babies and wanted to feel comfortable with the company whose food they fed their babies; accordingly, establishing relationships with parents and providing them with information were also objectives.

To achieve its communication objectives, Nestlé set up eight rest stops or "baby service stations" (Le Relais Bébé) during the summer months along France's main travel routes. The tradition of extended summer vacations in France meant that many people, including people with babies, would be driving along those roads. The rest stops offered travelers, without charge, everything they needed to change and feed their babies. Hostesses at the stops helped parents and, among other things, distributed hundreds of thousands of samples of Nestlé's baby food each summer.

Nestlé also established a toll-free telephone number staffed by licensed dietitians who answered questions about baby nutrition. It set up a direct-mail program, regularly sending baby-food samples, coupons, information, and related items to parents who indicated, in response to an initial mailing soon after a baby's birth, that they were interested.

France's leading baby-food company outspent Nestlé on conventional advertising by as much as seven to one during Nestlé's campaign, but Nestlé became the number two brand in France. Its share grew from 19 percent to 43 percent in less than seven years.

The strategic-role-first rule applies to field sales, too. Chapters 4 and 5 described a company that manufactured specialty products for use in construction. Those discussions explained that architects specified the products, but contractors at job sites had to apply the products correctly. The manufacturer's strategy therefore assigned its field sales force two different tasks. The salespeople called on architects to explain the products and encourage architects to specify them appropriately. They also spent time at job sites, especially for tricky applications, helping the contractors' employees use the products properly.

Having clearly identified these key sales jobs, the manufacturer's sales management could make sensible decisions about the sales force. It hired people who would be credible at construction sites. It trained its salespeople about the details of product application; it also trained them to give architects the information and support that those specifiers would find helpful. Its processes for evaluating salespeople considered not just sales dollars but also these tasks of education and customer support.

In another sales example, IBM's early strategy was to educate business customers, helping them to begin using computers. Many customers considered computers expensive and risky purchases, and IBM's strategy was to help them become more comfortable with computers as they gained value from them. IBM hired people for its sales force who promised to be good relationship managers. It trained them both about computers and about specific customer industries. Its policies kept the same salesperson or sales team on an account for a long time. These and other sales policies were selected to fit with the strategic role of sales.

MORE ABOUT SALES IN OUTSIDE-IN STRATEGY

When a company substantially changes its overall marketplace strategy in some way, its communication approach will often also have to change. Chapter 7 described how General Stair Corp. went from offering a largely undifferentiated product, prefab stairs, to offering stairs augmented by a guarantee and a service that determined when the stairs were needed. The change of strategy had to include a substantial redesign of the role of sales.

Changes in customers often drive changes in both marketplace strategy and communication. Traditionally, salespeople for pharmaceutical companies called on individual doctors to explain how drugs worked. As HMOs and similar organizations became more and more prominent, they exerted increasing control over doctors' choices of pharmaceuticals. The pharmaceutical companies began sending representatives to call on those organizations, providing information about both the efficacy and the cost-effectiveness of drugs. The change required that the companies change at least their sales training and in some cases also the types of people they recruited for their sales force.

Having sales policies that are clearly linked to sales strategy does not necessarily mean that either the sales or the overall marketplace strategy is outside in, however. A disguised case about one of the regional telephone companies created by the breakup of AT&T describes the company's mid-1980s sales strategy and tactics for ads in the Yellow Pages.[3] Managers said that they wanted salespeople to push customer companies to spend more and more on ads. They did not want salespeople to build rapport with customers, as they feared that relationships would make salespeople reluctant to push hard for higher sales. Accordingly, the managers randomly assigned individual salespeople to different accounts each year. It's not clear that this sales strategy made sense in customer terms, especially as competition arrived in the Yellow Pages business. Given the strategy, however, the tactics did fit.

What I call the *sales funnel* can help in thinking about and then explaining an important aspect of communication strategy. Consider a funnel drawn in cross section; think of prospects entering at the top and actual buying customers exiting at the bottom. The basic point of the funnel is that, alas, organizations must communicate with more prospects than they are able to convert into paying customers. In some situations, as shown at the left below, there are many more prospects than customers. In other cases, there are fewer prospects per eventual customer, as shown at the right.

Design of an explicit communication strategy often includes a decision about the basic funnel shape that fits a business and its customers. In its early days, Federal Express used an especially broad funnel, because promising prospects worked in many different offices and could not be identified effectively. It was preferable

prospects

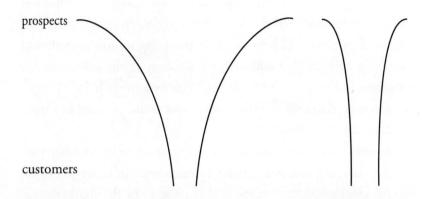

customers

for the company to communicate with many prospects and wait for the prospects to come forward when they were ready to turn into customers.

In other situations, especially when a company uses field sales, it is important to have a narrower funnel. One approach for doing so is to consider a relatively large number of prospects but to devise quick and inexpensive methods to screen or qualify those initial prospects, eliminating all but the seriously promising ones. For example, pharmaceutical companies have long used purchased information about pharmacy sales to determine which doctors are the most promising targets for sales calls about specific new products.[4]

Sometimes companies are lucky enough to have good methods for identifying the promising prospects from the outset. For example, the prospects might be companies that use a specific manufacturing process and have been sourcing a raw material from a supplier that has experienced quality problems.

One special point about salespeople and other company employees who have contact with customers: For a company to maintain an outside-in perspective, it is important to motivate those employees to notice and report back useful information about customers—their product needs, buying processes, and communication habits. This function of gathering information should normally be part of a company's definition of the sales role; for example, in Deming's TQC or total quality approach, salespeople were required to collect information that could be used in future product development.[5]

In some cases, one part of an organization treats another part of the same organization almost as a customer in order to obtain useful information about the real customers in the marketplace. In one company, a sales manager explained that the people who were most likely to know when a customer might be interested in buying a new piece of equipment were his own company's service people. Accordingly, he devoted some of his time and attention to his organization's service force, treating them as internal customers.

One specific communication error is so common that it should be highlighted. This error is to reverse the order of the steps when making decisions about sales management. In other words, the error is to hire a senior sales executive before deciding on the role that field sales should play in the marketplace strategy.

The error is common in start-ups, especially in technically-oriented start-ups. Typically, what happens is that technically-oriented founders know that they need sales expertise, know that they don't have that expertise themselves, and want to hire it as soon as possible. Such entrepreneurs have approached me for help in finding a sales executive—preferably immediately.

My response is to try to slow the process, first asking the entrepreneurs what specific kind of sales expertise and experience they need. For example, consider the founder of a company that planned to sell software for engineers to use in product design. I asked how the entrepreneur expected that customers would go about buying his product. Would large organizations buy it in bulk for use throughout their design groups? If so, he would want expertise in large sales—in selling to the complex decision-making units (DMUs) and decision-making processes (DMPs) typical of large software purchases. Or would individual engineers or groups of just a few engineers buy the product? If so, he would need expertise in making much smaller sales, efficiently and effectively, to engineers.

Entrepreneurs tend to be taken aback by such questions. In essence, the message is that there are many varieties of sales experience and that the entrepreneurs need to do enough analysis to decide what variety to hire. In other words, they need first to determine (as well as they can) the role of sales in their strategy, using insights about customers' needs and buying processes in defining the appropriate sales role. Only then can they sensibly go about hiring the appropriate sales expertise.

MATCH CUSTOMERS' COMMUNICATION PATTERNS

To repeat, communication approaches should fit within outside-in strategies and should match customers' communication needs and habits. For example, as discussed in Chapter 5, Nantucket Nectars believed that its target customers could be found at concerts, sporting events, and similar locations. Managers believed that targets would not pay much attention to broadcast advertising but would be open to trying new products and might notice a memorable product presentation. They consequently used mobile marketing squads in purple shirts driving purple Winnebagos to hand out samples of the products at appropriate events; the program achieved the strategic goals of generating trial usage and helping customers to remember to buy the purple-topped bottles of juice.

The founders of a company that marketed reflective fabric (which will be discussed at more length in Chapter 11) selected the market for runners' clothing as an initial target. They believed that their target customers were influenced by what they observed elite runners wearing. Many of the targets read specialized magazines for runners and looked for clothing in specialized catalogs. Accordingly, the founders placed their products in those catalogs and worked to be reviewed and covered by those magazines. They sponsored marathons and other races, incorporating their product into the official shirts or jackets for those events and including information about how customers could reach the company. For example, in one early communication success, the company teamed with an athletic-clothing manufacturer to supply (at cost) the official jackets for the Boston Marathon.

Managers at Sony Pictures Classics believed that many consumers decided to see a movie because someone they knew recommended it to them.[6] The company used this insight when it introduced the film *Crouching Tiger, Hidden Dragon* in 2000. Individuals who were considered influential were invited to early screenings of the film. For example, Sony managers got the magazine *Sports Illustrated for Women* to host a screening aimed at female athletes. Additional efforts targeted karate enthusiasts and other promising groups. The communication campaign was successful, and it cost only $7 million, roughly a third of what was spent on typical releases of Hollywood movies.

For many companies that serve business customers, trade shows are effective communication tools. There are numerous trade shows focusing on all kinds of industries and functions. Companies can participate as exhibitors; they can also have key employees give talks or participate in panel discussions in one of the information sessions included at many shows. Simple attendance at relevant trade shows can provide great value, too. Attendees arrive at trade shows in a frame of mind to accept new information, to learn about new products, and to talk with others.

Many managers, scientists and engineers, and other potentially interesting groups read specialized magazines aimed at particular industries, technologies, and market segments. Advertising in those magazines can be an effective and efficient way to match customers' communication habits. And response cards (bingo cards) in magazines can offer interested prospects a convenient way to identify themselves to the company for further discussion, to receive literature, to obtain a product trial, or for some similar purpose.

The preceding examples have emphasized the importance that customers frequently place on being able to try out a product. Recent technical advances, especially the Internet, have made trial uses of some products relatively easy. A software company can develop a restricted version of its product that nonetheless demonstrates some of its key capabilities and can make that version available over the Internet. Assuming that the company can solve the awareness problem and motivate prospects to pay attention and visit its site, it has an effective and relatively low-cost method of offering trial uses.

Often, customers are receptive to information they receive from specifiers or recommenders (such as architects or physicians) or channel partners (such as distributors). In such cases, it can be effective to give the recommenders or partners support literature that they, in turn, can give to actual customers. For example, the discussion of Lifeline's monitoring service for elderly people who remain in their own homes mentioned that Lifeline provided pamphlets to doctors and hospitals for distribution to prospective users and their families.

In all these cases, the basic idea is to begin with the strategic role of communication and then to select specific communication tools that can fit that role while matching customers' communication habits. As always with the outside-in discipline, the emphasis should be on customer benefits.

COMMUNICATE ABOUT CUSTOMER BENEFITS

This emphasis on customer benefits certainly applies to communication during the customer's initial purchase process. It also applies during usage. After they have purchased a product, customers often more or less forget about it, paying close attention only when something goes wrong. Having customers pay attention to what you do wrong but not what you do right can be frustrating and can damage your chances for getting future business. Careful communication can help correct the situation.

Some years ago, in working with a lumber-products company, I devised a communication approach that I have since used successfully with a number of companies in a variety of industries to address this problem. I call the device a *vendor report card*.

The basic idea is first to sit down with key members of a customer's DMU and agree on the criteria by which you and they will judge the quality of the job you do for them. Then, over time, you collect information relating to those measures, and you periodically review the information with the customer.

If they believe that you really will try to perform well on the dimensions that they specify, customers are often quite willing to devote time and attention to the initial discussions. The process gives you an effective way to get information about customer needs, and the periodic reviews provide the opportunity to focus the customer's attention on your successes as well as your failures.

Managers for the lumber-products company found that customers ranked the various criteria differently. For example, one customer explained that he preferred, of course, always to receive all the products he had ordered on one truck that arrived on time. He acknowledged that occasional problems were probably inevitable, but he emphasized that, if there were a problem, it was important that he receive a shipment on time, even if a few items were missing. Another customer also liked to receive complete shipments on time but viewed problem situations differently. He explained that incomplete shipments seriously disrupted his operations. If the order wasn't complete, he preferred that the supplier delay delivery until it was complete.

Thus, for the first customer, the lumber-products company would periodically report how many orders it had delivered that were both complete and on time and, in addition, how many orders had at least been on time. The reports to the second customer would list the number of orders that were both on time and complete and the number that were at least complete.

The periodic reports and accompanying discussions were great ways to be able to talk with customers about the benefits they had received. They were also effective tools for uncovering changes in customers' circumstances and preferences and for identifying new, measurable ways to serve customers better. In addition, the information about what each customer valued proved highly useful in guiding employees at the supplier, telling them what was most important in different customer situations.

A COMMUNICATION CHALLENGE: TUNED-OUT CUSTOMERS

Typical customer behavior creates another challenge for communication. Customers often notice and respond to a new communication tool in part simply because it is new and different. Coverage in the business press often contributes to the hype of a new technique. As the tool becomes more familiar, customers may tire of it, stop paying attention to it, and even actively avoid it.

The lesson here is that communication strategies will frequently have to change over time as fashions in customers' communication habits change. The underlying tasks that the tools are intended to accomplish may remain unchanged, but the choice of specific tools may require regular reassessment and adjustment. The second, more upbeat, lesson is that customers sometimes do respond well for a while to new techniques, so new communication approaches deserve careful consideration.

Internet banner ads are an example. Early banner ads apparently did generate respectable rates of click-through. Users quickly tired of the ads, however, and today's click-through rates for such ads are minuscule.

The problem is exacerbated by the high cost of many communication tools. TV time for one ad on the Super Bowl costs millions of dollars. A single ad on a popular prime-time TV show costs hundreds of thousands. The fully loaded cost of a single call by an industrial salesperson is typically hundreds of dollars.

As a result, companies have been scrambling to adjust their communication approaches and to find tools that are actually effective. Often, the efforts involve using well-known tools in new or more effective ways.

Because customers are often skeptical of paid advertising, there has been increased interest in public relations, where the idea is to get a credible third party to communicate to customers about you. The key is to offer journalists stories they find worth writing about and, without offending their sense of professional independence, to offer them enough information so that they will get right the details that matter to you. Entire books and entire marketing companies specialize in this area.

A closely related tool is event sponsorship. Consider the example of Goya Foods, a company that made food products used in Latin cuisines.[7] The Metropolitan Museum of Art in New York was planning an exhibition of the work of the artist Francisco Goya (no actual connection to the company). Goya Foods spent $245,000 to sponsor the event. Its name was displayed at the museum entrance and on printed materials for the exhibit. In addition, some of Goya's products were served in the museum cafeteria during the show. The museum obtained funding, which it badly needed. Assuming that Goya had decided that a key marketing task was to get new prospects to try the products, the sponsorship appears to have been an excellent choice of communication tool.

In the current communication environment, both large, established companies and start-ups have found it useful to experiment with communication tools. The discussion of scale in Chapter 6 described how dollarDEX.com, the Singapore-based Internet business, tried many small-scale communication experiments, carefully measuring the results provided by each tool. In the process, the company learned which tools were cost-effective (and should be retained) and which were not (and should be dropped).

Procter & Gamble, one of the largest advertisers in the world, has also been experimenting with new communication tools and reducing its reliance on traditional broadcast advertising.[8] For example, the company tried giving away rolls of Charmin toilet paper to discharged hospital patients, but that experiment didn't prove effective. Other experiments did.

Another P&G effort, aimed at young households attending family-friendly events, was considerably more successful. The company sent tractor-trailer-mounted bathrooms to such events in what it called the Charmin Pottypalooza tour. The bathrooms were equipped with running water, were nicely decorated and well maintained, and stocked Charmin toilet paper, Safeguard hand soap, and other P&G products. In early 2003, a P&G manager said that 2 million customers at more than 20 events had visited the bathrooms in the preceding year. Research showed that sales of Charmin to those customers had increased 14 percent. The company planned to introduce a second Pottypalooza.

We can expect companies to continue to try new and different communication approaches. Outside-in strategies and small-scale experiments should continue to lead the way.

CUSTOMERS, ADVERTISING, AND BRANDS

Although branding is often classified as part of product policy rather than communication, in fact branding overlaps the two categories. The topic of branding is discussed here rather than with product in Chapter 7 because of some unfortunate recent history, especially in dot-com companies, concerning the use of advertising to attempt to create brand equity.

First, take a broader view of branding. The topic has received substantial attention in business publications in the last decade or so. Reading that coverage has been something of a roller-coaster ride, with brands first being portrayed as endangered, then as powerful and effective, and then again as being in trouble.

Consider a few examples.[9] In July 1993, an article in *Business-Week* asked, "So is this the end of our long affair with premium brands?" It suggested that marketers seemed to be acting as if it were. Similarly, the next month *Fortune* ran an article about the amount of pressure that private labels were exerting on major brands. Although these articles focused on consumer packaged goods, the pessimism extended to the whole idea of branding. People questioned the willingness of customers to continue to pay premiums for branded products.

By 1996, the pendulum in the business press had swung the

other way.[10] In March, the headline of a *Fortune* article proclaimed, "The Brand's the Thing." It said that "companies like Coke, Microsoft and Disney are proving that having a strong name may be the ultimate competitive weapon." By 2000, the pendulum had swung again. An August 2000 article in *Business-Week*, headlined "Brands in a Bind," suggested that the bonds between customers and brands were loosening. We can expect that the pendulum will swing yet again.

Given such oscillating coverage in the press, it helps to step back and ask what has been and what is the basic role of brand for customers. A July 1994 article in the *Economist* noted the confusion in the press:

> Management gurus say variously that "the brand" is declining, dying, redefining itself or about to be resurrected.[11]

The article then proceeded to give a clear, customer-based explanation of the function of brand:

> The point of brand is, and always has been, to provide information. The form of that information varies from market to market, and from time to time. Some products make a visible statement about their users' style, modernity or wealth. . . . Others purport to convey reliability, say, or familiarity, or something else. Whatever the information is, however, the right question to ask is this: does the buyer still need or want it?

Thus, the fundamental question for outside-in analysis of branding is, "What information does the customer need that a brand could supply?" Assuming that brand will in fact be important in a specific situation, a second question should then ask what communication tool or tools would be most effective in providing the relevant information.

Sometimes the appropriate tool is advertising. In other cases, it is not. For example, customers may want to have a low-risk way to try the product. They may then become quite loyal to a brand that has provided them with a good trial experience.

The recent history that I find so troubling centered on the dot-com arena, although it extended to other areas as well. The basic thinking appeared to go something like this:

> Our product doesn't really offer much that is distinctive. But we need customers. So, we'll brand the product. We'll advertise our product heavily, and the advertising will make customers buy.

Actually, this version of the prevalent thinking may be overly kind, because it assumes there was in fact a product or service. A *Fortune* article looking back soon after many dot-com stocks crashed described the thinking this way:

> First build a "brand," the thinking went. Then get eyeballs. Then turn them into paying customers. Then figure out how to make a business of it.[12]

Such thinking (either version) was downright silly. And, especially because of the emphasis on broad advertising, it was extremely expensive.

One example of this phenomenon came from an entrepreneur who was starting a company that would provide an Internet-based service. She explained, explicitly and logically, her team's views of the organizations that would be their customers—of the relevant DMUs, of the needs and buying power of different members, and of the benefits that customers would value. The outside-in thinking was impressive.

Unfortunately, she then reported, in 2000, that she was under strong pressure from venture capitalists (VCs) from whom she hoped to obtain funding. The VCs were insisting that she spend millions of dollars on advertising to brand her service. She was convinced that brand name was not what would drive purchases, but that customers would want to try the service in some easy, low-risk way and would then use their initial experiences to decide whether to buy more. She did not believe that broad advertising was an effective tool for obtaining initial trial or for winning subsequent sales volume.

According to her customer picture, spending huge sums on advertising was foolish. "Brand the product with advertising" was a mantra in much of the VC community at the time, however, and the VCs were bound and determined that advertising was necessary. The entrepreneur never managed to find a strategy that both fit her customers and made potential investors happy. Her company failed.

Unrealistic expectations of what specific communication tools, especially advertising, can do are by no means confined to dot-coms. For example, a 2003 survey studied advertising and customer loyalty for fast-food chains.[13] The survey showed that advertising and customer commitment were not even correlated. Instead, customers cared about good food, polite service, and clean restaurants.

The CEO of Panera, one of the chains that had the most loyal customers, was quite clear about his understanding of customers: "Consumers are smart. It's the experience and how they relate to it." Yet many larger chains continued to advertise heavily. Achieving and maintaining an outside-in perspective is a challenge in communication, as it is elsewhere.

SUMMARY

Outside-in communication starts with customers' communication needs and habits as parts of customer pictures. The next step is to determine the roles of communication overall and of specific communication tools in outside-in strategies directed at those customers. Only then is it sensible to make specific decisions about how to use each communication tool so that it fits with customers' communication habits and plays the desired role in strategy.

The concept of the sales funnel can help in designing and describing communication strategy. The funnel summarizes the process of converting prospects into customers, showing roughly the relationship between the number of prospects and the number of buying customers.

Vendor report cards can be an effective tool for communicating with customers. They can help uncover the preferences and concerns of specific customers and can provide the basis for reminding customers of the benefits that a vendor has delivered to them. They can also help guide the execution of a marketplace strategy tailored to the needs of specific customers.

Often, customers respond to new tools but tire of those tools over time. That fact, together with the high expense of many traditional communication tools, has led managers in existing companies and in start-ups to search for new and effective communication approaches. Small-scale experiments can help identify the useful tools for specific situations.

Communication tools tend to become very fashionable and then to fade. Some of that pattern is created by customer behavior, but some is created by businesspeople and the business press, which may go through cycles, touting a tool (such as advertising for branding), then disparaging it, and then touting it again.

A more moderate approach is frequently preferable. For example, the key role of brand is to provide information to customers, and the relevant questions are, as usual, what information customers need and how they would like to receive that information.

OUTSIDE-IN ACTIONS

1. Recheck your customer pictures.

Make sure that they include the most important information about customers' communication needs and habits for both their purchase processes and their usage processes. Check that the pictures really capture the essence of customers' communication behaviors. If not, revise the pictures.

2. Recheck the communication portions of your strategy.

Verify that your statement of strategy explicitly includes the important aspects of your communication. Make sure that the role of communication is clear and that communication fits well into your consistent and coordinated outside-in strategy. If not, revise the strategy or, at least, the statement of strategy.

3. Translate that strategic role for communication into roles for specific communication tools.

Describe the role that field sales should fulfill in the strategy. Similarly, define the strategic role of advertising, the role of public relations, and the role of every other communication tool that you will use.

4. Decide on the details of your uses of those tools consistent with their roles in strategy.

For advertising, determine the advertising objectives, specific messages, choice of media, and so on. Determine specific sales policies, such as the types of people you should hire, the training you will provide them, the way to assign them to customers, how you will evaluate and compensate them, and so on. Make specific decisions for any other communication tools you will use.

5. **Be sure that your communication emphasizes customer benefits.**
Emphasize the things that matter most to customers. Consider using a vendor report card to formalize communication about benefits with individual business customers.

6. **Have realistic expectations about what a communication tool can accomplish.**
Recognize the limits, for example, on what advertising can do to establish brand identity. And, be aware that many customers tune out much of the communication to which they are exposed.

10

OUTSIDE-IN CHANNELS OF DISTRIBUTION
Channels for Customers and
Channels as Customers

Of all the elements in marketing strategy—the product line, price, promotion, and distribution—the last is the hardest to change.
—Raymond Corey

THE BROAD AREA OF distribution is a complex and challenging part of many marketplace strategies. When businesspeople decide whether to sell directly to customers or to use intermediaries such as distributors instead, they are in essence deciding what face their companies will present to customers. Sound outside-in design and execution of a distribution strategy therefore have the potential to play a key role in marketplace success. At the same time, however, establishing and maintaining a good distribution strategy are challenging tasks, and effecting needed changes in distribution is especially difficult.

As is true for each of the elements of marketplace strategy, distribution should be based on customers' needs and behavior, and it should fit with the other marketing tools to form a consistent and coordinated whole. If, for example, a company is developing a new product that will be sold through distributors, there may be substantial benefit from having a good understanding of the distributors' capabilities before the product design is completed. If initial evaluation shows that the distributors have only fair or poor abilities to repair complex products, then the product designers will want to create a product that does not require repair expertise from the channel, especially if prompt, accurate repair service is important to customers. They might build the product with individual modules that could be replaced rather than repaired in the event of malfunctions. They might also incorporate substantial self-diagnosis capabilities into the product.

This chapter begins by considering distribution in outside-in strategy, firmly based on customers and consistent and coordinated with the other strategic elements. It then discusses the question of whether channel intermediaries are themselves customers. It examines the difficulty inherent in changing distribution. Finally, it outlines recent developments in distribution that create both challenges and opportunities.

DISTRIBUTION CHANNELS TO FIT CUSTOMERS

The most basic decision for distribution strategy is whether to use direct or indirect distribution—whether to sell directly to customers or to involve intermediaries such as distributors. The outside-in discipline requires that the distribution decision begin with a consideration of customers. Several aspects of customers' needs and behavior influence the choice.

The most fundamental question is: Where and how do customers want to buy? Other questions help to explain and explore the answer to that first one: Do customers want to buy an assortment of products in one location, such as an industrial supply house or a supermarket? Do they require local availability and rapid delivery? Do they want to make frequent small purchases? Affirmative answers to such questions suggest serving customers through appropriate intermediaries such as distributors—using indirect distribution.

On the other hand, do customers require substantial amounts of sophisticated technical support? Do they buy large quantities at one time? Do they require customization? Do they value contact with the manufacturer, among other reasons in order to influence the designs of future products? Affirmative answers to questions such as these suggest selling directly to customers—using direct distribution.

An important related question is: What steps must be performed in order to serve customers well? Examples include presale customer education, help with choosing the specific product model or options, installation, postsale customer education, and repair services. Once these steps are clear, the manufacturer can assess the abilities of potential distribution partners, as well as the abilities of the manufacturer's own organization, to perform the necessary tasks.

Part of what makes channel decisions challenging is that, in most situations, some factors favor the choice of direct distribution while other factors favor indirect distribution. In other words, in most situations, distribution choices involve compromise. Explicit outside-in thinking provides the basis for making that compromise wisely. In addition, when indirect distribution is chosen, outside-in thinking helps in choosing specific intermediaries and in deciding what specific actions should be carried out by each channel member.

Sometimes the answers to the distribution questions lead to a mixed system, part direct and part indirect, as they did for Norton Company.[1] Norton was known for the skill with which it managed its distribution, and the distribution design it implemented in the 1960s remained a widely used example for decades.

Norton specialized in abrasives—grinding wheels and similar products. Customers in many industries used the wheels, sometimes in quantity in their production processes and sometimes just a few wheels at a time for MRO (maintenance, repair, and operations). Norton had a remarkably large product line—250,000 different wheels in the mid-1960s, of which only 35,000 were sufficiently widely used to be stock items. Norton managers believed that the huge number of products was mandated by customers' needs. Small changes in a wheel could create large changes (up to 50 percent) in productivity in a customer's grinding operation, yet the wheel accounted for only perhaps 5 percent of the cost of that operation. Customers thus received high benefits from having the best wheel for each job, and they insisted on receiving those benefits.

Norton used a mixed distribution system that differentiated between high-volume grinding wheels and low-volume grinding wheels. A customer that used enough of one specific wheel could order that wheel directly from Norton. All other orders went through distributors.

This strategy required close cooperation between Norton and its distributors. First, of course, there was the complexity created by the huge product line. In addition, customers needed help in deciding which specific wheel would work best for some purpose and then in using the wheel to best advantage. Norton provided training to employees of its distributors so that they could be the initial source of support. In addition, Norton's own salespeople and special sales engineers provided technical and product assistance to customers, sometimes independently and sometimes working with distributors. In fact, a majority of the salespeople's calls on customers were made at the request of distributors, sometimes jointly with employees of a distributor.

For an example in a very different environment, consider Coca-Cola.[2] As they worked to build a presence in China, the company's managers reasoned that customers might like Coke if they tried it but that they needed a convenient and comfortable way to buy the product. In Shanghai in 1996, Coke managers approached 14 neighborhood committees, the local watchdogs for the Communist Party. They worked out an arrangement under which the pensioners who staffed those committees stocked Coke in their offices and earned commissions on selling the product. The distribution channel proved effective at introducing residents of the neighborhoods to Coke.

Inadequate analysis of customers can lead to distribution mistakes. As will be discussed in more detail in Chapter 12, Accessmount was a start-up that developed a product to make the maintenance of ceiling-mounted lighting fixtures safer, easier, and less expensive. At first, because the product involved lighting (and even won awards at a major lighting trade show), Accessmount's founder worked hard to recruit and support distributors of lighting fixtures. Sales were disappointingly slow.

The founder then did some more outside-in thinking. He realized that the key early purchasers of his product would be the managers of the workers who performed maintenance in large buildings. Lighting distributors did not know those managers and certainly did not call on them regularly, but distributors of janitorial and sanitary supplies did. The founder shifted his emphasis to those "jan-san" distributors, who were a much better fit for his strategy. The lesson of the story is to emphasize the customer (needs, buying processes, and communication habits) rather than the product when making distribution decisions.

DISTRIBUTION IN MARKETPLACE STRATEGY

Distribution choices must, of course, fit well with the overall outside-in strategy. For example, the entrepreneur who developed the children's character Barney the dinosaur used good understanding of customers' buying processes to coordinate communication and distribution in her marketplace strategy.[3] A former schoolteacher, she developed the character in the late 1980s. She produced tapes of Barney and managed to place the tapes on consignment in retail stores that carried products for children. The problem was that people were not buying.

The founder reasoned that if she could get small children to view the tapes, the kids would then ask their parents to buy copies, and many parents would do so. In other words, trial usage (in this case, initial viewings by children) was key. She began sending free Barney videos to preschools and day-care centers located near retail outlets in which the tapes were available. She included notes in the video cases to tell parents where they could buy the tapes. This low-cost targeted communication campaign worked extremely well; sales in the stores climbed, and the founder signed up more stores. The strategy started Barney on the path to becoming a major force in children's TV, video, and toys.

Chapter 6 outlined the outside-in strategy of the clothing retailer Zara, which emphasized timely and frequently changing fashion at moderate, but not the lowest, prices. In this case, outside-in thinking drove what would normally be an intermediary to integrate backward, doing much of its own manufacturing as well as physical distribution and retailing.[4]

Zara's customer insights drove its decision to manufacture the majority of its own clothing, rather than outsourcing to obtain the lowest possible costs. Zara's founder emphasized time to market, along with identifying fashions that customers would want and changing merchandise in the stores often, as central to success. Zara knowingly accepted 15 to 20 percent higher manufacturing costs than its competitors. It was highly successful anyway, because customers valued its changing, fashionable merchandise, because its inventory costs were only a fraction (perhaps 50 or 60 percent) of those of competitors, and because it lost considerably less money on markdowns of mistakes.

Sometimes the choice of distribution strategy can have a wider effect on the marketplace strategy. Recall the example of White Wave's Silk soy milk, discussed in Chapters 4 and 5. Once they had finally created a product that fit well with customers' needs, the managers for Silk turned to the task of encouraging consumers to use the product more frequently. They used distribution channels as part of that effort.[5]

In 2003, White Wave's founder struck a deal to make Silk the exclusive soy milk for the entire Starbucks chain. In return, he agreed to formulate a special Silk blend for Starbucks, one that was tailored for espresso and chai beverages. An important part of the deal was that the Starbucks outlets would make clear to consumers that they were using the Silk brand. The Starbucks channel did not provide a large share of Silk's sales revenue, but it did contribute substantially to White Wave's efforts to communicate with customers.

Distribution choices can contribute to strategy in numerous other ways. They may, for example, help in implementing choices of market segments. The history of Dell Computer's channel strategies provides an illustration.[6] In 1991, the company established distribution agreements with selected retailers, including CompUSA and Staples. Dell expected the retailers to sell the products, while Dell itself managed after-sale service and support.

In 1994 Dell changed this strategy and exited the retail channel. Inventory control and channel management considerations were among the reasons for the move. Dell's entire strategy was based on just-in-time manufacturing (or, to be more exact, just-in-time assembly) under the Dell Direct Model. Dell assembled products only in response to specific customer orders. It managed its relationships with its own suppliers to keep its parts inventories extremely low while, at the same time, allowing Dell to ship products within at most a few days after they were ordered.

Retail channels fit poorly with the Dell Direct Model. They required inventory in the pipeline, and in a rapidly changing area such as personal computers that inventory could easily become obsolete. Dell and its channel partners had to agree on who would bear the costs of obsolescence. Similar problems occurred when there was a price cut on personal computers.

These inventory-related considerations were not the whole story, however. Retail customers created other problems for Dell. Many Dell transaction customers in 1994 purchased their personal computers over the telephone, speaking with Dell's internal salespeople. The customers who wanted to buy in a retail store instead included a disproportionate number of first-time personal-computer buyers.

Most first-time buyers lacked the confidence and knowledge to buy over the phone. They wanted to see the products, perhaps try them in the store, and get help in making their choices. Importantly for Dell, they frequently required extensive postsale support as they struggled to set up and then learn to use their new computers. Such support was expensive to provide, and Dell's channel arrangements meant that Dell itself had to provide it. When it exited the retail channel, in addition to improving its inventory situation, Dell effectively segmented the market, focusing on repeat and sophisticated purchasers and avoiding computer novices.

To be sensible, this change in distribution strategy required two additional important and, as it turned out, correct assumptions about customers. First, Dell could make the change because there were in fact enough repeat and sophisticated users in the market. Because Dell's main focus was elsewhere, on large corporate customers, there definitely were enough.

The second required assumption was more subtle. Dell had to assume that customers' choice of brand for their first personal computer did not dictate or strongly influence their choice for their second. In other words, the assumption was that at the time of their second or later purchase, customers looked around the marketplace and considered the costs and benefits of the models available at that time; they did not simply go to the brand they had purchased initially. This assumption meant that Dell could avoid the first-time purchases and still have a good chance of being selected for second-time ones.

In 2002 Dell made yet another change in distribution strategy.[7] It began offering unbranded personal computers to computer dealers in the United States. The reasoning was that some dealers acted essentially as the computer departments of small businesses. In doing so, the dealers often used so-called white boxes, or no-name computers. Dell wanted a share of that business.

At the same time, the new strategy was designed not to interfere with the basic Dell business model and not to recreate the previous problems with channel policies. In press coverage of the move, the head of Dell's small-business division stressed that there would be no inventory and no price protection. In addition, Dell recognized the need for partners who would provide the services that customers needed. The objective was to attract dealers that would provide customers with training, installation, repair, and other needed services.

This history of Dell's distribution strategy highlights the fact that manufacturers sometimes want to change their channel strategies over time as customers change. A later section will discuss the unfortunate fact that channel changes are often difficult to implement—far more difficult than were Dell's changes. First, however, let's take a closer look at the channel partners themselves.

CHANNEL MEMBERS: CUSTOMERS, PARTNERS, AND COMPETITORS

Many businesspeople say that their customer is the distributor or similar intermediary, not the end customer to whom the intermediary sells. Such comments are troubling. Yes, to some extent intermediaries are customers. At the same time, it is dangerous for businesspeople to act as if the intermediaries are their only or main customers. In doing so, they relegate much of their approach to the marketplace to other organizations whose interests are never perfectly aligned with those of the manufacturer.

First, suppose you sell through intermediaries who also carry products from your competitors. If a competitor understands your end customers better than you do and provides the intermediary with products and related services that are more attractive to customers than yours are, then surely that competitor will gain sales while you lose them, and its relative importance to the intermediary will increase.

If, instead, you sell through intermediaries who do not carry competitive products, then a competitor who creates a better offering for the ultimate customers will have its sales and those of its intermediaries increase. Both you and your intermediaries will suffer.

Thus, it's dangerous to act as if intermediaries are your only or main customers. At the same time, channel members are to some degree customers, and analysis of their needs and buying and usage processes provides important input for channel choices and for ongoing channel management.

Companies that rely heavily on intermediaries often spend a large amount of time and effort on understanding and supporting those channel members. It is sensible for them to do so. What is not sensible is devoting insufficient attention to the paying end customer or assuming that the manufacturer's interests are necessarily aligned with those of the intermediaries.

First, consider some examples of companies that relate well and sensibly to their intermediaries. Caterpillar has long used a worldwide network of dealers to distribute and service its construction and mining equipment.[8] Caterpillar managers believed that the dealers were essential to the company's strategy. The company sold large, expensive machines that customers used heavily in their operations. Breakdowns of those machines quickly translated into losses for customers. Caterpillar dealers provided not just sales but after-sale service and parts all over the world. A Caterpillar CEO once claimed that the company and its dealers combined to form the fastest and most comprehensive system for delivering parts that he had ever heard of. That system was central to reducing customer problems from downtime.

Caterpillar provided dealers with loyalty and with help. It refused to deal directly with customers. In 1996, the Caterpillar CEO wrote:

> It is not uncommon for our competitors to bypass their distributors and sell directly to the customer if they think a deal is important enough. We'd sooner cut off our right arm than do that.

Caterpillar provided its dealers with extensive business education and support tools. It helped to educate the next generations of the families that owned its dealerships, and it also helped the dealers implement management transitions. And so on. Caterpillar managers analyzed the needs of the dealers, treating them as customers and as partners. At the same time, the managers remained focused on the end customers, who would ultimately determine the success of both Caterpillar and its dealers.

Caterpillar had the advantage that it accounted for the bulk of the revenues of its dealers, who therefore were inclined to pay lots of attention to the company. Companies that sell to distributors and dealers for whom they are only a minor supplier face a more challenging task as they try to get attention and commitment. Analyzing the channel members as customers can help with that task.

Green Mountain Coffee Roasters provides an example.[9] Despite vocal concern from some of his board members, the company's founder decided to include service stations in the outlets for his product because he believed that end customers would value good coffee at those convenient locations. The trick was to make sure that the service-station personnel made the coffee properly and did not damage consumers' views of the Green Mountain brand.

The company set out to make the service stations more successful in selling coffee, serving the intermediaries' needs for increased revenues and profits as well as its own interests. Green Mountain augmented its product to the service stations, providing coffee machines, cups, banners, training, and other services and tools. The training was substantial, involving one- and two-day courses. End consumers got consistently high-quality coffee at numerous convenient locations. The service stations got sales and profits. By 2000, Exxon Mobil had become Green Mountain's largest customer, accounting for 17 percent of sales.

In these and many other examples, manufacturers sensibly treat intermediaries as part customer and part partner. At the same time, however, distributors are not simply customers or partners. In addition, they are also to some extent competitors.

Manufacturers and intermediaries compete for what is called *ownership of the customer*—in other words, to be the party that has the most knowledge of the customer and to whom the customer feels attached. Often, intermediaries are reluctant to share any more information about customers than necessary with the manufacturer; by withholding information, they are guarding their ownership of the customer.

Manufacturers and intermediaries also compete for the sales dollars of the end customers, arguing over who deserves how much. They argue over support levels, over which customers to target, and over many other issues. Thus, it makes sense to analyze intermediaries as customers, but the analysis should also probe for a clear understanding of the ways in which the intermediaries' interests and orientations conflict with those of the manufacturer. Managing the conflict is made even more challenging by the high level of inertia in the distribution part of strategy.

DISTRIBUTION IS A HIGH-INERTIA TOOL

To understand the problems with distribution that can be created by inertia, it helps to begin with a simplified look at the economics of direct sales and of indirect sales.

If the direct approach is at least an adequate match with customers' needs, it has some clear advantages. The manufacturer has more control over decisions concerning which customers to target, over the sales messages that are delivered to customers, over the mechanics of purchase and delivery, and over other aspects of the interaction with customers.

The problem with this approach, especially for resource-constrained entrepreneurs, is that it requires considerable up-front investment, in advance of cash flow from sales. The company must hire salespeople, provide them with offices and cars, hire sales management, and create any needed infrastructure such as physical distribution capabilities. The following simplified graph shows the situation, with substantial initial fixed costs and then some variable selling cost for each unit.

This picture is certainly not precise. The fixed costs are much

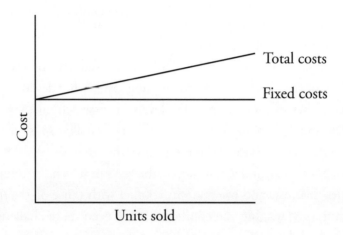

more likely to be a step function, with increments needed as sales rise. The graphic does, however, convey the general economics of direct sales well enough for comparison with indirect distribution.

With indirect distribution, the manufacturer faces substantially lower initial fixed costs. There will be some costs to establish the capabilities needed to work with and support the channel partners, but not nearly the fixed expense of direct sales. There will, however, be a more significant variable cost: the margin or commission paid to the channel partner for each unit sold. The following graph adds lines for indirect distribution to the preceding graph in order to provide a simple comparison of the two choices.

This graph highlights the fact that, under the critical assumption that customers will respond well to either approach, the economics favors indirect distribution early but direct distribution later. The problem is that channel changes can be difficult and dangerous. Distribution is a high-inertia tool.

Dell was lucky. The channel changes it wanted to make did not create serious problems in the marketplace. In a way, manufacturers for whom customer preferences allow only one realistic channel choice are also lucky. Others, however, find channel changes a serious problem.

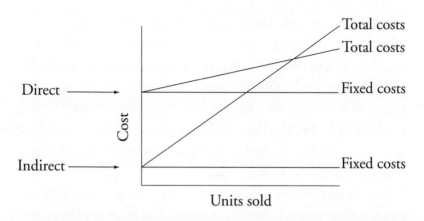

Consider a manufacturer of medical instruments that sold its first products to hospitals through several distributors.[10] Hospitals bought an enormous number of different items—everything from syringes to hospital gowns to reagents to medical instruments. For the large number of simpler items, the hospitals wanted to purchase through distributors, which provided an assortment of items and allowed the hospitals to purchase from a single source rather than from all the manufacturers of the individual items.

For especially complex equipment, however, the hospitals needed more knowledgeable sales and service people, and therefore suppliers sold directly to them. The initial products of the manufacturer in this example were at the edge of the capabilities of the distributors, but the distributors could handle them with some help from the manufacturer. The distributors had the great advantage of already knowing the customers, including the various members of their decision-making units (DMUs). They understood the hospitals' decision-making processes (DMPs). By using distributors, the manufacturer initially avoided the high fixed costs of setting up a direct sales force and getting to know the customers. That initial choice was successful and sales grew.

A few years later, however, the situation had changed. The

manufacturer had developed some newer, more complex instruments to meet additional needs of the hospitals. It tried having its existing distributors sell the first of the new products, but the distributors struggled, and there were very few sales. Managers expected that a direct sales force would be successful with the new products, whereas the distributors were not. They also realized that total sales had reached a level where the economics of selling direct had begun to be attractive.

The hurdle was in implementing the change. The hospitals that were the manufacturer's customers had been dealing primarily with the distributors, not the manufacturer, whose personnel would have to learn the DMUs and DMPs. The distributors would surely notice what was going on. Imagine the situation when the distributors were informed, or perhaps just guessed, that the manufacturer was changing its distribution approach. The distributors would have no incentive to sell products or to help during the transition. Worse, the distributors would have a substantial incentive to convince customers to buy other manufacturers' products if competitive manufacturers used those distributors and some incentive to punish the manufacturer by sending customers to other manufacturers even if those manufacturers sold direct.

Thus, changes from indirect to direct distribution are usually difficult. The manufacturer of medical instruments did manage to implement the change. It first increased its role in supporting sales by the distributor and in servicing the products. After it had established more ties with customers, it announced and rapidly implemented the channel change. It suffered disruption and lost sales in the process, however.

Dell's 1994 channel change dropped indirect channels, true, but Dell was in the fortunate position of not caring about keeping the customers that were served by the dropped partners. Dell's

2002 change to include new channel partners was not a major problem. Changes from direct to indirect are easier to implement because they do not involve the same level of conflict over ownership of customers.

Thus the concept of inertia, discussed in Chapter 6, is important in distribution strategy. Because distribution choices can be so difficult to change, it's advisable to take a long-term as well as a short-term view of distribution. Managers of a new business may in fact decide to emphasize the short term and choose indirect distribution, even though they would prefer direct in the long run. They should at least be aware of the implications for the future, however, and make the choice consciously. In some cases they can take actions that will make future changes a bit less difficult. They can, for example, choose to perform service themselves, thereby getting to know the end customers. In other cases, entrepreneurs will decide that having the right choice for the long run is so important that they will begin with the high-fixed-cost direct approach.

DISTRIBUTION TODAY—CHALLENGE AND OPPORTUNITY

Recent and ongoing changes in distribution channels are creating both challenges and opportunities. New technology and improved options for physical distribution make it possible to sell directly in situations that in the past could be handled only indirectly. At the same time, new technology and new methods have allowed some distributors and retailers to take substantially more control of the channels in which they participate.

Thus, intermediaries are gaining power in some marketplaces and losing power in others. The situation is made even more challenging by the fact that, in many markets, some forces are working to strengthen intermediaries, while other forces are working to weaken them. It is therefore not at all clear which channel players will be more powerful in the future.

In the travel industry, it is clear that the service providers, such as airlines, have gained substantial power relative to travel agents. Significant numbers of customers have begun to book their own travel over the Internet rather than using travel agents as they did in the past. Some cite the convenience of booking online. Many more say that they are price sensitive and believe that they can find better prices online.

Consequently, the airlines have been able to implement a series of reductions in the commissions they pay travel agents. In many cases, the agents now receive no commissions at all from the airlines for writing tickets. Some travel agencies may succeed in offering additional service to some customers and getting the customers to pay them for it. However, many, if not most, travel agents have gone or will go out of business.

Thus, new technology allowed the airlines to reduce or eliminate the role of their old channel partners. However, newer intermediaries have arisen in the travel market. Online sites have begun to offer customers access to many airlines at once, competing with the sites of the individual airlines. It is not yet clear whether direct sales by the airlines or indirect sales through the newer intermediaries will dominate the market.

Automobile-insurance companies in the United States have also used technology to gain power, in this case relative to companies that replace auto glass.[11] In 1990, Allstate began using computer connections to a large chain of glass installers. When Allstate policyholders called the insurer to report a cracked windshield or some similar problem, they were connected with the glass-installation chain, which arranged for and carried out the installation. Other insurers established similar systems.

Under these new arrangements, policyholders were spared the trouble of shopping for and evaluating potential glass-replacement companies. The insurers consolidated their purchases and no longer had to issue a check for each individual replacement. They also gained power relative to the glass-replacement companies and received substantially lower prices. In some cases, smaller independent auto-glass suppliers were not allowed to be part of the insurers' networks of preferred suppliers. In other cases, the smaller companies chose not to participate, presumably because of the lower prices and the technical requirements.

In other situations, intermediaries have used technology to gain power in their channels. The most obvious example is in retailing. A generation ago, the consumer-packaged-goods companies wielded great power. True, they needed and worked with retailers, but the manufacturers had better information and owned the powerful brand names. They had a tendency to tell the retailers what to do.

Times have certainly changed. Retailers, especially Wal-Mart, have used information technology to establish tight controls over their businesses. They appeal to consumers with low prices, pleasant service by discount-store standards, and excellent inventory management that keeps products in stock in the stores. Information technology lets the retailers know exactly which products are selling and which aren't, which products provide the most profit when placed in desirable locations such as the end caps of aisles, and other important information. Such understanding gives the retailer substantial leverage in negotiations with suppliers. The sheer volume of business done by Wal-Mart makes it an extremely powerful player, and the once-dominant packaged-goods companies cater to it.

Press coverage of the announcement of the acquisition of Gillette by Procter & Gamble (P&G) in 2005 highlighted just how enormous that change has been.[12] Some in the financial press speculated that the purpose of the acquisition was to create a manufacturer with enough clout to stand up to Wal-Mart. (The CEO of P&G disagreed, saying, "The power has shifted to the consumer.") Either way, Wal-Mart certainly was extraordinarily important to both manufacturers, accounting for 13 percent of P&G's sales and 17 percent of Gillette's. P&G alone had approximately 300 people in its Arkansas office, all working to serve Wal-Mart. Those employees were usually sent elsewhere after a few years in Arkansas; the retired head of the office commented that after a while they started to identify with Wal-Mart as much as with P&G. The situation had clearly come a long way from the days of manufacturer dominance over retailers.

In other industries, it is not yet clear whether the intermediaries will grow in strength or will weaken and perhaps disappear. The inertia in channel relationships makes the situation uncertain and often threatening for existing participants in many of these industries.

For example, consider the insurance industry. In the past, most insurance companies in the United States sold though agents. In some cases the agents were officially independent and could offer their customers products from different insurance companies. A little surprisingly given the terminology, even what were called dedicated agents often sold the products of more than one supplier. They might officially be dedicated to one insurance company, but in practice they dealt with many. Worse for the insurance companies, it was often the most effective agents who sold the most products from other suppliers.

The reality in insurance has been that many customers belonged more to the agent than to the insurance company. Customers knew the agent, not the company's employees. They often followed the agent's recommendations. If an agent stopped carrying the lines of one provider, many customers were happy to accept products from another carrier that the agent continued to handle. The customers valued the service and advice that the agent provided; a substantial number of them could not even name their insurance companies, but they did know their agents.

New technology for handling information and for communication are making it increasingly possible to conduct an insurance business directly with customers, but history and inertia make it extremely difficult for established insurance providers that have used agents in the past to change to the direct approach. Such circumstances are (and should be) unsettling and even frightening to established players in the industry, whose channel partners own the customer relationships.

The circumstances can also be good news for innovators, because they offer opportunities to new entrants. In the United Kingdom, an entrant named Direct Line used new technology and good marketing to become the largest car insurer in that country.[13] Direct Line's founders believed that most customers didn't like having to buy car insurance, although they were required to do so. The founders set out to offer an easy purchase process and attractive prices. Their strategy combined state-of-the-art computer technology and telephone selling (initiated by the customer, not by some insurance salesperson) with the brand symbol of a little red telephone on wheels. That symbol was intended to help prospects notice and remember the company and to create an atmosphere of friendliness and service. As the *Economist* observed, Direct Line changed the way Britain's insurers do business. The company has been highly successful.

Chapter 2 discussed the notion that business opportunities often exist when there are problems with existing methods of satisfying customer needs. In the insurance industry, past practices have created substantial inertia. The few established players that have always dealt directly with their customers and new entrants are the ones that are most likely to be able to use advances in technology to connect with customers. Existing companies that have sold primarily or exclusively through agents find it far more difficult to do so.

Similar analysis of other marketplaces can uncover other opportunities for successful new strategies based on new direct methods of distribution. The changes will often be substantially easier for new entrants.

SUMMARY

Outside-in distribution should, of course, rest firmly on a foundation of customer analysis. Key questions are where and how customers want to buy and also what steps are needed to serve customers well. In most situations, some factors favor direct distribution, while other factors favor indirect, so the choice of a distribution method involves compromise.

Distribution choices must be consistent and coordinated with the other elements in an outside-in marketplace strategy. Distribution can help with a variety of marketplace tasks—everything from communication with customers to market segmentation.

Channel intermediaries are at the same time customers, partners, and competitors of a manufacturer. It does make sense to analyze the intermediaries as customers, but it does not make sense to lose sight of the paying end customer. It makes sense to treat intermediaries as partners in some ways, but it also makes sense to be aware of (and deal actively with) the ways in which the interests of the intermediaries conflict with those of the manufacturer.

In situations in which outside-in analysis does not clearly dictate a choice between direct and indirect distribution, economics generally favors an indirect approach, with low fixed and higher variable costs, when sales volume is low. As sales grow, the direct approach, with higher fixed but lower variable costs, increases in attractiveness. The problem is that businesspeople cannot easily select the more economically attractive approach at each stage, using indirect distribution first and then switching to direct distribution. There is substantial inertia in distribution, and changes from indirect to direct distribution are especially difficult.

Advances in information technology and improved capabilities in physical distribution have made and continue to make new distribution methods feasible in a variety of marketplaces. The inertia faced by established players in those markets makes it difficult for them to implement new models. Frequently, changes are introduced instead by new entrants. There are substantial opportunities involving channel changes for innovators to explore.

OUTSIDE-IN ACTIONS

For Existing Businesses

1. **Explicitly analyze distribution choices from the outside in.**
   Explain how and where customers want to buy. Describe the steps that must be performed in order to serve customers well.

2. **Compare your existing channel arrangements with those customer needs and behaviors.**
   Identify areas that need improvement, where the existing arrangements do not fit well with customer needs and behaviors. Then decide how you (or intermediaries if you use them) could make appropriate changes.

3. **If you use intermediaries, analyze those intermediaries.**

First, consider them as customers and partners. Try to identify ways in which you could satisfy more of the intermediaries' needs. Also analyze your intermediaries as competitors. Consider the ways in which your interests and theirs conflict. Explore what you might do about those problems.

4. **Consider how new distribution methods might work in your market.**

Do what you can to improve your strategy to protect against such threats. (The key, of course, will be to find ways to serve customers better than new entrants would be able to do.) Especially if you use direct distribution while some of your competitors use indirect, try to find ways to use new methods more effectively in the marketplace than they can.

For New Businesses

1. **Explicitly analyze your distribution choices from the outside in.**

Explore how and where customers want to buy. Define the steps that must be performed in order to serve customers well. Identify the factors that favor direct distribution and the factors that favor indirect.

2. **Next, chose your distribution strategy in light of customers' needs and behavior.**

Make sure that the choice is consistent and coordinated with the rest of your marketplace strategy. Consider inertia in making the choice. Be especially cautious about starting with indirect distribution if it appears that direct distribution will be the better long-term choice.

3. **If you decide to use intermediaries, analyze those channel members both as customers and as competitors.**

   Determine how you can motivate them to do what you need them to do. Explore the ways in which their interests and yours conflict, and consider what you might do about those conflicts.

4. **See if you can exploit new distribution methods.**

   Look for opportunities in serving customers with new or changed distribution (enabled by new information technology and new options for physical distribution).

11

RESEARCHING CUSTOMERS

Continuously Improving the Customer Pictures

*Personally, I would much rather talk with three homemakers
for two hours each on their feelings about, say, washing
machines than conduct a 1,000-person survey on the same
topic. I get much better insight and perspective on what
customers are really looking for.*
—Kenichi Ohmae

THE DISCUSSION OF RESEARCH in the marketplace has been delayed until this late point in the book because, unfortunately, research can never really provide enough information to resolve the uncertainty and eliminate the risks in marketplace strategy. And, as noted repeatedly earlier in the book, the best opportunities invariably involve high levels of uncertainty that cannot be eliminated before going to market.

Consequently, this book has emphasized rigorous outside-in thinking, using a combination of intuition, hypotheses, and whatever hard information is available. The idea has been to get as much insight as possible from the available information, even though we never have as much information as we would like.

It is, however, usually possible to gather some useful information.

Even though we can't eliminate the risks, we can usually reduce them, sometimes substantially. This chapter turns to the question of how to do so effectively.

Most of the following discussion considers clearly identified efforts to research customers. Helpful as they can be, such deliberate activities are not the only way to gather useful information about customers. In addition, the outside-in discipline calls for efforts to learn about customers all the time, in everything you do.

Many activities, including but not limited to those that directly involve customers, can provide insights and information for improving customer pictures. Many different employees of a company see and hear things that can contribute. The outside-in discipline requires a customer reason for everything you do in the marketplace. Effective use of this discipline requires working continuously to improve your customer pictures and then the strategies and actions based on them.

Thus, we should begin by emphasizing that the purpose of research in the outside-in discipline is to improve customer pictures and then, in turn, to improve strategies and actions. Deliberate research of the sort emphasized here is one method of achieving this purpose, but by no means the only one.

REALISTIC EXPECTATIONS FOR CUSTOMER RESEARCH

As discussed in Chapter 2, I believe that many businesspeople are deterred from using the outside-in approach because they quickly realize that they can't learn nearly enough about customers. The outside-in discipline requires that they persevere despite their lack of knowledge. It is important to begin any research with a clear understanding and acceptance of this essential inadequacy of information and with realistic expectations for the research.

There are several reasons that we can't get all the information we would like to from customers. A short list of reasons is:

- Customers won't tell us.
- Customers can't tell us.
- We can't or won't listen.

Businesspeople often pay considerable attention to the first reason, customers' unwillingness to tell us what they could tell us if they chose to. That reason does occur in some situations. A *New York Times* article at the time of the O. J. Simpson murder trial in the 1990s observed that people were reluctant to admit that they read tabloids such as the *National Enquirer:*

> Only occasionally, they say, and only when they stumble upon it near the checkout at the local Safeway. Of course, they say, they don't believe what they read in it. And of course, they never, never buy it, though each week 3.5 million Americans do—nearly half a million more than before the Simpson story broke.[1]

People are frequently reluctant to reveal their income. Managers are understandably reluctant to reveal sensitive details of their strategies. On balance, however, the first reason is normally the least problematic of the three.

In most situations, and especially in researching big new opportunities, the second reason is a far more serious problem. If a new product is intended to change fundamentally how customers do something, then it should not be a surprise that customers often have difficulty imagining how they would use the product. It should be even less of a surprise that, in such situations, customers cannot come up with descriptions of truly new products that they might like.

Otherwise excellent authors have suggested that this second problem is a reason not to do customer research. In his otherwise very useful publications, Clayton Christensen wrote that listening to customers is fine for smaller, more incremental developments, but that for really big changes it is a mistake that has gotten numerous previously successful companies into serious trouble. He advocates, as one of his four laws or principles, "Markets That Don't Exist Can't Be Analyzed."[2]

I strongly disagree. Such markets cannot be analyzed with precision. Customers cannot predict how truly new products will affect them. But the markets and customers can and should be analyzed with rigor, and information from customers is one important input to that analysis. Customers can tell us what they do now and, frequently most important, what they don't like about the current situation. They can give us useful information about their current processes for evaluating and buying new products. Their input does not dictate strategy, of course, but it is often highly informative.

Similarly, in an otherwise very good article, Dorothy Leonard and Jeffrey Rayport wrote:

> Market research is generally unhelpful when a company has developed a new technological capability that is not tied to a familiar consumer paradigm. If no current product exists in the market that embodies at least the most primitive form of a new product, consumers have no foundation on which to formulate their opinions.[3]

The authors then proceeded to describe a thoroughly sensible, though elaborate, methodology for observing customers in their own environments. I would certainly call their method a form of market research, and I believe the problem with the statement just quoted is that it rests on a faulty definition of market research.

Yes, there is a lot of bad market research in the world. Really good researchers have always understood the limits to the information that customers can provide, and they have designed and conducted their research realistically and usefully. They do not ask customers to dictate product design or other elements of strategy. They do not ask customers for information that the customers cannot provide. They do get as much useful information as they practically can from customers, and they combine that information with other insights.

The third potential problem with customer research is that we, the users of the information, can't or won't listen. Innovators who are enthusiastic about their new technologies or great product concepts find it very difficult to hear messages that are less upbeat—that question the level of real customer need, that emphasize difficult problems in fitting into a customer's existing operations, or that reveal the opposition of some key member of the customer's decision-making unit (DMU). Managers of existing businesses find it very difficult to hear that customers have problems with their approaches, especially if those approaches fit well with past customer needs and behavior. Actually hearing the messages that the marketplace is in fact able to provide can be a challenging task.

SENSIBLE CUSTOMER RESEARCH

The discussion so far leads to some initial suggestions for successful research in the marketplace. First, especially in situations with a lot of newness, use research methods that probe and explore; avoid formal questionnaires. I strongly agree with Kenichi Ohmae's statement at the start of the chapter that a few in-depth conversations with customers are preferable to a large-scale survey on the same topic.

This philosophy is even more important in product areas that are less familiar to customers than washing machines. In essence, this approach emphasizes potentially useful depth over almost-certainly-superficial-and-often-misleading breadth. There is far too much emphasis on sample size in market research. In what appears to be an attempt to obtain statistically significant results, researchers may collect basically irrelevant information. It may be helpful to recall that statistical significance is really primarily a measure of sample size, not a measure of meaningfulness, as people mistakenly assume.

One additional corollary is this advice: Don't outsource your customer research. Do it yourself. Intelligent probing and exploration with prospective customers is an enormously important learning process. Don't educate outside consultants or market-research professionals rather than yourself and your own organization. Here entrepreneurs often have an advantage over managers in larger organizations. Cash constraints lead them to do more of their own research.

Numerous entrepreneurs and managers have performed useful and effective customer research. For example, Joyce C. Hall was the inventor of the modern greeting-card business and the founder of Hallmark Cards.[4] He began early in the twentieth century by selling postcards. He then added greeting cards, such as Christmas cards and valentines.

From the start, Hall monitored the sales of each item in his product line and dropped cards that did not sell well. This use of quantitative information was innovative at the time. Hall went further and used qualitative information, too.

His basic objective was to understand why customers did or did not purchase cards. Standing outside stores that carried his products, he would watch customers through the windows. He would then approach customers as they left the stores, asking some why they had bought cards. He asked others why they had not bought—what they had wanted but had failed to find.

These observations led Hall to the insight that customers bought cards that expressed personal feelings they felt they could not convey by themselves. The customers needed help in maintaining emotional connections with friends and relatives. Hall's insight about customers' needs and behavior became the basis of Hallmark Cards. The company's emphasis on understanding customers' needs for help with expressing emotions continued long after Hall's leadership ended.

In a more recent example, in 1993 Louis Gerstner became CEO of IBM, a company that, despite its proud and successful history, was performing very poorly. Gerstner spent his first months traveling all over the world to meet with and listen to IBM's customers. He then proceeded with a multiyear effort that made IBM successful again.[5]

These examples suggest another fundamental principle for effective outside-in customer research: Try to use every activity as a source of customer information. Don't depend exclusively on more formal, deliberate research efforts to learn about customers. And, try to involve as many people in your organization as possible in noticing and then communicating information about customers.

For example, in the late 1990s a cochairman of the consumer-products company Unilever explained that when he made business trips he took time out to visit the homes of real customers:

> "I usually ask them to show me how they clean their clothes. One woman in Thailand was kind enough to show me how she washed her hair," he says. "I always ask to look in the fridge—not so much looking for my products, but just to get a sense of what people are buying."[6]

In another example, also from the 1990s, managers at John Deere & Co. began sending workers from their assembly lines out into the marketplace.[7] Those workers might explain new products to farmers and to Deere's dealers. They might teach customers and dealers how to maintain the products. They might simply spend a day visiting a local farm, watching and talking with the farmer. Deere managers debriefed the workers after every trip and then tried to incorporate their increased customer knowledge into Deere's strategies and actions.

Programs of contacts between senior managers and everyday customers can also contribute. The successful turnaround at Tesco included a program called TWIST, for Tesco Week in Store Together.[8] In TWIST, each corporate manager spent time in a store, assigned to a specific relevant task. The executive in charge of logistics and information technology spent a week stocking shelves. The CEO worked at a cash register. In other companies, senior executives regularly spend time answering phone calls from customers. Such activities can be important in helping a company stay in touch with its customers' needs and behaviors.

More formal, deliberate customer-research projects can also make sense. Any discussion of research projects should begin with a clear statement of why, in general, marketplace research makes sense. I believe that the only reason to design and execute a research program is to improve your actions in the marketplace—to improve the design and execution of your marketplace strategy. If the information you could possibly collect does not have at least some potential to change and improve your decisions and actions, then that information is not worth collecting.

Yes, managers in existing organizations are pressured to collect information for a variety of less-than-sensible reasons. And yes, entrepreneurs sometimes collect otherwise irrelevant information because potential or actual investors demand it. But I believe that people should not be required to waste their time on such efforts. The following discussion will concentrate entirely on the topic of information that is actually useful for outside-in strategy.

Three factors combine to determine whether some real-world information should, in fact, be gathered through research. First, ask whether the lack of knowledge (the uncertainty) that exists without the information has a large effect on your ability to be effective and successful. In other words, ask how much that uncertainty really matters and how much better off you would be if you could reduce it. Second, ask how much real-world information can do to reduce the uncertainty. Unfortunately, there are usually a number of important uncertainties that you would love to resolve, but for which the information that is actually obtainable cannot provide much help. Third, ask how much time and effort it would take to obtain the real-world information.

The value of collecting potential information rests on adequately favorable answers to all three of these questions. (For the mathematically oriented, the value can be described conceptually as the product of three partial derivatives: the partial of the objective function with respect to some uncertainty, the partial of the uncertainty with respect to obtainable information, and the partial of that information with respect to cost.)

Chosen well and used effectively, imprecise information about customers can still prove useful. The 7-Eleven Japan subsidiary of the retailing company Ito Yokada provides an example.[9] 7-Eleven Japan operated convenience stores. Because those stores were very small, managers focused strongly on having the right amounts of the right products on the shelves at the right times. Information from the point-of-sale terminals in the stores was central to that effort. In addition to the expected data about time of day and products purchased, the terminals captured a bit of information about each customer, because the sales clerks keyed in a few variables—the customer's gender and a guess at his or her age.

True, such information provided only a crude demographic segmentation of customers, yet it was enough to provide value. It showed how much of which products was purchased by children after school, what was purchased at dinner time by salarymen, and so on. Managers in the stores and at headquarters analyzed the information closely and used it to tailor the multiple daily deliveries to each store. 7-Eleven Japan's financial results stood high above those of the competition.

POTENTIAL SOURCES OF INFORMATION

Several types of sources can sometimes provide useful information. It is always wise to begin by checking secondary sources—trying to find useful information in publicly available books, articles, and reports. Good business libraries contain a wealth of information. With the Internet, the supply of easily available information has exploded. Public statements, marketing literature, and Web sites of the marketers of any products and technologies that compete with or are complementary to yours are also promising sources.

As the foundation of eventual marketplace success, customers are, of course, critical sources of information. The overall principle is to ask them useful questions that they can in fact answer. As stated earlier, often the most helpful questions concern customers' current choices and behavior and, especially, their current problems. As noted in Chapter 3, potential initial customers for Federal Express could not have defined the service that would ultimately prove so successful, but they could definitely have described their problems with the U.S. Post Office. With a good questioner and listener, many could also have described their frustration with the mail room of their own organization (and thus made clear the importance of having early Federal Express couriers pick up deliveries in individual offices, not in the mail room).

Thinking about the entire DMU can lead to other promising sources of insights. The idea for Gillette's Oral-B Indicator toothbrush came from an examination of publicly available information and from discussions with dental hygienists and dentists. The technical researcher who led the effort explained that consumers were not able to describe their preferences for toothbrushes well. Secondary research showed that although U.S. consumers bought more toothbrushes per capita than consumers in any other country, on average Americans replaced their toothbrush only every three years.

Discussions with dental-care professionals then established that old toothbrushes did not clean adequately and suggested that many consumers did not think to replace their brushes frequently and did not know how to tell when a toothbrush was worn out. Using knowledge from earlier experience with textiles, the Oral-B research team developed the Indicator, a toothbrush with a blue stripe across the ends of the bristles. The stripe faded with use, giving the consumer a clear reminder to buy a new brush.

Whenever practical, it is a good idea to observe customers as well as to question them, watching especially for problems and for the ways in which customers currently deal with those problems. With business customers, one important function of beta sites is to allow observation of how a new product fits or does not fit with customers' needs and processes.

Observation can be highly effective with consumer products, too. Intuit, the company that developed the financial software Quicken, had members of the Junior League in Palo Alto, California, try out early versions of its product, with the founder and other company employees looking on. That early observation of customers' use let the developers get the initial product design right for the market.[10]

Intuit continued to emphasize observation.[11] In its Follow-Me-Home program, the company asked people who had just purchased the product from retailers to allow Intuit representatives to go home with them and watch them unwrap, install, and use the software. The Intuit representatives were expected to watch and not interfere until the end of their visits, at which time they could offer help or advice.

Experimentation is sometimes feasible. Work with beta customers provides some room for experiments. In other cases, especially with more straightforward aspects of their strategies, companies can actually try more than one approach in the marketplace and see what works. For example, Staples has used catalogs with different prices for the same product.[12] (In this case, Staples decided to retain the price variability, sometimes sending catalogs with different prices to the same customer. Observant, price-sensitive customers found the lowest price. Many others did not.)

AN OVERALL APPROACH—RESEARCH IN STAGES

There is a basic frustration in designing and conducting useful research, especially in situations with considerable newness. When they start to research a specific area of customer needs or a specific marketplace, most people feel that they don't know enough to know what they need to know. In other words, they feel they don't have enough information to decide what information they need to collect. The situation sounds like a Catch-22; it is a potential endless loop.

The answer, I believe, is what I call *market research in stages*. Even when you feel dreadfully ignorant, you normally know—or can intelligently hypothesize—a little. The idea is to force yourself to do whatever analysis you can, even though the process feels extremely uncomfortable. As demonstrated with an example in the next section, I believe that if people really push themselves, they generally find that they know, not enough, but more than they think they do. The idea is to use the initial, halting analysis to decide which information (that can be collected with acceptable amounts of time and expense) is most critical for the next decisions that you must make and the next actions that you must take.

Next comes collection of that information, followed by thorough analysis to extract every possible bit of insight from it. That analysis provides the basis for another round of deciding what information is most important for the next actions and decisions, collecting the additional information, and extracting every possible bit of insight from it. The process continues. At each stage, your objective is to make some of the most pressing decisions and then to proceed to the next ones.

The following diagram summarizes the process of market research in stages.

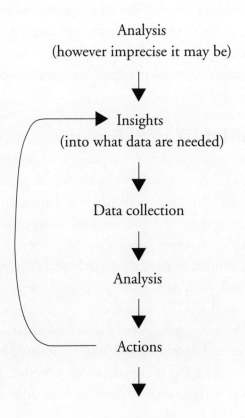

Analysis
(however imprecise it may be)

Insights
(into what data are needed)

Data collection

Analysis

Actions

One clear implication of this discussion is that marketplace research should consist of several (perhaps many) rounds of data collection, interspersed with analysis. In a way, this conclusion should be obvious. If you start out not knowing much, then you are certainly not in a position to design your entire data-collection effort at the outset. Instead, it makes sense to do the best you can in an initial round of research. The results of that first round should put you in a position to do a better job of collecting the information you need in a second round. The second round should let you do an even more informed job in the third. And so on.

Yet, in practice, people do try to design a single, comprehensive data-collection step. Doing so is frequently not sensible. This problem is especially likely to occur in large companies, where budgeting processes drive managers to specify their plans in detail at the outset in order to obtain the approvals needed to proceed. This is an area in which entrepreneurs, not shackled by counterproductive approval processes, have a clear advantage.

A RESEARCH EXAMPLE

In the 1990s, a group of entrepreneurs set out to form a new technology-based company. The basic idea in marketing is, of course, to begin with customers' needs and then proceed to design a product and other components of strategy to meet those needs. In practice, however, especially when new technology is involved, it is common to have a new technical development come first. The developers then look for groups of customers who would value products based on the new technology. The entrepreneurs in this example followed the second pattern.

A researcher had developed a new ink that could be applied to fabrics (and other surfaces) to make them reflective. The new ink had important performance advantages over other methods of producing reflectivity. Treated fabrics wore and laundered well. The ink could be applied to fabric in the same way that other inks and dyes were applied. It could be made in any color. It did not change the texture of the fabric.

Under normal conditions, fabric that had been treated with the ink looked like any other fabric. When it was struck by light from a bright source, however, the treated fabric reflected the light and was highly visible. The ink was relatively expensive; it might, for example, add $25 to $30 to the retail price of an adult's jacket. The founders applied for (and eventually acquired) a patent for the invention.

The founders faced the critical decision of what market to enter first with their new ink. In actuality, they considered a range of possible applications, including clothing. Their initial research led them to select the broad area of clothing. They next had to decide which of many possible clothing markets to address first. Because most people have more familiarity and comfort with clothing markets than with the other possible areas for application of the new ink, this discussion considers the second-round choice, deciding among possible clothing applications, rather than the initial choice of clothing. The general principles for analysis are the same.

Through secondary research, the founders identified the key steps and players in the apparel industry. Mills made yarns (from natural and synthetic materials) and wove them into raw fabrics. Converters took the raw fabrics and applied finishes that might alter their appearance or feel. Next, printers applied any prints that were desired by the apparel manufacturers; the new reflective ink would be applied at this stage.

Apparel manufacturers then designed and made the actual garments. This part of the industry was fragmented, with over 18,000 businesses in the United States. The average workforce was only 52 people per business, and only 4 of the companies had sales of over \$1 billion. For the mainstream apparel business, apparel manufacturers sold to retail outlets, such as department stores, specialty stores, discount stores, and catalog businesses, which in turn sold to consumers. There were also other distribution methods toward the end of the chain, such as bulk sales to institutional customers.

The founders' next job was to decide which part of the apparel market to target first. They were not knowledgeable about that market, and the choice was, obviously, a crucial one for them.

Let's turn to the task of deciding what research in the marketplace the founders should do next—whom they should talk with and what they should ask. Many people's initial reaction is that they don't have nearly enough information at this point to design research (or, alternatively, that they know so little that they must try to learn everything they can). At the same time, they understand that, in reality, the founders did have to decide what research would be realistic despite having such limited initial information. The following discussion is intended to demonstrate that if they push themselves enough, people will in fact be able to be rather specific about what to do.

Most people decide (as the founders did) that they must first consider the attractiveness of the product to different groups of end users. Others in the chain, such as printers and apparel manufacturers, will definitely have to be studied soon, but they will be interested only if end-user demand will be sufficiently strong. Moreover, some of the intermediaries will differ for different end-user groups.

So, people start by identifying possible end-user markets within apparel. They think about potential customers who would welcome reflectivity after dark, and they come up with all kinds of possibilities: sports clothing (for runners, for bicyclists, for walkers), clothing for safety workers such as firefighters or police officers, clothing for construction workers who must work outside at night, jackets for children, Halloween costumes, fashion items for club wear, and numerous others. The founders did similar, though more extensive, brainstorming.

The next job is to do as much pre-data-collection analysis of the various end-user groups as possible. For purposes of illustration, let's consider only two: runners and safety officers (firefighters and police officers).

Despite their initial feelings of ignorance, many people in fact know quite a bit about runners, in part because many of them either run or have spouses or other relatives or friends who are runners. Some runners are extremely serious and run regularly, while others take a more casual approach. Busy people who cannot always run during daylight hours will sometimes run in the dark. Such people include many who are busy with their careers and have enough money to buy special running gear—and who are, in fact, quite prepared to invest money in their running clothes.

Especially the more serious runners are likely to shop in running specialty stores and through specialized running catalogs. They are very particular about the products they buy, and they do not want to use equipment that fits their needs poorly and does not perform. Runners get information about products from several sources. They respect and often copy the product choices of elite runners. They read about equipment in running magazines and catalogs. They discuss products with the salespeople in the running specialty stores, who are often serious runners themselves. Concentrations of runners can be found at races, both marathons and shorter events. At such locations, runners notice what others, especially the elite runners, are wearing.

So far, the picture of this customer group sounds promising. There are good locations and communication approaches for reaching the runners, and the runners are willing to spend money on their clothing. One challenge, of course, is that the product must really perform well, in the opinion of runners in general and especially of the elite runners. Therefore, if the founders decided to pursue this segment, they would want to conduct serious research to get the product right. Given the difficulty of getting accurate reactions to verbal descriptions of products, it would be advisable to create prototype runners' clothing for research subjects to try and to discuss.

A bit more thought uncovers another special challenge in the runner's market. The whole idea of the ink is that treated fabric looks just like ordinary fabric in daylight. How, then, are runners, shopping on Saturday mornings in running specialty stores, to know why a treated jacket costs $25 or $30 more than another jacket that looks essentially the same? It does not seem feasible to start a trend of shopping in the dark.

So, research about the runners segment would include consideration of the communications task—the job of conveying the product's benefits to customers in the real retail world. There will be many things to study later, but getting the product right and figuring out whether it will be possible to communicate its benefits seem appropriate for initial emphasis; if those challenges are not surmountable, the runners segment is not a good choice.

Most people know considerably less about the market for clothing for police officers and firefighters, but probing finds that many do know some key things. Most police officers and firefighters in the United States work for cities and towns. The cities and towns specify the designs of their police and fire uniforms. Thus, the good news is that purchases of such products will be large ones, not the one-jacket-at-a-time pattern typical of the runners segment. Furthermore, it seems that reflectivity would be valued for some, although not all, police and fire applications. And there may be organizations, such as unions, that would be willing to push for improved safety.

On the other hand, the DMU for these purchases is likely to be complex, with several participants with different roles. Various towns and cities will have their own decision-making processes (DMPs) for buying. Those processes are likely to take a long time.

The next keys to understanding the police and fire market would be to assess the attractiveness of reflectivity to this market and also to learn more about the DMUs and DMPs. Those DMUs and DMPs could be prohibitively long and complex, far too long for a cash-starved start-up.

Once you have done this type of initial analysis, the next question is whether you are ready to choose one of these two segments over the other. Some people are ready to choose police and fire because of the size of the purchases. For those people, the next key decisions concern ways of targeting the segment. The initial analysis suggests that they should proceed to study desirable product designs and the DMUs and DMPs.

Others select the runners, because of their willingness to spend money, the relative ease of finding them, and the expectation that their buying processes will be short. To consider how to target that segment, these people would proceed to work at getting the product right and figuring out the communication challenge.

Some people, however, are not yet ready to choose. A key insight is that they do not get off the hook of having to do thoughtful analysis. For them, the next decision is which segment to pursue. To make that choice, they will have to study the pros and cons of both markets. Thus, they will have to study the same issues as the people who choose police and fire and also the same issues as those who choose runners. With the additional information, they would then choose one of the segments for further exploration.

The actual entrepreneurs proceeded through this type of process as they created Reflective Technologies, Inc. They conducted their market research in stages. One of the founders, looking back, described the process as being like peeling an onion. The founders decided to start with the runners market. They studied product needs and communication. As they peeled additional layers, they also studied other members of the apparel chain.

The founders did not abandon other possible clothing applications. In fact, they eventually sold to many end-user markets, ranging from training jackets for the U.S. Army for use at West Point to clothing for children. Initially, however, runners proved a good target. They provided sales revenue soon. By contrast, it took the founders four years to complete their initial sale to West Point. That sale was substantial, to be sure, but the DMP was so long that had the company targeted that market first it would have run out of cash long before it realized revenues.

The Reflective Technologies story offers a suggestion for another promising source of useful information. From the start, the founders were interested in the possibility of branding their ink. They wanted to require manufacturers who used it to apply labels clearly identifying the reflective material by name (which was eventually chosen to be Illuminite). The developers of Gore-Tex had followed a similar branding strategy. They had required manufacturers that used their product to attach hang tags about Gore-Tex. The Gore founders were also familiar with the problem of communicating nonvisible benefits in retail environments such as specialty running stores. (The Gore founders argued that, in fact, their task of convincing customers of the benefits of Gore-Tex was even more difficult than the corresponding task for Illuminite.) The Gore founders were generous with time and advice for the Reflective Technologies team; one of them joined the Reflective Technologies board. The encouraging lesson is that, if you can find other innovators who are further along with an idea that is closely analogous but not competitive with yours, they may be a willing and highly valuable source of information and advice.

It's important to note that it is always conceivable that information and understanding obtained at a later stage of research will make entrepreneurs back up and reverse their earlier choices. The Reflective Technologies founders uncovered one such potential show-stopper. It turned out that they could not find any printers who were interested in and capable of working effectively with the new ink; they decided that the printers were entirely focused on cost and efficiency and were not sufficiently interested in new ideas.

The founders decided that if they proceeded they would have to sell treated fabric rather than ink. In other words, they would have to either apply ink to fabric themselves or subcontract and supervise someone who would carry out that task. Doing so would be challenging, and the founders debated whether they could manage to do so successfully. Although they eventually decided that they could, it is not at all inconceivable that they would have decided that they could not. If so, they would have had to back up and choose a different application.

This example illustrates the application of customer research in stages. The idea is to push hard to use everything you know for sure plus your intuition and your explicit hypotheses. You formulate your strategy in steps, making key initial decisions, at least tentatively, and then proceeding to use more analysis and additional data collection to make the next decisions. Sometimes you back up, changing earlier decisions on the basis of newer information. You peel layer after layer from the onion.

TYPES OF RESEARCH

As noted previously, early in the process of designing a marketplace strategy, especially one with substantial newness, large, formal questionnaires do not work. Instead, useful data collection requires probing discussions with customers and others. Much later, when the uncertainty is substantially reduced, formal questionnaires may sometimes be appropriate. The following diagram summarizes the situation.

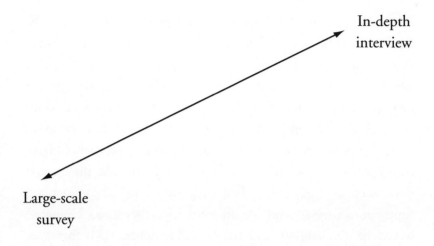

In-depth
interview

Large-scale
survey

The invisible horizontal axis in this picture represents the amount of information obtained from each respondent in the research. The vertical axis gives the cost per respondent. In-depth interviews cost more for each subject but also provide more information per respondent. A large-scale survey costs less per subject but also gives less information per respondent.

The usual logical progression is to start at the upper right, with in-depth interviews (or with observation), and then to proceed toward the lower left, as long and as far as makes sense and is worth the effort. Often, especially in entrepreneurial situations with tight cash constraints, most of the research will remain on the upper part of the line.

An encouraging recent trend in market research is to apply observation techniques that come from cultural anthropology.[13] The idea is that good observers will notice things that prospective customers would not notice or report. For example, a cultural anthropologist turned market researcher was helping to design a broadcast video and audio system for a hospital. Her observations revealed that surgical staff members told jokes during operations, apparently to relieve the tension. She suggested that the product should have a clearly visible indicator to tell surgeons that the audio was on (so that they could avoid having their jokes broadcast throughout the hospital). She noted that interviews would have been unlikely to uncover the practice of telling jokes during surgery.

COMMON MISTAKES IN RESEARCHING CUSTOMERS

There are numerous mistakes that people can and do make in researching customers. This section singles out four.

Researchers sometimes ask about subjects that customers know and can easily discuss, whether the information is useful or not. It is, of course, sensible to ask customers about topics on which they can provide useful information. On the other hand, many interview plans almost automatically ask about details of a customer company's size, number of employees, breadth of product line, and similar easy-to-supply information, even if that information is not germane to the next set of key actions and decisions.

Second, researchers frequently prejudice their research results through the questions they ask. UPS is a well-known presence in the United States, with its brown delivery trucks and its brown-clad drivers who hustle to deliver packages. Speed has long been a central measure at UPS, with time-and-motion studies used in efforts to make its people work as quickly as possible. The company assumed that delivery time was the most important criterion for customers, and its research asked customers about the delivery times they experienced and any ideas they had for reducing those times. Some customers dutifully responded with ideas.

Finally, however, UPS reportedly asked more broadly what customers wanted from the company. Significant numbers of people wanted the drivers to slow down and take the time to talk with them, to provide practical advice about shipping. UPS added some slack time to each driver's schedule, along with incentives for drivers to use the slack time effectively.[14]

Similarly, experiments designed to gather information can have too narrow a focus. The developers of an early software product for personal computers did not know what to charge. The product didn't sell at an initial price of $395. The company began an experiment. It moved the price to $50 and then raised it $20 per week until it met resistance from customers in the form of lower sales. During this time, the company did not advertise; the only publicity was a small editorial reference in *PC Week* magazine. The experiment led to a price of $89.95.[15] The problem with this experiment was the implicit assumption that price was the key determinant of sales. True, price mattered, but testing price in the total absence of a communication strategy does not seem sensible.

The third major problem area involves not listening to the results of the research. Committed entrepreneurs and managers, who believe strongly in their products or their technologies, find it very difficult to hear negative messages from the marketplace. Similarly, they may resist following clear implications of their research.

In the early 1980s, Levi Strauss managers considered offering tailored men's clothing—jackets, dress pants, and even three-piece suits. They used data from hundreds of questionnaires to segment the men's clothing market. They invited men who they thought were in their target segment to participate in focus groups, one of which has been preserved as part of a TV show about the project. The participants were quite clear that Levis meant jeans, not suits. The company went ahead with the new product line anyway. It failed.[16]

The fourth problem is treating customer research as something to do once or twice, or perhaps occasionally—something separate from normal business activities. The worst examples of this problem occur in businesses that have their research done by others. As noted earlier, I advise people not to outsource their research. The problem can also occur in companies that do their own research but use occasional big research projects followed by long periods of no research at all.

Ongoing research is needed, in part, because we never know as much as we usefully could about customers; there is always room to improve customer pictures and the strategies based on them. It is also needed because things change. Customers change over time. Their needs may change. Their buying processes may change. Their communication habits may change. The competition may change, so that customers face changed alternatives in the marketplace.

It is therefore essential to continue to gather information about customers, seeking more and more timely understanding of them. Then, of course, it's essential to use that new understanding to update and improve your outside-in strategy. The discussions of Unilever and John Deere earlier in this chapter provided examples of the ongoing collection of information about customers by many different people in a company. Experiments can also help. Chapter 6 talked about scale, noting that small-scale experiments can sometimes provide low-cost, low-risk ways to try out marketplace approaches and learn more about customers.

Constant, ongoing customer research was a central activity for Zara, the clothing retailer, whose strategy rested on rapidly changing, moderately priced fashion.[17] The company employed hundreds of designers, part of whose job was to find the newest trends. The designers went to fashion shows; they followed fashion magazines; they went to fashionable restaurants and bars. And they listened to customers, who, according to one designer, "know better than anyone what they want." Another designer described the role he and his colleagues filled: "We're like sponges. We soak up information about fashion trends from all over the world."

Managers in Zara's stores were also essential for collecting information. Part of their job was to provide data every day about what was selling and what wasn't. In addition, they sent to headquarters whatever they could learn about their customers' tastes and desires and about their own insights into what customers would value. This constant stream of customer information provided the foundation for Zara's nimble and successful strategy.

SUMMARY

Research about customers can never really provide enough information to resolve the uncertainty and eliminate the risks in marketplace strategy. Sensible research can, however, contribute a great deal. It is important to ask customers about topics on which they are able to provide useful information. Often, observation of customers can provide information that customers couldn't articulate. It is also important to listen to the research results, not prejudging the answers and not ignoring unwelcome ones.

Companies with the outside-in perspective continuously observe and learn more about customers. They involve many different employees in those efforts. They also conduct more formal, deliberate research about customers. The reason to conduct such research is to improve your actions in the marketplace. If information does not have at least the potential to change and improve your decisions and actions, then that information is not worth collecting.

In a specific situation, especially one involving substantial newness, the sensible first step is to explore secondary sources. Primary research then begins with in-depth interviews and observation. Only when the situation is far better understood does it make sense even to consider proceeding to large-scale survey research.

There is a potential Catch-22 in market research. When they start to research a specific area of customer needs and behavior, most people feel that they don't have enough information to decide what information they need to collect. Conducting market research in stages addresses this problem: beginning with initial probing analysis of whatever information, insights, and hypotheses the researcher can muster at the start, proceeding to insights about what information is needed next and to data collection, and then looping back to more analysis, further insights, and more data collection.

Good research continues indefinitely. It provides information that helps in updating customer pictures, which, in turn, provide the basis for improving outside-in strategies over time.

OUTSIDE-IN ACTIONS

1. **Do your own customer research.**

2. **Focus your research on key topic areas.**

   Choose areas where your lack of knowledge has a large impact on your chances of success and where you believe that with acceptable expenditures of time and money you could gather actually obtainable information that could increase your knowledge significantly. Emphasize those areas in both your continuous information-gathering and any more formal research projects.

3. **Make researching customers an ongoing, important activity for your organization.**

   Involve as many people from your organization as you can in learning directly about customers and the marketplace. Create mechanisms for capturing the new information. Write down the results, both to communicate them to others and to provide a record for use in the future. Also, obtain information from secondary sources when you can, using the parts you find credible and helpful.

4. Use information to improve your customer pictures and strategies.

Continue to use new information to improve your understanding of customers, incorporating it into your customer pictures and then improving your strategy on the basis of the new understanding. Focus on the areas you've selected for emphasis, but also be open to learning about other topics.

5. Conduct your market research in stages.

At each stage, push yourself to extract as many insights as you can.

Write down the results, both to communicate them to others and to provide a record for use in the future.

Use the information to improve your customer pictures and then, as appropriate, to adjust your strategies.

Then decide what research to do next: what information would be most useful as you make the next decisions or take the next actions in the marketplace.

Collect the information.

Return to the first step in this cycle.

12

CHOOSING MARKETS, CUSTOMERS, AND PARTNERS
Key Tasks for Many Entrepreneurs

There is only one valid definition of business purpose: to create a customer.
—*Peter Drucker*

WITH AN OUTSIDE-IN perspective, customers and their needs come first. Businesses and their marketplace strategies—their products and prices, their communication and their distribution—are designed to satisfy customer needs and match customer behavior. And a variety of successful businesses have in fact been built from the start with this outside-in perspective.

There is, however, another very common pattern for the very beginning of a business, especially in high technology. In practice, technological developments occur in a variety of sometimes serendipitous ways. Often, scientists or engineers develop some promising new technology without having a customer application clearly in mind. They may not be thinking of business at all as they pursue research on technology, often in an academic setting. If they do decide to investigate commercial applications for their work, the developers, often joined by businesspeople, then face the task of figuring out how they could bring that technology to some market successfully. In my experience, this technology-first pattern has been the rule rather than the exception in high-tech start-ups.

With the technology-first pattern, entrepreneurs are faced immediately with the task of identifying the initial markets in which to apply their technologies. The key for them is to adopt an outside-in perspective as soon as possible, even if they didn't start with one. Once they at least tentatively choose their initial target market, they face the additional task of choosing the types of customers within that market and the specific customers on whom to focus their efforts.

Even entrepreneurs who start with an outside-in perspective face this last task to some degree; even if they have designed their strategies starting with customers' needs and behaviors, they must select the specific customers for their initial emphasis. The process is clearer and easier in such cases than it is with the technology-first pattern, but it still requires careful attention.

Thus, selection of an initial market is a key task for the technology-first entrepreneur. Selection of initial customers within a target market is important for innovators in general. This chapter discusses the outside-in approach to those topics. It then also considers the choice of partners, another topic that is frequently of special relevance for entrepreneurs.

This discussion uses the term *entrepreneur* to mean anyone who is starting a new business, regardless of whether that business is a stand-alone start-up or a new business within a larger existing organization. In other words, it uses the term *entrepreneur* to include what is sometimes called an "intrapreneur."

CHOICE OF INITIAL MARKET

The Reflective Technologies example discussed in the previous chapter followed the pattern of technology first, market selection later. The discussion demonstrated the overall approach to choosing an initial market, shifting to an outside-in perspective as soon as possible.

The basic idea is first to think broadly and creatively about markets in which the technology could conceivably provide customers with lots of value. Then use whatever you know or can surmise about the possible markets to select some of them for further exploration. Use initial rounds of market research to investigate key aspects of those markets, with the objective of making at least a tentative choice. Then use additional rounds of research to probe more deeply into the target market. If some of that subsequent research finds an insurmountable obstacle, back up and consider other potential targets.

There are several sources that can help in the initial brainstorming about ideas for markets. It can be useful to talk with people who already know and understand the technology—or perhaps similar technologies. It is generally wise to work hard to look more broadly, however. Start by articulating as clearly as possible the types of performance benefits that the new technology seems capable of providing to possible customers. Then try to think creatively about what markets might appreciate those potential benefits. And, talk with people who have insights into such markets.

Once you have a list of possible markets, the key to making good choices among them is to use the right criteria in evaluating the alternatives. The preceding chapter's discussion of Reflective Technologies emphasized an outside-in approach, considering customers' needs and their buying processes. The criteria for comparing the runners and the firefighters-and-police-officers markets that were used implicitly in that discussion were strength of customers' needs, ability to find the customers, ability to communicate with the customers, whether the customers had money to spend, the customers' buying processes or decision-making processes (DMPs), and the decision-making units (DMUs).

The speed with which Reflective Technologies could begin to generate actual revenues was far more important than the eventual size of the market. The firefighters and police, armed forces, and industrial markets were each far larger than the runners market, but the DMPs in those markets were long and complicated, and the entrepreneurs would have run out of cash long before realizing sales from them.

The founders of Reflective Technologies used an explicit set of criteria in evaluating the possible markets they identified. One of the founders recalled the following list: value delivered to the end customer, speed to positive cash flow, speed of market penetration, ultimate market size, market pricing and profitability, Reflective Technologies' fit in the industry supply chain, competitive advantage, likely competitive responses, ability of the market to lead to related markets, impact on company valuation, and impact on investors' exit strategy.

He initially described these factors as being more or less in order of importance; on second thought, he said that size belonged farther down the list. In any case, notice that customer issues are paramount—how valuable the product is to customers and how long it will take for them to purchase. Even the first of the criteria about competitors, competitive advantage, is about the relative attractiveness to customers of Reflective Technologies' products and of competitors' products.

The following are a few specific aspects of customer behavior that are not mentioned explicitly in the previous list (although they are included implicitly):

- The complexity of the buying processes in this market
- The duration of the buying processes
- The amount of money customers in the market have to spend

More importantly, it's best not to treat this or any other list as a mechanical checklist. Yes, a checklist approach in the previous chapter would have identified the runners market as having a relatively short time to initial revenues, because runners are willing to spend money on their gear, shop regularly, and value useful innovations. The checklist approach would not, however, have been likely to uncover the key challenge of demonstrating product benefits in lighted stores or to note the key roles of elite runners. It's not impossible for those issues to have been identified with a checklist, but it's unlikely.

Frequently, in using a checklist people have the mindset that they are trying to fill in all the boxes. Once they have something in each of the boxes, they stop. With word pictures of customers, the emphasis is instead on depth and richness in describing key characteristics of customers and their behavior.

SHOULD MARKET SIZE DETERMINE THE CHOICE?

The topic of estimating market size makes me want to get up on a soapbox. My problem is that I've seen far too much emphasis on supposed market sizes, with far too little emphasis on other concerns. To oversimplify a bit, in the late 1990s, it seemed as if all one had to do to raise money with a business plan was say that a market was very large, produce some impressive résumés, and present pro forma numbers. (I am obviously not being entirely fair here, but the general point has considerable validity.)

The plans did not talk about the strength of the needs, the

buying processes, communication challenges, time to purchase decisions, and other customer-related topics. And it doesn't make much sense to discuss market size without looking carefully at these topics. For example, the founders of Reflective Technologies knew that there were many more walkers than there were runners, but the runners market was clearly more attractive. For the most part, walkers do not devote nearly the same amount of attention or the same amount of money to the clothing they use during that activity.

Although I am therefore reluctant to spend much time on the topic of estimating market size per se, I acknowledge that it deserves a bit of attention. There are two reasons that entrepreneurs size markets. The first is to learn something useful about potential markets. The second is to make it appear that they know something useful. The first reason is fine and sensible. The second can be important, but I'm not happy about that fact. Given that other considerations that are more closely related to specific customers are so much more important, I recommend spending only a limited amount of time on market sizing.

Published sources can provide estimates of size. The U.S. Department of Commerce collects and publishes potentially useful information. Research firms conduct studies and publish reports that contain estimates. The estimates from these sources often have the great advantage that they give credibility to business plans, but they should be approached with some caution.

In the late 1990s, essentially all Internet-related business plans included estimates from Jupiter Communications or Forrester Research. A 1999 *New York Times* article provided a sobering description of how those companies prepared their forecasts.[1] Its author argued that Jupiter and Forrester had "transformed themselves into prediction factories, supplying the world with a steady stream of airy, context-free, yet reassuringly precise predictions" of market sizes. The article went on to report that executives at the research companies had firmly rejected suggestions that they provide ranges of numbers rather then single point estimates and that they did not track the accuracy of their own past estimates. Nevertheless, the forecasts were an accepted part of market selection and planning.

Other methods can help entrepreneurs create their own estimates of market size. One approach is to size the market by analogy—to use historical sales patterns for products that can be considered similar. A classic example was the use of sales data from the introduction of microwave ovens to suggest likely adoption rates for more recent products.

The key to using analogies well is to be sure to check all relevant aspects for similarity. Normally, analysts look only at similarities in technology and product. Other considerations are at least as important. First, were the customer needs similarly strong, and were customers similarly aware or unaware of their situations? In addition, the entire marketplace strategy, not just the product, is relevant. A historical pattern of sales was determined by the strength of the customers' needs, the specific product, the effectiveness of gaining awareness, the ability to help customers with their processes for evaluating the product, and so on. If the previous product was part of a weak overall strategy, the analogy is likely to underestimate the prospects of the new product. If the previous product had an especially smart strategy and the new strategy does not devote adequate attention to anything other than the product, the analogy will be far too optimistic.

Another sizing method is to ask prospective customers about their purchase intentions or about the probability that they would buy a product. One problem with this approach is that, even for products they understand well, customers frequently do a poor job of predicting their own behavior. For that reason, analysts sometimes adjust downward the customers' statements about their probabilities of purchasing.

If a new product is significantly different from what customers have known in the past, and especially if it requires them to change some of the ways in which they do things, then customers often have at best limited abilities to predict their behavior. In such situations, education will normally be an important part of the seller's marketing strategy. To ask potential customers to say whether they would buy before exposing them to the educational communication is putting the cart before the horse.

There are other methods. Some people have used formal models for sizing markets. For example, marketers of consumer packaged goods have used formal trial-and-repeat models to build up total demand. They predict how many customers will try the product in each time period, how many of those will repurchase, and how much they will buy when they do. The models then use some straightforward arithmetic to calculate estimates of market size.

As noted earlier, my first suggestion is not to spend too much time on such estimates but instead to emphasize more important questions, such as value to customers and the customers' buying processes. On the other hand, despite the frequent overemphasis on specific estimates of market size, sensible efforts to size markets can be helpful. They can serve as a relatively quick screen, helping you to eliminate potential markets that are clearly not large enough to be worth pursuing. As long as the sizing doesn't take too much time and energy, and as long as the analysis goes on to consider other issues for markets that pass the initial screen, such uses of market sizing are sensible.

The founder of a company called Accessmount provides an example. After recognizing a market need, he had developed a system for safely accessing ceiling-mounted lighting fixtures for purposes such as changing light bulbs or cleaning. The Accessmount System consisted of a special base for lighting fixtures and a tool on a long pole. Standing safely on the floor, the user raised the pole and inserted the pronged tool into the special fixture base. The tool grabbed and disconnected the fixture (both mechanically and electrically) so that the user could lower it to ground level for cleaning or bulb changing. The pole and tool were then used to raise the fixture and to reestablish both mechanical and electrical connections with the base.

Accessmount's founder reasoned that the system would be especially valuable for fixtures in locations that would otherwise be dangerous to access; lighting fixtures over flights of stairs were the most obvious example. He explained that he wanted to have some idea of the market size, not to use as a precise prediction, but merely to serve as a screen or hurdle for his idea. He reasoned that if very conservative estimates indicated that the market was large enough to give him a viable business opportunity, he could sensibly proceed with his venture.

He figured out that the tax assessor's office in a city had good data on the types of buildings in that city, including information on the number of stories in each building. Combining the information he got from some municipal assessors' offices with some educated guesses to translate the data about buildings into estimates of numbers of fixtures, he established relatively quickly that this particular application market was indeed large enough to be interesting. Similar simple methods let him find rough but conservative estimates for other possible applications.

Having thus decided that the potential market seemed large enough to be worth pursuing, he then stopped trying to estimate market sizes. Instead, he proceeded to more in-depth research, using interviews with prospective customers and other knowledgeable people, working to understand customer needs and buying processes as the basis for selecting specific approaches to the market.

As an example of the challenges in forecasting market size for truly new products, let's return to Federal Express in the 1970s. Suppose that we had first explored prospects' needs and then had described the planned service to them. Suppose we then asked them if they would use it. My prediction is that many, although not all, managers and professionals and their support-staff members would have said that they were interested. The following imaginary response might have been typical:

> Yes, I definitely would be interested. I had a real problem last April, and I certainly could have used your help getting a report to Chicago on time. And, I bet I could use the service again next month, about the middle of October. I know we're going to face a crunch then.

In other words, many prospects would have been interested, but almost no one would have been able to predict the extent to which businesspeople would come to depend on Federal Express.

How then could the founder of Federal Express have predicted market size? Just as the founders of McDonald's did when they adopted a fast-food format (see Chapter 4), he could have considered trends in the marketplace. Companies seemed to be doing business over wider and wider geographic areas. The pace of business seemed to be increasing. People really were dissatisfied with the mail service. In the end, however, it would have been impossible to obtain sound, precise estimates of market size. Expressed customer dissatisfaction and apparent marketplace trends were promising, but they did not translate clearly into numbers.

CHOICE OF INITIAL CUSTOMERS

Once they know their target market (either because they have started with the market or because they have started with the technology and then selected a market), entrepreneurs face the additional task of choosing initial customers. In practice, it's often hard for them to resist spending time (often large amounts of time) on any potential customer who will talk with them. Nevertheless, a more disciplined approach to the selection of initial customers can be far more effective.

Salespeople and managers in existing businesses, under pressure to meet revenue targets, face a similar issue. They are anxious for sales. It seems wrong for them not to talk with anyone they can.

But doing so is not wise. Fundamentally, the problem is that businesspeople have only a finite amount of time and are usually under time pressure. We might think of them as having limited time budgets. It makes sense for them to spend those budgets wisely—on the potential customers who are most likely to become actual customers. And, among the people who are likely to buy, it makes sense to spend time on those who are most likely to buy soon with lower required investments from that limited time budget. (And note that the people in a customer company who have the most available time are sometimes people who simply aren't very busy, and they may not have much responsibility and may not be able to buy.)

In general, ideally, the best initial customers:

- Will get especially high value from the entrepreneur's offering.
- Are relatively easy to find.
- Are relatively easy to inform or educate.
- Will make purchase decisions relatively quickly.
- Will help the innovator learn more about the product, its value to customers, and methods for marketing it successfully.
- Will lead naturally to additional customers.

Obviously, in practice, one doesn't often find initial customers who meet all of these criteria simultaneously.

The real world adds a variety of complications. In many markets, it is tempting to try to find people who like to buy new things as initial customers. There are, in fact, clear innovators in some markets. In many medical markets, for example, there are some clear opinion leaders, and selling to those leaders is often a sound strategy.

In other markets, innovators may have importantly atypical needs, including, in some cases, the need to do something new and different for the sake of doing something new and different. Mainstream customers may have markedly different attitudes toward new and different things, placing much more emphasis on quantifiable benefits and potential risks. In particular, innovators may not be good references for other customers.

The company Wildfire Communications provides an illustration.[2] Wildfire developed and marketed the Wildfire Assistant (generally called simply "Wildfire"), an intelligent electronic assistant with a female voice that combined the functions of a secretary, a receptionist, a switchboard, a Rolodex, and an automated voicemail system. Wildfire used a natural-speech interface and maintained a directory of contact names and numbers that could be accessed or dialed with voice commands. It could route phone calls to a user at any specified location. It could interrupt calls to tell the user who else was phoning. It could accept and execute instructions from a user to remind him or her to place calls or take other actions. And so on.

The company's founder had set out to reinvent the telephone and to create an application that would spread like a wildfire. A case study about Wildfire quoted *Information Week*, which called the product "the hottest, hippest new must-have [technology] for the upwardly mobile professional." The case study cited rave reviews from what it characterized as opinion leaders who had used the product. One said that after using Wildfire for two months he could no longer live without it. Another said that Wildfire was exactly what you'd want in the perfect executive assistant.

The problem was that these innovators were not representative of the wider market. The company tried selling Wildfire to companies with large numbers of mobile professionals. It tried to interest communication carriers in buying the product to sell to their end customers. It tried to get manufacturers of personal computers to include a version of the Wildfire software with their machines. The product was not successful in the United States and was eventually sold to an English communication provider (which was subsequently acquired by France Telecom) that was interested in eventually using the underlying technical capabilities.

Discussions in Chapters 7 and 8 suggest further ideas relevant to customer selection, both for entrepreneurs and for managers of existing businesses. Chapter 7 considered the topic of product augmentation, pointing out the tendency of selling companies to give customers more and more augmentation without considering whether each element of augmentation was actually valued by a specific customer or what it cost to provide each element. The end of Chapter 8 discussed the idea of creating and then using simple measures of the attractiveness of individual customers.

Both start-ups and existing businesses will be better off, of course, if their customers are profitable. The benefits that a customer will perceive your offering as providing, the ease or difficulty of selling to the customer, and the amounts of service, support, and other augmentation that the customer will need are related measures that help determine whether a customer will be profitable for you. Understanding those measures helps with customer selection.

A COMMON TRADE-OFF IN CHOOSING INITIAL CUSTOMERS

The discussions of Reflective Technologies noted that the speed and complexity of the DMP can be central in the choice of initial markets. Similar considerations can be used in selecting initial target customers within a single market. For example, in selling a technical product that will be used by engineers, entrepreneurs sometimes face a choice between targeting companies in which individual engineers can make their own purchases or targeting companies in which the purchase decisions are made centrally. The advantage in selling to individual engineers is that the buying process will be shorter and simpler. The advantage in selling to the more centralized purchaser is that each sale will be much larger.

For example, a company named InPart developed a searchable database of digitized three-dimensional designs for standard mechanical parts.[3] The database was available online. It was intended for use by product designers and engineers who used 3-D CAD (three-dimensional computer-aided design) programs. The discussion in Chapter 8 of actually doing benefit pricing outlined some of the relevant numbers. Without a usable library, the engineers had to create their own versions of the designs of standard parts to use with their CAD programs. InPart managers determined that a typical engineer created 10 standard part designs each month, spending two hours per design. That time cost money; in addition, the users found the process tedious. The InPart database would reduce time, cost and tedium.

Some organizations control and try to standardize the choices of software and related products and services for their engineers. In such organizations, end users, engineering management, information technology professionals, finance or accounting managers, purchasing agents, and other senior managers might all be involved in a significant new purchase. The DMP would almost certainly be complex, with formal evaluations of possible purchases that emphasize their economic benefits to the organization. On the other hand, once such a customer decides to buy, the sales volume would be large. To sell to such customers, InPart would have needed experienced field salespeople who could understand and address the complex DMUs and DMPs.

In organizations in which individual engineers can make their own decisions, the processes would be very different. Engineers might learn of new products from colleagues, from specialized magazines, or at trade shows and professional conferences. Once they were aware of InPart's offering, good prospects in this type of company would almost certainly have wanted to try it out. Their evaluations would have emphasized the potential of the product to reduce the drudgery of creating designs. If they liked the trial use, they would then often have been ready to buy. Thus, the buying process would have been short. Key tasks for InPart would have been to generate the needed awareness and then to provide easy trial uses of the product.

As noted earlier, the trade-off here is between a longer time to a larger sale and a shorter time to a smaller sale. Entrepreneurs face similar trade-offs in many other marketplaces. The better choice in a specific situation will depend on the relative strength of the benefits to the individual purchaser and the benefits to the corporate customer; the buying processes and the ease or difficulty of accomplishing the needed tasks of awareness, evaluation, and decision; and the amount of cash available to the entrepreneur (and the resultant level of time pressure).

WHY NOT FIND PARTNERS?

At the beginning of a new venture, entrepreneurs face an enormous, perhaps overwhelming, number of tasks. Often, jobs related to understanding, gaining access to, and getting to know customers are especially daunting. It is therefore not at all surprising that entrepreneurs almost automatically are attracted to the idea of finding partners, especially partners who already know the relevant customers and markets.

On the one hand, partners can sometimes be highly effective. On the other hand, there is a long history of problems with partnerships and strategic alliances, both in entrepreneurial situations and in other business contexts. It is therefore essential to have clear, explicit, and realistic objectives, first for selecting partners and then for working effectively with them.

First, a few words about terminology. Entrepreneurs (and others) tend to use the term *partner* to cover a broad spectrum of arrangements. They may mean another organization whose interests are sufficiently aligned with the entrepreneur's that it will be helpful without being paid—perhaps a consulting firm that will recommend the product because it contributes to the results the consultants are trying to achieve for their clients. Alternatively, when they say "partner," entrepreneurs may actually mean their immediate customers (such as the apparel manufacturers that bought Reflective Technologies' reflective fabric to make clothing items for the runners market) or other companies between themselves and the end consumer. Or, entrepreneurs may mean something in between.

The following discussion uses the term *partner* to cover all these situations. The basic point of the discussion applies to all of them.

There are two basic questions in evaluating a potential partner:

- Does the potential partner have the necessary capabilities?
- Does the potential partner have adequate motivation?

The idea is to start by determining the marketplace tasks that must be accomplished if you are to be successful. Next, identify the tasks that a potential partner might be able to carry out. Then ask whether the partner in fact has the capabilities to carry out those tasks in the way you want them carried out. And finally, ask whether the partner would be motivated actually to use its capabilities in that way.

The first implication of these questions is that entrepreneurs must figure out what the necessary capabilities are *before* they can sensibly recruit partners. Thus, they cannot outsource the creation of their rigorous outside-in strategies to partners. Instead, they need to do enough thinking about and analysis of their end customers to create customer pictures and strategies which, in turn, will let them discover what are the key tasks and skills that must be performed in the marketplace. They can then consider looking for partners to perform some of the needed tasks.

Unfortunately, it often turns out that potential partners who have appropriate capabilities do not have adequate motivation to work with an entrepreneur, while highly motivated potential partners lack essential capabilities. In particular, it is frequently tempting to look at the largest, most effective company in an industry and think that its capabilities would make it a wonderful partner but then to find that the company is slow or unwilling to participate.

The founders of Reflective Technologies (RTI) faced this problem. As explained earlier, they decided that the runners market was an attractive initial target because of the strength of the value proposition, the speed with which they could begin generating revenues, and related factors. They then needed to find manufacturers of running clothes that would work enthusiastically with the new reflective fabrics. Almost automatically, they thought of highly visible brand names such as Nike.

Looking back later, they recalled that they had expected managers at Nike to be enthusiastic about and receptive to such an exciting innovation. To their shock, they found that Nike was approached by so many innovators with great new ideas that the company had an 800 number for innovators to use.

After considerable effort, the Reflective Technologies founders finally did succeed in holding discussions with appropriate Nike managers and did find interest. The problem was that those Nike managers were not interested in doing all the work required for marketplace success. They expected RTI to develop and champion its own benefits and to solve key problems, such as that of demonstrating reflectivity in a lighted store. They wanted to talk about exclusivity. Moreover, Nike's adoption and product-design processes took a lot of time, and the RTI founders wanted cash revenues as soon as possible.

As a result, the founders did not select Nike as their initial partner. Instead, they kept the conversation with Nike open, but they also found a smaller manufacturer of running apparel that was known in the industry for being innovative. That company did not have the enormous capabilities that Nike did, but it was far more motivated to use the capabilities it did have to get Illuminite products to market.

Even with this innovative partner, RTI had to perform some of the jobs that a naive analysis might have assigned to the partner. It turned out that even in specialty runners stores, it required substantial attention and support to get salespeople to understand, display, and explain Illuminite products the way RTI wanted them to. The company assigned some of its own salespeople to help support the retail stores, whose personnel welcomed the attention. RTI's manufacturer partner was less happy about having others dealing directly with its retailer customers, but RTI managers felt that the partner would not offer adequate support on its own.

As products with Illuminite began to sell in the stores, Nike became ready to market products that used RTI fabric. The founders were delighted to have Nike as a partner and even managed to handle the problem of exclusivity with Nike and with other large manufacturers. When necessary, they did grant exclusivity, but they did so only for limited time periods and for specific products or geographic areas, so that their own growth was not unduly restricted.

GETTING PARTNERS TO PARTICIPATE

Chapter 10 described distributors as part customer, part partner, and part competitor. The same is true of so-called partners in many situations. It helps to analyze them both as customers and as partners. It's also essential to recognize and deal with the ways in which they are competitive. A start-up in Singapore provides an illustration.

In 1999, four entrepreneurs founded dollarDEX.com, which they described as an online financial superstore. The basic business concept was to provide customers with a choice in shopping for financial products. By 2000, the dollarDEX.com Web site allowed customers to shop online for home mortgages, car loans, and seven types of general and life insurance. Other financial products were added subsequently. To simplify the presentation, this discussion considers only home mortgages.

The founders' analysis revealed that without dollarDEX.com, the process of obtaining a home mortgage was often unpleasant. Applicants for housing loans typically visited bank branches to apply for (and sometimes negotiate) mortgage loans. The process was time-consuming. Applicants had to visit during a bank's business hours, not at the applicants' convenience. They had to fill in essentially the same form for each bank. The terms and other information from different banks were often difficult to compare. The process could be intimidating; applicants might feel more like supplicants than like customers. In addition, housing loans were complex. While borrowers frequently focused entirely on the interest rate on a loan, in fact there were a variety of features that differentiated one home loan from another—processing fees, pre-payment rules, and responsibility for the bank's legal fees, for example.

The environment in Singapore seemed especially favorable for an online solution. The population was highly computer-literate. The government was itself a heavy user of the Internet, and it had identified information technology businesses as especially desirable for the future economic health of the country. Also, the dollarDEX.com founders believed that the inefficiencies and resultant high prices in Asia's financial-services markets helped to create an attractive opportunity.

The basic dollarDEX.com value proposition was to give the customer a choice, a better deal, and a better shopping experience. Customers would fill out a single application—online, at their convenience. Through dollarDEX.com, they would have access to all of dollarDEX.com's partners, the financial institutions that would provide the loans or insurance products. Thus, dollarDEX.com would give customers a stronger position in negotiating with financial institutions, would bring the relevant information together in one place, and would help customers sift through the clutter of information.

The basic mechanism would be a reverse auction—reverse because it began with the customer's requirements. A potential mortgage borrower would begin by specifying his or her loan requirements and filling out the online loan application at the dollarDEX.com Web site. The partner banks would receive notice of the application and would have two days to reply if they were interested. They could submit their bids using a dollarDEX.com platform. The basic terms of each bid would be disclosed to all partners; however, competing banks would not be told either the identity of the bidder or any special features that were offered. (The dollarDEX.com founders explained that this design was intended to focus competition on features and innovation rather than price.) The partners would pay dollarDEX.com a fee for each bid they submitted.

On the one hand, the founders of dollarDEX.com argued that they would coexist rather than compete with the financial institutions. The site would provide neutrality, which end customers wanted. The institutions would gain additional customers without incurring the high costs of acquiring them through other means. The managers of dollarDEX.com prepared quantitative arguments to show that they would provide net benefits to the partners. They found, however, that potential partners were resistant, and the selling process was a long one. Partners recognized that dollarDEX.com was designed to give more power to customers.

Banks and other financial institutions did eventually participate. Some more innovative and less established companies emphasized the benefits of access to customers and signed up earlier. The more conservative established financial institutions were much slower to join. They were concerned that dollarDEX.com would reduce their power in the marketplace. As dollarDEX.com became established and as its volume of business grew, however, the more conservative players decided that they had to participate.

This dollarDEX.com example suggests a principle for working with partners. Be realistic about the interests and motivations of potential partners. They will act when action is good for them, not when it is good for you. Often, it's useful to try to find nondominant but highly capable companies that will derive a clear, substantial competitive advantage from working with you. Look for open-minded and innovative companies and managers. At the same time, be realistic about what partners can and cannot (and will and will not) provide.

SUMMARY

When entrepreneurs start with a technology rather than a target market and a set of needs, they face the critical task of selecting the initial market in which to apply their technology. The most important criterion is the value they can provide to customers in candidate markets. The duration and complexity of the customers' DMPs and the customers' financial resources are normally also high on the list of relevant considerations. Market size is a factor, although it is often overemphasized in practice. Published information can provide a useful starting point for sizing a market. A variety of formal methods can also contribute.

Once they know their target market, entrepreneurs face the additional task of choosing their initial customers. Ideally, the initial customers should derive high value from the entrepreneur's offering, should be easy to find and to sell to, and should be able to help the entrepreneur learn about and reach additional customers. In practice, there are trade-offs among these characteristics. Entrepreneurs frequently face trade-offs between customers who will provide larger sales but take a long time to purchase and other customers who will buy quickly but in smaller amounts.

Managers of existing businesses also face choices about how much of the time and resources of their organizations should be applied to a specific customer. Conscious analysis of the attractiveness of individual customers can contribute to sound choices.

Entrepreneurs frequently want to attract partners to help them, and partners can sometimes be highly effective. Good selection of partners requires consideration of both their capabilities and their motivations. Many partners are part customer, part partner, and part competitor, and choosing and working with them successfully requires being aware of and dealing effectively with all three roles.

OUTSIDE-IN ACTIONS

1. Use clear, explicit, customer-focused criteria in selecting markets.

Work to be creative in identifying potential markets.

Identify customer-focused criteria that seem most important in evaluating the attractiveness of different markets.

Use the criteria to choose a market and explore it further.

If you find an insurmountable obstacle as you do that exploration, go back and select a different market.

2. Don't overemphasize market size.

When appropriate, use relatively quick and simple measures of market size. Be sure not to let analysis of market sizes get in the way of sufficient careful analysis of critical questions such as the strength of customer needs.

3. Actively select customers.

Resist the temptation to talk to all possible prospects.

State explicitly the criteria you will use to judge the attractiveness of different potential customers.

Identify the most promising prospects.

Implement a mechanism to ensure that you and your organization really do use customer attractiveness to guide decisions about how you spend your time and resources.

4. **Evaluate potential partners.**

   Consider partners only after you are sufficiently clear about what you need to get done in the marketplace.

   Define the marketplace tasks that must be carried out if you are to be successful.

   Identify potential partners that could carry out some of those tasks.

   Evaluate both the capabilities and the motivations of any potential partners to carry out the needed tasks.

   Pursue only those potential partners that have both capabilities and motivation.

13

THE OUTSIDE-IN CORPORATION

To start out with the customer's utility, with what the customer buys, with what the realities of the customer are and what the customer's values are—this is what marketing is all about. But why, after forty years of preaching Marketing, teaching Marketing, professing Marketing, so few suppliers are willing to follow, I cannot explain. The fact remains that so far, anyone who is willing to use marketing as the basis for strategy is likely to acquire leadership in an industry or a market fast and almost without risk.
—Peter Drucker

THIS STATEMENT COMES FROM Peter Drucker's 1985 book *Innovation and Entrepreneurship*. He defined marketing as the entire business seen from the customer's point of view; thus, for decades he had been preaching, teaching, and professing the outside-in perspective. The frustration in his statement is almost palpable. At the same time, his message clearly contains both the bad news and the good news that are at the core of this book.

Businesspeople have fallen into a bad habit of inside-out thinking. We've been told that the inside-out habit is a bad one. Individual highly successful businesspeople have attributed their success to focusing on customers. Experts such as Drucker have argued repeatedly for the outside-in viewpoint. But achieving and maintaining an outside-in perspective has proved to be remarkably difficult. That's the bad news.

The good news is that the bad news creates an opportunity. If you do manage to achieve and maintain an outside-in perspective while others in your marketplace do not, you gain a competitive leg up. The purpose of the outside-in discipline presented in this book is to let you achieve and maintain that perspective—to lead an outside-in corporation.

Drucker has stated the benefits of outside in very strongly indeed. I usually say that the outside-in discipline increases your chances of success and gives you a competitive leg up. Drucker says that you are likely to become an industry leader—and to do so quickly and almost without risk. Perhaps Drucker is right and I have understated the benefits of creating and maintaining an outside-in corporation. I hope so.

This chapter briefly revisits the bad news and the good news. It then presents a few additional tools for implementing the outside-in discipline. Finally, it summarizes the steps you can take to create and implement outside-in strategies, basing them firmly on customers, updating and improving them over time, and using them to guide a truly outside-in corporation.

THE BAD NEWS AND THE GOOD NEWS

The bad news continues. As one example, consider information technology (IT). High-tech suppliers prospered at the end of the twentieth century, as companies invested heavily in technology and the Internet boom generated demand. But then the dot-com bubble burst. In addition, senior executives in many customer companies apparently decided that they had had enough of spending large amounts on technology without realizing clear, quantifiable value for their organizations.

Growth and in some cases sales of the high-tech suppliers declined. Customers were reluctant to buy. Then it suddenly seemed as if many of the suppliers were talking about customers—about understanding customers' needs and then satisfying those needs.

In January 2004, a commentary in *BusinessWeek* noted that in the past, suppliers of IT products and services had often been driven by their own engineering departments rather than by customers' needs. It said that the downturn in high tech had changed that (inside-out) engineering-driven pattern for the better. It was telling, however, that the title of the commentary was, "Why High Tech Has to Stay Humble." Even more telling was the subhead: "The Industry Can't Forget the Key Lesson of the Lean Years: Put Customers First."[1]

The author's worry seems to be well founded. Information technology suppliers may have made progress toward outside in. But achieving and maintaining an outside-in perspective has proved difficult.

If anything, outside in has become more important. Customers seem to be gaining even more power, and they seem to be increasingly ready to use that power. The IT industry provides an example.[2]

In April 2004, customers, observers, and many industry participants were shocked when Sun Microsystems and Microsoft announced a 10-year agreement resolving Sun's antitrust case against Microsoft and providing that the companies would cooperate to make it easier for customers to use their products together. There had been a long-standing, well-publicized feud between Sun and Microsoft. Sun CEO Scott McNealy had been known for his strong and pointed criticism of Microsoft and of Bill Gates.

Coverage in the business press gave credit for the agreement to pressure from customers:

> That the truce finally came together last week shows how sweeping changes are forcing technology giants to

acknowledge a new reality: Customers have more power than ever before over their suppliers and have little patience for the bitter rivalries of the industry's youth.

The *Wall Street Journal* went on to explain that Sun and Microsoft had suspended their talks in December 2003 but they had then faced continued pressure from customers. GM's chief technology officer said that he had explained to the two suppliers how much pain it caused customers when their products did not work well together. The talks resumed and resulted in agreement. Asked about his startling change in attitude toward Microsoft, McNealy's response was:

The customer is in charge.

Before proceeding to the good news, let's look briefly at one more factor that contributes to the bad news. The business world in general and the business press in particular seem susceptible to what I call the "technique-of-the-year syndrome."

Some business technique becomes fashionable. Its proponents herald the benefits of the new technique and almost always roundly criticize the techniques that went before. Soon, it seems as if all the major business publications are writing about the new technique. One or more consulting companies build thriving practices implementing the new approach for clients—perhaps revising the clients' organizations, perhaps changing their processes, perhaps doing both.

After a while, stories about disappointing results begin to appear. The new technique is not meeting the extravagant expectations that people had for it. Businesspeople sour on it and may abandon or water down their efforts to use it. Someone presents an even newer technique. Its proponents herald its benefits. And the syndrome continues.

Let me be very clear: I'm not against new business approaches. They can be very helpful when they are used sensibly. I hope you identify and benefit from many useful ones. The problem is the feast-or-famine cycle that throws out older techniques and overemphasizes new ones. The syndrome gets in the way of achieving and maintaining an outside-in perspective. It focuses on one (often internally focused) technique at a time. It would be much more effective to combine only the relevant aspects of a variety of techniques and to use them to execute strong strategies in the marketplace, satisfying customers and earning profits in the process.

Thus, there is continuing bad news. There is also good news. Chapter 1 told the good-news stories of Dell Computer and of the turnarounds at IBM and McDonald's and Tesco. Peter Drucker's claims for the great benefits of outside-in strategy are more good news; so many businesses are run from the inside out that the truly outside-in corporation has a big advantage.

Consider a few more examples. A study published in 2004 asked CEOs how they spent their time.[3] The study's authors wanted to identify differences between the time allocations of the CEOs of the best-performing companies in their sample and the time allocations of the CEOs of the worst-performing companies. They calculated the percentage of his or her time that each CEO spent in face-to-face contact with customers. To the authors' surprise, the initial results were 18 percent for the best-performing companies and 15 percent for the worst-performing; the difference was small.

The authors then interviewed the CEOs to probe this surprising result. They found that although the percentages were similar, the activities that made up typical CEO-customer contacts were not. The CEOs of the worst-performing companies socialized with customers at cultural or sporting events. In contrast, the CEOs of the best performers spent the contact time talking business—asking customers how well their company was serving those customers and how it could do better.

In other words, the CEOs of the best-performing companies spent their contact time trying to understand their customers better and to implement and improve outside-in strategies. Their companies benefited, registering the best performances in the sample. Achieving and maintaining an outside-in perspective promotes success in the marketplace.

The outside-in discipline contributes both to major strategic decisions and to smaller marketplace actions. For example, Barnes & Noble grew from a single store in 1971 to a major force in retailing on the basis of insights into customers.[4] In particular, the CEO believed that to many customers, shopping for books was entertainment and a social activity. He thought customers wanted to browse in bookstores, often staying for long periods of time. They would value clean and available rest rooms. People wanted finding books on topics that interested them to be easy. Those with children wanted stores that would help them engage the kids in books and in reading. The CEO believed that customers would notice and be influenced by flashy displays and posters in the stores. He believed that many people wanted to buy fashionable books by trendy authors, feeling that the books they purchased were statements about themselves. People wanted access to bookstores in the evenings and on weekends, including on Sundays, when bookstores had traditionally been closed.

In the late 1980s, the CEO began to implement a strategy based on his customer picture. He chose visible, upscale, suburban locations and built large stores. He designed the stores to look rather like libraries. His were the first bookstores to remain open on Sundays. The stores had clean rest rooms and comfortable chairs available for reading. They included displays and posters about books and authors. There were book-related activities for children. And so on. The outside-in strategy was obviously a large success.

An outside-in perspective drove specific merchandising decisions at Home Depot.[5] In exploring attitudes about water heaters, Home Depot managers asked customers what brand of heater they owned. GE ranked third on the list, even though GE did not make water heaters. The Home Depot managers concluded that GE would be a strong brand. They convinced Rheem, which did make water heaters, to manufacture a heater exclusively for them, and they convinced GE to allow the use of its name in exchange for a royalty payment and the after-sale service and parts business. The heater was a success in the stores.

The bad news really does create opportunity. Companies whose CEOs demonstrated a more outside-in perspective performed better than companies whose CEOs did not. The outside-in discipline can guide both major strategic moves and specific actions. It shows the outside-in corporation the way to competitive advantage.

A FEW MORE OUTSIDE-IN TOOLS

At this point, let's turn to a few tools that are important (essential, really) to implementing outside-in strategies successfully, to improving those strategies over time, and to maintaining an outside-in perspective.

The first tool is both simple and extremely powerful in the outside-in discipline. It is writing—recording both your customer pictures and your outside-in strategy.

Writing down your customer pictures and your outside-in strategy serves two purposes. First, it communicates your logic to other people. Some of those others will be able to contribute to your thinking, helping you improve your customer pictures and your outside-in strategy.

Moreover, in an outside-in corporation, everyone understands—really understands—that customers are the key to success. Everyone understands the outside-in strategy well enough to execute his or her role effectively. Obviously, communication is needed to achieve that understanding.

The second purpose of a written outside-in record is a bit less obvious but every bit as important. It is to communicate with yourself and others, in the future.

Things change. Customers change. So do competitors. So does the business environment. Your understanding of customers changes. As things change, the outside-in discipline requires that, over time, you update your customer pictures and then your strategy. To do so, you need first to remember your previous outside-in thinking, so that you can revise it.

Without a written record, people find it extraordinarily difficult to reconstruct past reasoning accurately. In my work with businesses, I've asked about past decisions and found it remarkably hard to get clear explanations of why the decisions were made as they were. Usually, some of the participants have moved on to different companies, or at least to different positions. Even those participants who remain are generally unable to recall their past thinking without having intervening events color their memories.

The answer to this problem is to write down your thinking right after you do it. The written record then gives you a clear starting point for improving your customer pictures and the strategies based on them.

The next tool for the outside-in corporation is measures to use in monitoring and guiding the implementation of strategy. Even with rich customer pictures leading rigorously to an outside-in strategy, implementation is hardly automatic. It obviously requires considerable effort and attention to see to it that the strategy is executed properly.

Asked how they would tell whether their strategy is in fact working well, many people say that they would look at market share or profits. These measures are certainly important, but they are not useful for guiding day-to-day execution. They report events too long after the fact. And, they are aggregate measures that do not point clearly to specific actions to be taken to make any needed strategic adjustments.

Instead, managers need more immediate measures that link more directly to the key tasks for successful execution. The measures should provide information that will guide specific actions. In particular, the information must be sufficiently timely for the company to be able to act on it.

There should be only a few key measures. True, businesses will have lots of other information to consider and analyze, but there should not be a long list of measures to guide day-to-day execution. The logic here is analogous to the discussion of focus in Chapter 6. People cannot concentrate on too many things at once. If you try to concentrate on a long list of things, you generally end up actually concentrating on none of them.

The measures should be chosen to guide the key immediate action areas in the outside-in strategy. In some situations, for example, generating trial use of a new product is critical. Managers of such businesses would need measures to guide, evaluate, and perhaps change the methods they were using to generate trial. Other managers, who were selling into large company decision-making units (DMUs), would select measures that indicated whether the long selling processes were in fact progressing and that could help guide those processes. And so on.

Dell Computer's strategy attached considerable importance to the quality of the customers' experiences when they dealt with Dell. As of 1999, the company had 16 million individual customer contacts per week. To monitor and manage those contacts, Dell tracked three major measures of the customer's experience:

- "Ship to target" measured how often an accurate order reached the customer on time.
- "Initial field incident rate" measured how often something went wrong after delivery.
- "On-time, first-time fix" measured how often service people arrived on time and fixed the problem on their first visit.[6]

Dell did collect other data, but it emphasized these three measures. Presumably they reflected the characteristics of customers' experiences that Dell managers believed were most salient to customers, while, at the same time, they were tied closely to actions that Dell employees could take and manage.

Clear communication of the strategy and explicit quantifiable objectives were central to the turnaround at Tesco.[7] Employees were told that the purpose of Tesco was "to create value for customers to earn their lifetime loyalty." To make the overall strategy come to life throughout Tesco, the organization used a device called the "steering wheel." Each manager had a steering wheel that identified the key measures that should be used to evaluate his or her performance. It is especially noteworthy that one measure on a manager's steering wheel evaluated how well his or her subordinates understood that part of the organization's performance on the key measures of its particular wheel.

The next tool for the outside-in corporation addresses the combinations of data, hypotheses, and intuitions that form the foundation of outside-in strategies. As stated repeatedly in preceding chapters, we never have as much hard data about customers as we would like. Outside-in strategies, especially strategies that involve considerable newness, always have a lot of hypotheses and intuitions in their foundations, and some of those hypotheses and intuitions will turn out to be incorrect.

The outside-in discipline includes continuing efforts to improve the customer foundation, using increased knowledge to correct some of the faulty hypotheses and intuitions and then adjusting the strategies accordingly. It helps if you pay special attention to carefully selected parts of that foundation.

There will surely be some surprises as you implement a strategy. Some of those surprises can be handled relatively smoothly. Others may call into question the basic logic of the strategy. I suggest identifying, as part of the design of the strategy, what I call *red flags*. These are possible indications from the marketplace that would signal that the strategy must be seriously reevaluated and perhaps fundamentally changed.

Identifying red flags involves asking two questions:

- Which of my assumptions are especially likely to be seriously inaccurate?
- Which assumptions are especially central to the logic of my strategy?

Any assumptions that appear in the answers to both questions are candidates to be red flags.

There are two keys to using the red flags effectively. One is to limit their number. Having been explicit about many uncertain things in the process of designing an outside-in strategy, you will find it tempting to create a long list of assumptions that could be wrong and that appear important. The problem is that a long laundry list of potential danger signs is less effective in practice than a short list of key red flags. (The logic is analogous to the logic about focus and about measures.) The second key is to monitor the red flags regularly so that they really do serve as warnings.

The final and essential tool for the outside-in corporation is ongoing contact with customers. One goal of that contact is to spread understanding of customers and focus on customers throughout the corporation. The other goal is to gain more and more understanding of customers in order to improve customer pictures and strategies.

As suggested by the discussion of CEOs of top-performing companies, it's important to work actively to gain understanding of customers through customer contacts. Here are three simple but powerful topics that can be the basic outline for useful conversations with customers:

- What do you like best about our performance as a supplier?
- What do you like least about our performance?
- As specifically as you can, please tell us what we could do better.

It's important for senior managers to encourage customer contacts, to spend time with customers themselves, and to talk repeatedly about the importance of customers. For example, the new CEO of a major food-products company was working to increase the customer orientation of his organization. He led groups of executives on observation trips to supermarkets. It seemed as if every time he spoke, he included information about customers' changing eating habits in his conversation. He focused strongly on customers, and he thereby sent strong messages to others in the company that they should do so, too.

Outside-in corporations see to it that many different employees have contact with customers. As Chapter 11 pointed out, customer contacts by the CEO were a central part of the turnaround at IBM. Customer contacts by assembly-line workers were effective for John Deere. Other companies will find it useful to encourage purposeful customer contacts by a wide range of employees. In any case, as Deere did, they will find it important to create mechanisms to capture and use the insights from such customer contacts.

In most companies, many customer contacts occur in the normal course of business, without special planning. Used effectively, those contacts can be a gold mine of information about customers. It helps to notice whom customers talk to and whom they are comfortable with. For example, at Disneyland and Disney World, the employees who receive the most inquiries (and, by implication, are the most likely to receive information about customer problems) are the garbage collectors; Disney employs lots of them, and customers find them highly approachable.[8] Good outside-in implementation should include collecting and using the information that those garbage collectors gather.

STEPS IN THE OUTSIDE-IN DISCIPLINE

Start with Rich, Explicit Customer Pictures

Success in the marketplace comes from customers with needs that you can satisfy with your offerings. In particular, the offerings must be sufficiently valuable to customers that they will decide to buy something rather than live with the status quo and will then choose your offering rather than whatever else is available. Customer pictures therefore begin with customers' needs. They also include key aspects of the customers' behavior, especially the ways in which customers become aware of, evaluate, and decide to purchase new products. They include customers' communication habits and details of customers' processes and environments for using products. With business customers and occasionally with consumers, the pictures should present the various members of the relevant DMU. Often you will want to consider more than one customer segment and will therefore want to construct multiple customer pictures.

Recognize That You Will Never Know Enough about Customers—but Proceed Anyway

There will never be enough hard data to provide a complete foundation for rich customer pictures. Especially if what you are doing is a big departure from what has been done in the past, the hard data will be sketchy. As a result, initial customer pictures necessarily are based primarily on intuition and explicit hypotheses. That's fine. It's not comfortable to confront the extent to which you are depending on intuition and hypotheses, but it is far better to confront it than to ignore it.

Discuss the Customer Pictures and Improve Them

Get reactions to your initial customer pictures from other people. They may have insights that can help you improve the pictures. And, articulating your thinking is generally useful in and of itself.

Write Down the Customer Pictures

The written record provides the basis for communicating your logic to others in your organization. It also gives you a starting point for reassessing and improving your analysis over time, as you learn more through experience in the marketplace. It is almost impossible to remember consistently and accurately what your thinking was in the past unless you have written it down.

Define Your Outside-In Strategy

Select a consistent and coordinated set of choices for the marketplace tools (product, price, communication, and distribution) to address the needs of one or more segments of customers, as presented in your customer pictures. Your strategy should follow clearly and logically from your customer pictures.

Check Your Strategy for Rigor

The mark of sound, rigorous outside-in thinking is that once the customer pictures are presented and accepted, the decisions about strategy seem almost obvious—the reaction to them should be, "of course." There should be a clear, explicit customer reason for everything you do in the marketplace.

If you can't find a clear, explicit customer reason in your customer picture for some part of your strategy, go back. If you believe that there is a reason but you omitted it from your picture, revise the picture. On the other hand, if you believe in parts of the picture that conflict with the strategy, then fix the strategy. Continue until you have a fully supported outside-in strategy.

Identify a Few Key Areas for Focus

The entire list of tasks to be accomplished in order to execute the strategy will be long, but people who try to focus on a large number of different tasks at the same time generally wind up focusing on none. Instead, identify the few areas of the strategy that have the highest combination of importance and difficulty. Focus on them.

If Possible, Use Scale to Your Advantage

You will inevitably not have as much information as you would like when you make important business decisions. When possible, try to make smaller moves that let you experiment and learn.

True, you won't always be able to use smaller-scale decisions to reduce risk and promote learning; some large decisions have to be made all at once. Pressures to generate results and potential competitive pressures can also push you toward getting the big decisions settled. In the long run, however, it does not make sense to rush into large wrong decisions if you don't have to, and when you have the option to do so, using smaller-scale decisions can help a great deal.

Pay Attention to High-Inertia Tools

Brand image takes a long time to establish and a long time to improve. Large price increases are extremely difficult to implement. Channel relationships are hard to change. Other marketplace tools may also entail high levels of inertia. Be sure to take some time away from the press of immediate concerns to devote to your high-inertia tools. Planning well in advance for them pays off handsomely.

Choose a Few Key Measures to Guide Execution of the Strategy

Choose a small number of measures that focus on the key action areas in the strategy. Make sure that the measures are clearly linked to specific actions, telling you what needs attention and suggesting appropriate actions.

Identify and Monitor Red Flags

Red flags are possible indications from the marketplace that the strategy should be seriously reevaluated and perhaps fundamentally changed. Identify assumptions that are both especially likely to be inaccurate and especially central to your outside-in thinking. Select a small number of red flags and monitor them regularly.

Write Down Your Strategy

It turns out to be virtually impossible to reconstruct past business logic accurately after the fact. If the logic has not been written down, managers' memories of it will be influenced by what has happened in the interim. They will have forgotten some of the details and the reasoning. Without clear statements of the previous logic, they will find it much more difficult than necessary to use new insights to improve their customer pictures and their strategies.

Use Other Business Tools and Techniques That Can Contribute

Avoid the one-fashion-at-a-time trap. Look for tools and techniques that could help, especially in the areas that you've singled out for focus. Use those techniques and tools to implement and support your outside-in strategy.

Communicate the Pictures and the Strategy—Clearly and Often

Chapter 2 noted that many businesspeople complain that they cannot delegate as much as they would like. They wind up being excessively busy, and it is difficult for their businesses to achieve the desired success. The major problem is frequently that employees do not have an adequate understanding of the basic logic of the business. Customer pictures and explicit strategy statements linked to those pictures promote the needed understanding. Communicate your outside-in logic repeatedly, so that it becomes an integral part of the company, familiar to and regularly used by employees.

Assume That Things Will Change

If you start out with less hard customer information than you would like, then you certainly hope that your level of understanding of customers will change. Customers themselves change. So does technology. Competitors act. Other forces affect the marketplace. Actively planning to notice and evaluate such changes works better than ignoring them until they become serious problems.

Continue to Gather Information

New information is integral to the process of outside-in change. Over time, the amount of actual hard data underlying a strategy should increase. New information provides the basis for identifying and implementing needed changes in customer pictures and the strategies based on them.

Information about customers is most important. Talk with customers. Observe them. Give salespeople and others who have contact with customers the motivation to notice and report useful information. Think carefully about who might contribute.

Work to give everyone in your organization an outside-in perspective. Give them opportunities to interact with customers and to learn more about customers. Create mechanisms to capture and use their insights.

Actively Question Your Past Logic

Regularly review your past customer assumptions and pictures and your strategy. Update them (in writing) when appropriate.

Communicate the changes repeatedly. As needed, revise your decisions about your key areas for focus, your key measures for execution, and your red flags. Communicate those changes repeatedly. Continue the process.

Make Outside In a Habit—Both For You and For Your Organization

The rigorous outside-in discipline advocated in this book is frequently not easy or comfortable. It does, however, offer the promise of better strategy design, better communication of the strategy to others, and better ability to adapt when things change. Those benefits substantially increase the probabilities of success in the marketplace. And customers are the key.

NOTES

Preface

1. Peter F. Drucker, *The Practice of Management*, 1954, p. 50.
2. Jeffrey A. Krames, *What the Best CEOs Know*, 2003, p. 32.

Chapter 1

1. Jeffrey A. Krames, *What the Best CEOs Know*, 2003, p. 59.
2. Ibid., p. 113.
3. Ira Sager, "How IBM Became a Growth Company Again," *BusinessWeek*, Dec. 9, 1996, pp. 154–162.
4. Jeffrey A. Krames, *What the Best CEOs Know*, p. 115.
5. Pallavi Gogoi and Michael Arndt, "Hamburger Hell," *BusinessWeek*, Mar. 3, 2003, pp. 104–108; Daniel Kruger, "You Want Data with That?" *Forbes*, Mar. 29, 2004, pp. 58–60; Kate MacArthur, "Big Mac's Back," *Advertising Age*, Dec. 13, 2004, pp. S-1–S-8.
6. Ira Sager, "How IBM Became a Growth Company Again."
7. Jeffrey A. Krames, *What the Best CEOs Know*, p. 115.
8. Daniel Kruger, "You Want Data with That?"
9. Kate MacArthur, "Big Mac's Back," p. S-1.
10. "Leahy's Lead," *Economist*, Aug. 11, 2001, p. 53; www.Tesco.com/companyhistory; David E. Bell, "Tesco Plc," Harvard Business School Case 9-503-036.

11. Peter F. Drucker, *The Practice of Management*, 1954, p. 37.

12. Peter F. Drucker, *The Practice of Management*, p. 39.

13. Theodore Levitt, "Marketing Myopia," *Harvard Business Review*, 1960, reprinted with retrospective commentary in Sept.–Oct. 1975.

14. B. Charles Ames, "Trappings vs. Substance in Industrial Marketing," *Harvard Business Review*, Jul.–Aug. 1970.

15. Edward B. Roberts, *Entrepreneurs in High Technology: Lessons from MIT and Beyond*, 1991.

16. Jeffrey A. Krames, *What the Best CEOs Know*, p. 56.

Chapter 2

1. Jeffrey A. Krames, *What the Best CEOs Know*, 2003, p. 34.

2. Diane Brady, "Will Jeff Immelt's New Push Pay Off for GE?" *BusinessWeek*, Oct. 13, 2003, pp. 94–98; "Special Report: The Best and Worst Managers of the Year," *BusinessWeek*, Jan. 10, 2005, p. 56.

3. *The Charlie Rose Show*, Feb. 11, 2005.

4. Peter F. Drucker, *The Practice of Management*, 1954, p. 39.

Chapter 3

1. Jeffrey A. Krames, *What the Best CEOs Know*, 2003, pp. 34–35.

2. V. Kasturi Rangan and Susan Lasley, "Rohm and Haas (A): New Product Marketing Strategy," Harvard Business School, Case 9-587-055.

3. "Xerox Corporation—The 9200," in Barbara Bund Jackson, *Computer Models in Management*, 1979, pp. 334–346.

4. Stephen Baker, "And Now, Designer Motor Oil?" *BusinessWeek*, Sept. 19, 1994, p. 58.

5. Gary Loveman and Jamie O'Connell, "Merry Maids," Harvard Business School Case 9-396-076.

6. Nathan Tyler Productions, "In Search of Excellence," aired on WGBH Boston, 1985.

7. *Fortune*, Sept. 9, 1983.

8. Philip Kotler, *Marketing Management: The Millennium Edition*, 2000, p. 17.

9. Barbara E. Bund, "Exercise: Federal Express Then and Now," 2003.

10. Kenichi Ohmae, "Getting Back to Strategy," *Harvard Business Review*, Nov.–Dec. 1988.

Chapter 4

1. Gary Samuels, "Help Thy Customer, Help Thyself," *Forbes*, Dec. 18, 1995, pp. 196–197.

2. Louis Lavelle, "Inventing to Order," *BusinessWeek*, Jul. 5, 2004, pp. 84–85.

3. Peter F. Drucker, *Innovation and Entrepreneurship*, 1985, p. 228.

4. David Halberstam, *The Fifties*, 1993, pp. 155–158.

5. Steven Demos with Catherine Fredman, "Got Soy?" *Hemispheres*, Aug. 2001, pp. 21–26.

6. H. Kent Bowen and Sylvia Sensiper, "Lifeline Systems, Inc. (A)," Harvard Business School Case 9-698-025.

7. Mercedes M. Cardona, "Affluent Shoppers Like Their Luxe Goods Cheap," *Advertising Age*, Dec. 1, 2003, p. 6; "The Big Picture," *BusinessWeek*, May 24, 2004, p. 13; John Helyar, "The Only Company Wal-Mart Fears," *Fortune*, Nov. 24, 2003, pp. 158–166.

8. David Green, "Learning from Losing a Customer," *Harvard Business Review*, May–Jun. 1989.

9. Robert A. Guth, "M-Commerce: Mobile and Multiplying," *Wall Street Journal*, Aug. 18, 2000, p. B1.

10. Leigh Buchanan, "Death to Cool," *Inc.*, Jul. 2003, pp. 82–104.

11. Jaclyn Fierman, "The Death and Rebirth of the Salesman," *Fortune*, Jul. 25, 1994, pp. 80–91.

12. Barbara Bund Jackson, "Build Customer Relationships That Last," *Harvard Business Review*, Nov.–Dec. 1985; Barbara Bund Jackson, *Winning and Keeping Industrial Customers*, 1985.

13. Barbara E. Bund, Dell Computer Corporation, 1998.

14. Barbara Bund Jackson, *Winning and Keeping Industrial Customers*.

Chapter 5

1. Joel Kurtzman, "Advertising for All the Little Guys," *Fortune*, Apr. 12, 1999, p. 162L.

2. Robert Berner, "Why P&G's Smile Is So Bright," *BusinessWeek*, Aug. 12, 2002, pp. 58–60.

3. Roy S. Johnson, "Home Depot Renovates," *Fortune*, Nov. 23, 1998, pp. 200–212.

4. Deborah Ball, "Italian Challenge: Water Everywhere, But Not on the Go," *Wall Street Journal*, May 23, 2005, p. A1.

5. Ian C. MacMillan and Rita Gunther McGrath, "Discovering New Points of Differentiation," *Harvard Business Review*, Jul.–Aug. 1997.

6. Barbara E. Bund, Dell Computer Corporation, 1998.

7. William C. Taylor, "Companies Find They Can't Buy Love with Bargains," *New York Times*, Aug. 8, 2004, p. BLL5.

8. Christina Cheddar Berk, "Silk Soy Milk Looks to Strengthen Healthy Image with National Ads," *Wall Street Journal*, Apr. 21, 2004, p. B4B.

9. Davis Bestor, "The North Face: Channel Issues," Stanford Business School Case M193.

10. John Cassidy, *dot.con*, 2002, p. 110.

11. V. Kasturi Rangan and Gordon Swartz, "MathSoft, Inc. (A)," Harvard Business School Case 9-593-094.

Chapter 6

1. Al Ries and Jack Trout, *Marketing Warfare*, 1986, p. 172.

2. Richard S. Tedlow, *New and Improved*, 1996, pp. 115–117.

3. Alvin J. Silk and Mary Shelman, "RiceSelect™," Harvard Business School Case 9-595-033.

4. Neil H. Borden, "The Concept of the Marketing Mix," *Journal of Advertising Research*, Jun. 1964.

5. Barbara Bund Jackson, *Winning and Keeping Industrial Customers*, 1985, p. 182.

6. William Echikson, "The Mark of Zara," *BusinessWeek*, May 29, 2000, pp. 98–100; Jane M. Folpe, "Zara Has a Made-to-Order Plan for

Success," *Fortune*, Sept. 4, 2000, p. 80; Carlta Vitzthum, "Just-in-Time Fashion," *Wall Street Journal*, May 18, 2001, p. B1; Richard Heller, "Galician Beauty," *Forbes*, May 28, 2001, p. 98; Miguel Helft, "Fashion Fast Forward," *Business 2.0*, May 2002, pp. 61–66.

7. James Surowiecki, "The Most Devastating Retailer in the World," *New Yorker*, Sept. 18, 2000, p. 74.

8. David E. Bell, "Tesco Plc," Harvard Business School Case 9-503-036.

9. David E. Bell and David Vennin, "Toupargel," Harvard Business School Case 9-594-003.

10. Erick Schonfeld, "How Much Are Your Eyeballs Worth?" *Fortune*, Feb. 21, 2000, pp. 197–204.

11. Patricia Sellers, "eBay's Secret," *Fortune*, Oct. 18, 2004, pp. 161–178.

12. Joseph Pereira, "Sneaker Company Tags Out-of-Breath Baby Boomers," *Wall Street Journal*, Jan. 16, 1998, p. B1.

Chapter 7

1. Kathleen K. Wiegner, "Buggy Whip Chips," *Forbes*, Jan. 7, 1991, pp. 285–286.

2. Frederick E. Webster, Jr., "Perdue Foods, Inc.," Harvard Business School Case 9-574-799.

3. George Stalk, Jr., and Alan M. Webber, "Japan's Dark Side of Time," *Harvard Business Review*, Jul.–Aug. 1993.

4. John Markoff, "The Chip on Intel's Shoulder," *New York Times*, Dec. 18, 1994, p. 6E.

5. Jim Carlton and Stephen Kreider Yoder, "Humble Pie: Intel to Replace Its Pentium Chips," *Wall Street Journal*, Dec. 21, 1994, p. B1; John Markoff, "Intel's Crash Course on Consumers," *New York Times*, Dec. 21, 1994, p. D1.

6. Jeffrey A. Krames, *What the Best CEOs Know*, 2003, p. 120.

7. Tim Smart, "Jack Welch's Encore," *BusinessWeek*, Oct. 28, 1996, pp. 155–160.

8. "General Electric: The House That Jack Built," *Economist*, Sept. 18, 1999, pp. 23–26.

9. James C. Anderson and James A. Narus, "Capturing the Value of Supplementary Services," *Harvard Business Review*, Jan.–Feb. 1995.

10. Christopher W. L. Hart, "The Power of Unconditional Service Guarantees," *Harvard Business Review*, Jan.–Feb. 1988.

11. Joshua Hyatt, "Guaranteed Growth," *Inc.*, Sept. 1995, pp. 69–78.

12. Sarah Schafer, "Have It Your Way," *Inc. Tech* no. 4, 1997, pp. 56–64.

13. Faith Keenan, Stanley Holmes, Jay Greene, and Roger O. Crockett, "A Mass Market of One," *BusinessWeek*, Dec. 2, 2002, pp. 68–72.

14. Peter Burrows, Geoffrey Smith, and Steven Brull, "HP Pictures the Future," *BusinessWeek*, Jul. 7, 1997, pp. 100–109; Pui-Wing Tam, "Fill 'er Up, with Color," *Wall Street Journal*, Aug. 3, 2004, p. B1.

15. Barbara Bund Jackson, *Winning and Keeping Industrial Customers*, 1985, pp. 149–152.

16. Pui-Wing Tam, "Fill 'er Up, with Color," *Wall Street Journal*, Aug. 3, 2004, p. B1.

17. Barbara Bund Jackson, *Winning and Keeping Industrial Customers*, 1985.

18. "DEC's About-Face," *Datamation*, Sept. 1, 1987, p. 9; Susan Kerr, "X.400 E-Mail Standard Picks Up Steam in the U.S.," *Datamation*, Dec. 15, 1987, pp. 24–26; Peter H. Lewis, "E-Mail Searches for a Missing Link," *New York Times*, Mar. 12, 1989, p. 6F.

19. Norm Alster and Lori Hawkins, "Trouble in Store for Data-Storage King?" *BusinessWeek*, Dec. 4, 2000, pp. 122–126; Daniel Roth, "Can EMC Restore Its Glory?" *Fortune*, Jul. 22, 2002, pp. 107–110; Steve Hamm, "Why High Tech Has to Stay Humble," *BusinessWeek*, Jan. 19, 2004, pp. 76–77.

20. Michael E. Porter and Nancy Taubenslag, "Rockwell International (A)," Harvard Business School Case 9-383-019.

Chapter 8

1. Brent Schlender, "Sun's Java: The Threat to Microsoft Is Real," *Fortune*, Nov. 11, 1996, pp. 165–170.

2. Howard Banks, "Profitless Prosperity," *Forbes*, Nov. 6, 1995, pp. 64–66.

3. Benson P. Shapiro and Craig E. Cline, "Cumberland Metal Industries (A),(B),(C) and (D)," Harvard Business School Cases 9-578-170 through 9-578-173.

4. Brian O'Reilly, "They've Got Mail," *Fortune*, Feb. 7, 2000, pp. 101–112.

5. Emily Thornton, "Fees! Fees! Fees!" *BusinessWeek*, Sept. 29, 2003, pp. 99–104.

6. Rita Koselka, "It's My Favorite Statistic," *Forbes*, Sept. 12, 1994, pp. 162–176.

7. Laurie J. Flynn, "Sun to Introduce New Pricing Strategy for Its Software," *New York Times*, Sept. 16, 2003, p. C9.

8. Andrew E. Serwer, "How to Escape a Price War," *Fortune*, Jun. 13, 1994, pp. 82–90.

9. Rick Brooks, "Unequal Treatment: Alienating Customers Isn't Always a Bad Idea, Many Firms Discover," *Wall Street Journal*, Jan. 7, 1999, p. A1.

10. Robert S. Kaplan, "Kanthal (A)," Harvard Business School Case 9-190-002.

Chapter 9

1. "Cabot Corporation," in Glen L. Urban and Steven H. Star, *Advanced Marketing Strategy*, 1991, pp. 368–386.

2. Stan Rapp and Thomas L. Collins, *Beyond MaxiMarketing*, 1994, pp. 135–142.

3. "Central Bell Publishing, Inc.," in Glen L. Urban and Steven H. Star, *Advanced Marketing Strategy*, 1991, pp. 194–213.

4. John W. Verity, "Taking a Laptop on a Call," *BusinessWeek*, Oct. 25, 1993, pp. 124–125; Sheryl Gay Stolberg and Jeff Gerth, "High-Tech Stealth Being Used to Sway Doctor Prescriptions," *New York Times*, Nov. 16, 2000, p. A1.

5. Andrea Gabor, *The Man Who Discovered Quality*, 1990, pp. 208–209.

6. John Lippman, "How Sony Marketers Gave 'Crouching Tiger' an Early Leg Up," *Wall Street Journal*, Jan. 11, 2001, p. A1.

7. Christie Brown, "Goya O'Boya," *Forbes*, Feb. 26, 1996, p. 102.

8. Jack Neff, "P&G Brings Potty to Parties," *Advertising Age*, Feb. 17, 2003, p. 22.

9. Zachary Schiller, "Procter & Gamble Hits Back," *BusinessWeek*, Jul. 19, 1993, pp. 20–22; Patricia Sellers, "Brands: It's Thrive or Die," *Fortune*, Aug. 23, 1993, pp. 52–56.

10. Betsy Morris, "The Brand's the Thing," *Fortune*, Mar. 4, 1996, pp. 72–86; Nanette Byrnes, Dean Foust, Stephanie Anderson Forest, and William C. Symonds, "Brands in a Bind," *BusinessWeek*, Aug. 28, 2000, pp. 234–238.

11. "Don't Get Left on the Shelf," *Economist*, Jul. 2, 1994, p. 11.

12. Jerry Useem, "dot-coms: What Have We Learned?" *Fortune*, Oct. 30, 2000, pp. 82–104.

13. Shirley Leung, "Fast-Food Firms' Big Budgets Don't Buy Consumer Loyalty," *Wall Street Journal*, Jul. 24, 2003, p. B4.

Chapter 10

1. E. Raymond Corey and William E. Matthews, "Norton Company (A)," Harvard Business School Case 9-570-001.

2. Richard Tomlinson, "The China Card," *Fortune*, May 25, 1998, p. 82.

3. Carl Shapiro and Hal R. Varian, *Information Rules*, 1999, p. 88.

4. Richard Heller, "Galician Beauty," *Forbes*, May 28, 2001, p. 98; Miguel Helft, "Fashion Fast Forward," *Business 2.0*, May 2002, pp. 61–66

5. Janet Adamy, "Behind a Food Giant's Success: An Unlikely Soy-Milk Alliance," *Wall Street Journal*, Feb. 1, 2005, p. A1.

6. Barbara E. Bund, Dell Computer Corporation, 1998.

7. Gary McWilliams, "In About-Face, Dell Will Sell PCs to Dealers," *Wall Street Journal*, Aug. 20, 2002, p. B1.

8. Donald V. Fites, "Make Your Dealers Your Partners," *Harvard Business Review*, Mar.–Apr. 1996.

9. Luisa Kroll, "Entrepreneur of the Year: Java Man," *Forbes*, Oct. 29, 2001, pp. 142–145.

10. Benson P. Shapiro and Edward Bullard, "Newport Instrument Division," Harvard Business School Case 6-576-035.

11. Zachary Schiller and Wendy Zellner, "Making the Middleman an Endangered Species," *BusinessWeek*, Jun. 6, 1994, pp. 114–115.

12. James Surowiecki, "The Customer Is King," *New Yorker*, Feb. 14 & 21, 2005, p. 104; Sarah Ellison, Ann Zimmerman, and Charles Forelle, "P&G's Gillette Edge: The Playbook It Honed at Wal-Mart," *Wall Street Journal*, Jan. 31, 2005, p. A1.

13. "Death by a Thousand Cuts," *Economist*, Apr. 19, 1997, pp. 75–76; Carolyn T. Geer, "The Little Red Telephone Is Ringing," *Forbes*, Feb. 23, 1998, pp. 106–110.

Chapter 11

1. David Margolick, "The Enquirer: Required Reading in Simpson Case," *New York Times*, Oct. 24, 1994, p. A12.

2. Clayton M. Christensen, *The Innovator's Dilemma*, 1997, p. xxi.

3. Dorothy Leonard and Jeffrey F. Rayport, "Spark Innovation through Empathic Design," *Harvard Business Review*, Nov.–Dec. 1997.

4. David Owen, "Card Tricks," *New Yorker*, Apr. 19 & 26, 2004, pp. 106–114.

5. Ira Sager, "How IBM Became a Growth Company Again," *BusinessWeek*, Dec. 9, 1996, pp. 154–162.

6. Deborah Orr, "A Giant Reawakens," *Forbes*, Jan. 25, 1999, pp. 52–54.

7. Kevin Kelly, "The New Soul of John Deere," *BusinessWeek*, Jan. 31, 1994, pp. 64–66.

8. David E. Bell, "Tesco Plc," Harvard Business School Case 9-503-036.

9. Gale Eisenstodt, "Information Power," *Forbes*, Jun. 21, 1993, pp. 44–45.

10. Michael Oneal, "Scott Cook Wants to Control Your Checkbook," *BusinessWeek*, Sept. 26, 1994, pp. 100–102.

11. John Case, "Customer Service: The Last Word," *Inc.*, Apr. 1991, pp. 89–93.

12. Scott Woolley, "I Got It Cheaper than You," *Forbes*, Nov. 2, 1998, pp. 82–84.

13. Katie Hafner, "Coming of Age in Palo Alto," *New York Times*, Jun. 10, 1999, p. E1.

14. David Greising, "Quality: How to Make It Pay," *BusinessWeek*, Aug. 8, 1994, pp. 54–59.

15. Kelly Walker, "Software Economics 101," *Forbes*, Jan. 28, 1985, p. 88.

16. WGBH Boston, "Not by Jeans Alone," *Enterprise Series* Episode 109, 1981.

17. Carlta Vitzthum, "Just-in-Time Fashion," *Wall Street Journal*, May 18, 2001, p. B1; Miguel Helft, "Fashion Fast Forward," *Business 2.0*, May 2002, pp. 61–66.

Chapter 12

1. Jim Frederick, "The Virtual Science of High-Tech Forecasting," *New York Times Magazine*, Dec. 19, 1999, pp. 70–73.

2. Jeffrey F. Rayport and Mary Conner, "Wildfire Communications, Inc. (A)," Harvard Business School Case 9-396-305.

3. Joseph B. Lassiter III, Michael J. Roberts, and Jon M. Biotti, "In-Part," Harvard Business School Case 9-898-213.

Chapter 13

1. Steve Hamm, "Why High Tech Has to Stay Humble," *Business-Week*, Jan. 19, 2004, pp. 76–77.

2. Robert A. Guth and Don Clark, "Behind Secret Settlement Talks: New Power of Tech Customers," *Wall Street Journal*, Apr. 5, 2004, p. A1.

3. Patrick Barwise and Seán Meehan, "Don't Be Unique, Be Better," *MIT Sloan Management Review*, Summer 2004.

4. Myron Magnet, "Let's Go for Growth," *Fortune*, Mar. 7, 1994, pp. 60–72.

5. Bruce Upbin, "Profit in a Big Orange Box," *Forbes*, Jan. 24, 2000, pp. 122–127.

6. Scott Kirsner, "The Customer Experience," *Net Company*, Fall 1999, pp. 12–38.

7. David E. Bell, "Tesco Plc," Harvard Business School Case 9-503-036.

8. Stephen S. Tax and Stephen W. Brown, "Recovering and Learning from Service Failure," *Sloan Management Review*, Fall 1998.

INDEX

About the Author

BARBARA E. BUND, PH.D., is a senior lecturer at MIT Sloan School of Management. Credited by Philip Kotler with popularizing the term *relationship marketing*, Bund has also taught at Harvard and is the author of *Winning and Keeping Industrial Customers* as well as other books and articles.